The Law of Comparative Advertising:
Directive 97/55/EC in the United Kingdom and Germany

D1326191

The Law of Comparative Advertising: Directive 97/55/EC in the United Kingdom and Germany

Ansgar Ohly
Max-Planck Institute for Foreign and
International Patent, Copyright and
Competition Law, Munich
and Michael Spence
St Catherine's College, Oxford

·HART·
PUBLISHING

OXFORD – PORTLAND OREGON
2000

Hart Publishing
Oxford and Portland, Oregon

Published in North America (US and Canada) by
Hart Publishing
c/o International Specialized Book Services
5804 NE Hassalo Street
Portland, Oregon
97213-3644
USA

Distributed in the Netherlands, Belgium and Luxembourg by
Intersentia, Churchillaan 108
B2900 Schoten
Antwerpen
Belgium

Distributed in Australia and New Zealand by
Federation Press
John St
Leichhardt
NSW 2000

Hart Publishing Ltd is a specialist legal publisher based in
Oxford, England.
To order further copies of this book or to request a list of other
publications please write to:

Hart Publishing, Salters Boatyard, Folly Bridge, Abingdon Rd,
Oxford, OX1 4LB
Telephone: +44 (0)1865 245533 Fax: +44 (0)1865 794882
e-mail: mail@hartpub.co.uk

British Library Cataloguing in Publication Data
Data Available
ISBN 1 84113-117-2 (cloth)

Typeset by Hope Services, Clifton Hampden, Abingdon
Printed in Great Britain
by Biddles Ltd, Guildford and King's Lynn

Contents

Contents

1

Introduction

Although the harmonisation of unfair competition law has been on the agenda of the European Commission since the early 1960s, it has yet to be achieved.[1] The task of discerning common standards for competition across Europe—of proscribing 'unfair business practices in the market place'[2]—seems almost Herculean.[3]

It is our conviction, however, that common standards for competition in the European market can be found and that the harmonisation of European unfair competition law is not impossible. But if harmonisation is to succeed, European lawyers will need to look beyond the confines of their own familiar legal systems. In particular, the lawyers of the United Kingdom and Germany will need to find common ground in unfair competition regulation. For this reason we have undertaken—as

[1] For a historical overview see F. K. Beier, 'The Law of Unfair Competition in the European Union—Its Development and Present Status' [1985] *EIPR* 284 and G. Schricker, 'European Harmonization of Unfair Competition Law—A Futile Venture?' [1991] *IIC* 788.

[2] W. R. Cornish, *Intellectual Property* 3rd edn. (London, Sweet & Maxwell, 1996) at 13.

[3] For a comparative overview see A. Kamperman Sanders, *Unfair Competition Law* (Oxford, Clarendon Press, 1997) and A. Ohly, *Richterrecht und Generalklausel im Recht des unlauteren Wettbewerbs—ein Methodenvergleich des englischen und des deutschen Rechts* (Cologne, Carl Heymanns, 1997). The European Commission has started a new initiative in this area. On the basis of comparative legal and economic research, the Commission presented a Green Paper on Commercial Communication in May 1996 (COM(96)192 final). The comments made by the EU Member States and by interested circles are summed up in the document CAB 15/0012/98—EU. See F. Henning-Bodewig, 'Das Grünbuch der EU-Kommission über die "Kommerziellen Kommunikationen" ' *GRUR Int.* 1997, 515.

academic lawyers working in those two countries—to consider possible future principles for a European law of unfair competition. This study represents a first step in our project.

We have chosen to begin with comparative advertising because the topic draws together at least three of the most important themes in unfair competition law. These themes are that a trader ought not to succeed in competition (i) by misleading consumers, (ii) by denigrating a competitor, his goods or services, or (iii) by taking unfair advantage of a competitor's goodwill. A comparative advertisement may well fall foul of all three of these standards. Comparative advertising has great potential to mislead. Comparative advertising consisting of critical claims ('A is better than B') is prone to denigrate a competitor. Comparative advertising consisting of claims of equivalence ('A is as good as B') is prone to take unfair advantage of a competitor's goodwill. Comparative advertising is an interesting place to begin discussion of unfair competition law—and an interesting place for the European Union to have begun the project of its harmonisation—because it raises some of the most important and difficult themes of the subject.

This study outlines the history of the law of comparative advertising in the United Kingdom and Germany and proposes a model for reading Directive 97/55/EC ('the Comparative Advertising Directive').[4] The Directive is in many ways a difficult piece of legislation, uncertain in its scope, in places too obviously the result of political compromise, and problematic in its potential effects. Although welcomed as a liberalising measure, the Directive restricts permissible comparative advertising in the United Kingdom and does not go as far as some might have hoped in liberalising comparative advertising in Germany. Our model is an attempt to make sense of a potentially very confusing document. We offer a reading of the Directive that, we hope, is both faithful to its apparent purpose and allows it to operate in a principled and coherent way.

[4] Directive 97/55/EC of the European Parliament and of the Council amending Directive 84/450/EEC concerning misleading advertising so as to include comparative advertising OJ 1997 L290/18. See App. IV.

In outlining this model we do not tackle the question whether the law relating to comparative advertising ought to have been harmonised. It may well be argued that advertising is a context in which the principle of subsidiarity ought to have been given full effect.[5] Advertising has a function in shaping contemporary culture. The reception of a particular advertisement is highly culturally determined. An advertisement that might be amusing to an Englishman might be offensively denigrating to a German and vice versa. However, our intuition is that differing regimes of advertising regulation across the European Union unnecessarily increase costs for firms and that the creation of a truly single market, particularly with the advent of electronic commerce, requires that common standards for advertising be found.[6] This study simply accepts that the European Union has chosen to harmonise the law in relation to comparative advertising and sets out to offer a reading of its attempt to do so that is both logical and capable of implementation.

[5] Article 5(2) EC. Articles of the European Community Treaty are cited using the numbering adopted in the Treaty of Amsterdam.

[6] See also P. Spink and R. Petty, 'Comparative Advertising in the European Union' (1998) 47 *ICLQ* 855 at 856 and 875.

2

Comparative Advertising in the United Kingdom

Advertising, including comparative advertising, has been regulated in the United Kingdom in three ways. First, the Committee of Advertising Practice and the Advertising Standards Authority have provided for the self-regulation of advertising in all media excluding television and radio. This system of self-regulation is arguably the most important form of advertising regulation in the United Kingdom. Self-regulation and the industry-focussed system of statutory regulation governing advertising in television and radio are seen as preferable to more traditional legal regulation, because they distance the government from the control of speech and reduce the danger that the freedom of speech will unnecessarily be curtailed. Second, the common law has restrained advertising that constitutes passing off, injurious falsehood or defamation. Third, the legislature has created a complex system of civil and criminal actions to regulate advertising. It has also regulated the use of trade marks in advertising. While self-regulation has been the most important form of advertising regulation generally, and is thus the system of regulation with which this survey shall begin, trade mark law has probably been the most important constraint on comparative advertising practice.

This three-layered system of regulation is Byzantine in its complexity and uncertain in its effects. Simply to describe how the system works is a lengthy task. Moreover the reader may well be left, like many consumers and traders, uncertain whether any particular advertisement would or would not be unlawful and on what grounds. Nevertheless, the United Kingdom regulatory regimes must be set out, because they provide the context in which the Comparative Advertising Directive will be interpreted.

1. Self-Regulation

Self-regulation, which has a long tradition in United Kingdom commerce,[1] plays an essential role in advertising practice.[2] The two most important codes of advertising self-regulation are the British Codes of Adertising and Sales Promotion.[3] These lay down standards for advertising in all media other than television and radio and provide sanctions for their enforcement. The first British Code of Advertising Practice was introduced in 1961 and reflected the principles of the International Code of Advertising Practice issued by the International Chamber of Commerce.

The Advertising Code ('AC') and Code of Sales Promotion ('CSP') are monitored by the Committee of Advertising Practice ('CAP'), which consists of representatives of 22 participating media and advertising organisations, and the Advertising Standards Authority ('ASA'), which consists of individuals, at least half of whom are unconnected with the advertising business and who are chosen by the Chairman of the authority to reflect a diversity of backgrounds. CAP devises and amends the Codes and offers pre-publication advice on advertising. ASA investigates complaints received from any source and can identify problems in advertising through its own research and operate to resolve them. If a complaint is upheld, CAP and ASA jointly adminster a range of sanctions against the offending

---

[1] The first voluntary codes were introduced to regulate some professions at the end of the 19th century: see L. Brandmair, *Die Freiwillige Selbstkontrolle der Werbung* (Cologne, Carl Heymanns, 1978) at 35ff.

[2] G. Miracle and T. R. Nevett, *Voluntary Regulation of Advertising* (Lexington, Lexington Books, 1987), I. S. Blackshaw and G. Hogg, 'Comparative Advertising and Product Disparagement' [1992] *Media Law & Practice* 294 and L. Brandmair, *Die Freiwillige Selbstkontrolle der Werbung* (Cologne, Carl Heymanns, 1978) at 35ff.

[3] *British Codes of Advertising and Sales Promotion* 10th edn. (1999) See App I.

advertiser. As a first step, the advertiser is asked to withdraw the advertisement or to amend it. If the advertiser refuses to comply, the violation is brought to the attention of the relevant media associations, which, as a rule, refuse to publish the disputed advertisement. CAP and ASA also issue regular reports in which offenders are identified by name, expel members for violations of the codes and refer members to the Office of Fair Trading, the responsibilities of which are outlined below.[4]

AC and CSP are built upon four general principles: (i) that all advertisements should be legal, decent, honest and truthful, (ii) that all advertisements should be prepared with a sense of responsibility to consumers and to society, (iii) that all advertisements should respect the principles of fair competition accepted in business, and (iv) that no advertisement should bring advertising into disrepute.[5]

There are several specific rules of the AC that will directly impact on comparative advertising practice. Under rule 19.1, comparisons with a competitor's product are allowed 'in the interests of vigorous competition and public information'. Such comparisons should, however, be 'clear and fair'.[6] 'The elements of any comparison should not be selected in a way that gives the advertisers an artificial advantage.'[7] Under rule 3.1, an 'advertiser must hold documentary evidence to prove all claims, whether direct or implied, that are capable of objective substantiation'. Rule 20.1 provides that 'advertisers should not unfairly attack or discredit other businesses or their products' and, under rule 20.2, broken or defaced products may only be used in the illustration of comparative tests. Finally, rule 21.1 provides that 'advertisers should not make unfair use of the goodwill attached to the trade mark, name, brand or the advertising campaign of any other business'.

---

[4] See below at 16–17.
[5] *British Codes of Advertising and Sales Promotion* 10th edn. (1999) at 7.
[6] *Ibid.*, rule 19.2.
[7] *Ibid.*, rule 19.2.

2. Common Law[8]

(Comparative advertising is permissible at common law only as
long as it does not amount to passing off, injurious falsehood or
defamation.)

(a) Passing Off

In order to prove a case in passing off, a plaintiff must show (i)
that the products or services the plaintiff supplies to the public
enjoy a particular 'goodwill' in that they are recognised in the
market to be distinctively associated with him, (ii) a misrepresentation which, it is reasonably foreseeable, will damage that
goodwill, classically the misrepresentation that the defendant's
goods or services are those of the plaintiff, and (iii) actual damage to the plaintiff's goodwill or, in the case of *quia timet* relief,
the probability of such damage.[9]

Comparative advertising will not normally run the risk of
passing off, because the aim of such advertising is to distinguish
the goods or services of the advertiser from those of his competitor. Nevertheless, it is possible that a comparative advertisement might fail adequately to do so. One case in which it did
was *McDonald's Hamburgers Ltd.* v. *Burger King (UK) Ltd.*[10] In
this case Burger King had advertised one of its hamburgers with
the slogan, 'It's Not Just Big, Mac'. Whitford J, assisted by survey evidence, concluded that a majority of those at whom the
advertisement was directed would assume that the 'Big Mac'
was available at Burger King as well. On this basis Burger King

---

[8] The law outlined in this section is, of course, strictly the common law of
England rather than the United Kingdom. The law of Scotland and Northern
Ireland is not, however, substantially different and this section may be read as a
guide to the law of passing off, injurious falsehood and defamation in the United
Kingdom as a whole.

[9] See, for example, *Erven Warnink BV* v. *Townend & Sons Ltd.* [1980] RPC
31 at 93, *per* Lord Diplock and *Reckitt & Colman* v. *Borden* [1990] RPC 340 at
406, *per* Lord Oliver.

[10] [1986] FSR 45 See also *Kimberley-Clark Ltd.* v. *Fort Sterling Ltd.*, Ch. D,
21 Apr. 1997, Laddie J, unreported.

were found to have passed off their product as produced by McDonald's.

(b) Injurious Falsehood

If a comparative advertisement contains incorrect information about a competitor's goods, then the tort of injurious falsehood, also known as malicious falsehood, trade libel or slander of goods, may apply. This tort can be brought against any type of false claim; there is no limitation that the claim be made in the course of trade, nor does the tort require the existence of competitive relations between the plaintiff and the defendant.[11] However, the scope of injurious falsehood is rather narrow. Indeed, in any case also involving the use of a registered trade mark, an action for injurous falsehood is unlikely to be more successful than a claim for infringement of the trade mark. To plead both causes of action has therefore been criticised as wasteful.[12]

There are three requirements of the tort of injurious falsehood, each of which merits particular consideration. These are (i) that there has been a falsehood, (ii) that it was made maliciously, and (iii) that the plaintiff has suffered special damage.[13]

Consider first the requirement that there has been a falsehood. Two aspects of the falsehood requirement are particularly pertinent to the application of the tort to comparative advertising.

The first is the so-called 'one meaning' rule. This rule is that the statement about which complaint is made must be false on its 'ordinary and natural meaning', of which there can be only one. The fact that the statement could reasonably be interpreted by a substantial number of readers or listeners in a way that would render it false is insufficient.[14] The purpose of this rule is

[11] See, for example, *Kaye* v. *Robertson* [1991] FSR 62.

[12] *Cable & Wireless Plc* v. *British Telecommunications Plc* [1998] FSR 383 at 385, *per* Jacob J. This is because use of a competitor's trade mark to refer to his goods will *prima facie* constitute infringement. See below at 22.

[13] For a summary of the tort see *Kaye* v. *Robertson* [1991] FSR 62 at 67, *per* Glidewell J.

[14] See, for example, *Vodafone Group Plc* v. *Orange Personal Communications Services Ltd.* [1997] FSR 34.

difficult to understand, but it probably flows from the entitlement to a jury and the role of damages in defamation proceedings. However, as juries are no longer a part of injurious falsehood trials and the award of damages in injurious falsehood has rather different purpose from that which it has in the law of defamation, this relic of the relationship between injurious falsehood and defamation ought arguably to be abolished.[15]

The second aspect of the falsehood requirement which is particularly pertinent to the field of comparative advertising was given classic expression in the decision in *White* v. *Mellin*.[16] In *White* v. *Mellin* it was held that the statement must relate to the goods of the plaintiff. A false claim in relation to the defendant's own goods is not actionable. The courts have argued both that the general public is sceptical of advertising claims and that too close a scrutiny of comparative advertisements could confer an official 'seal of quality' on the product found to be superior, a 'seal of quality' that could itself be used for advertising purposes.[17]

This theoretically precise borderline between inaccurate claims about a trader's own products and claims about his rival's products becomes blurred in comparative advertising. A claim that one product is superior to another necessarily implies a claim that that second product is inferior to the first. But the courts have nevertheless shown confidence in their ability to draw the distinction. In *White* v. *Mellin* itself, the House of Lords dismissed an action brought by a baby food manufacturer against a retail trader who had affixed stickers to the manufacturer's products claiming that the trader's own products were considerably more nutritious.[18] Even the reproduction of a chemical comparison test suggesting that the defendant's colours were equal to or better than those of the plaintiff was

[15] This argument is made by Jacob J in *Vodafone Group Plc* v. *Orange Personal Communications Services Ltd.* [1997] FSR 34 at 38.

[16] [1895] AC 154. This decision was recently affirmed in *Schulke & Mayr UK Ltd.* v. *Alkapharm UK Ltd.* [1999] FSR 161.

[17] *White* v. *Mellin* [1895] AC 154 at 165, *per* Lord Herschell LC.

[18] *Ibid.*

considered in *Hubbuck* v. *Wilkinson* to be mere puffing of the defendant's own goods.[19] However the courts do seem prepared to categorise comparative statements as statements directed against the plaintiff's goods where a reasonable man would 'take the statement as being a serious claim'.[20] This will generally be true in the case of a substantiated statement, but not in the case of the mere claim that the defendant's products are 'better' than those of the plaintiff.[21] The more precise the claim is, the more likely it is that it will constitute an injurious falsehood.[22]

The second requirement for the action of injurous falsehood is that the defendant must have published the statement 'maliciously'. The term 'malice' has proved notoriously difficult to interpret.[23] Malice will definitely be established where it can be proved that the defendant either knew, or was reckless whether, the statement was false.[24] It may also be possible to prove malice regarding a statement that the defendant believed to be true, if it can also be established that he made the statement intending to injure the plaintiff.[25]

The third requirement for the action of injurious falsehood is that the plaintiff must show 'special damage'. Section 3 of the Defamation Act 1952 abrogates this requirement of proof of special damage wherever:

(a) . . . the words upon which the action is founded are calculated to cause pecuniary damage to the plaintiff and are published in writing or other permanent form or (b) . . . the said words are calculated to

[19] [1895] All ER 244. See, in particular, the judgment of Sir Nathanael Lindley MR at 247: '[i]t is not unlawful to say that one's own goods are better than other people's'.

[20] *De Beers Abrasive Products* v. *International General Electric Co of New York* [1975] FSR 323 at 329, *per* Walton J.

[21] *Ibid.*, at 329.

[22] *Vodafone Group Plc* v. *Orange Personal Communications Services Ltd.* [1997] FSR 34 at 39.

[23] 'This term has caused more confusion in English law than any judge can hope to dispel': *Shapiro* v. *La Morta* (1923) 40 TLR 201 at 203, *per* Scrutton LJ.

[24] See, for example, *McDonald's Hamburgers Ltd.* v. *Burger King (UK) Ltd.* [1986] FSR 45 at 61 and *Kaye* v. *Robertson* [1991] FSR 62 at 67.

[25] *Wilts United Dairies Ltd.* v. *Thomas Robinson* [1957] RPC 220 at 237.

cause pecuniary damage to the plaintiff in respect of any office, profession, calling, trade or business held or carried on by him at the time of the publication.

It is generally agreed that the requirement that the statement be 'calculated to cause pecuniary damage' to the plaintiff is an objective one and that any statement of which this is the probable effect will be actionable.[26]

It can be seen from this exposition of the requirements of injurious falsehood that the action is of a relatively narrow scope. Its effectiveness as a weapon against comparative advertising is even further reduced by the courts' approach to interlocutory injunctions in injurious falsehood cases.

The courts are reluctant to grant an interlocutory injunction to restrain an injurious falsehood if the defendant intends to plead justification.[27] The only situation in which an injunction will be granted readily is that in which no jury could consider the statement to be true.[28] Like the 'one meaning' rule, this reluctance was originally a consequence of the role of juries in deciding defamation cases. However, since *Bestobell* v. *Bigg*[29] the courts' reluctance to grant interlocutory injunctions in injurious falsehood cases has been justified by reference to the defendant's freedom of speech.[30] The impact of an injunction on the defendant's freedom of speech is treated as a part of the balance of justice under *American Cyanamid* v. *Ethicon*.[31] Where an action in malicious falsehood is successful, however, damages will be available even if the plaintiff has relied on section 3 of the

[25] For example, this was conceded by the parties in *Emaco* v. *Dyson Appliances Ltd.* 16 January 1999, Chancery Division, Parker J, unreported. See also *Customglass Boats* v. *Salthouse* [1976] RPC 589 at 603.

[26] *Bestobell Paints Ltd* v. *Bigg* [1975] FSR 421 at 430ff.

[28] *Kaye* v. *Robertson* [1991] FSR 62 at 67, *Compaq Computer Corporation* v. *Dell Computers Corporation Ltd.* [1992] FSR 93 at 100.

[29] [1975] FSR 421 at 431.

[30] *Consorzio del Proscuitto di Parma* v. *Marks & Spencer* [1990] F5R 530 at 536–8, [1991] RPC 351; *Compaq Computer Corporation* v. *Dell Computers Corporation Ltd.* [1992] FSR 93 at 104; *MacMillan Magazines Ltd.* v. *RCN Publishing Co. Ltd.* [1998] FSR 9 at 15.

[31] [1975] AC 396.

Defamation Act 1952.[32] Indeed, aggravated damages may well be available.[33]

(c) Defamation

Comparative advertising may sometimes also constitute defamation. In order for an action in defamation to lie a comparative advertisement would have to contain a statement which might tend 'to harm the reputation of [the competitor] so as to lower him or her in the estimation of the community or to defer third parties from associating or dealing with him or her'.[34] Defamation can protect trading companies as well as individuals.[35]

If a trader harmed by comparative advertising can bring an action in defamation, he will have two advantages over a trader who can bring an action only in injurious falsehood. First, rather than needing to prove the statements contained in the advertisement to be false, he need only prove that they had a tendency to lower his reputation. The defendant then bears the burden of raising one of the defences to defamation, such as that the statements were statements of opinion regarding a matter of public interest (the defence of 'fair comment') or that the statements were statements of fact and were true (the defence of 'justification'). Second, because juries are normally available in defamation trials, damages awards are often large. Such damages are not restricted to actual lost income, but can include compensation for damage to goodwill.[36]

However, notwithstanding these two advantages of the action for defamation, a trader harmed by comparative advertising needs also to remember four limitations on the application of the

---

[32] *Joyce* v. *Sengupta* [1993] 1 All ER 897.

[33] *Ibid.*, at 910–11, *per* Sir Michael Kerr.

[34] This definition is drawn from the American Law Institute's Restatement (Second) of Torts §559, but it has been commended as 'a workable test consistent with the [English] case law' (P. Milmo and W. V. H. Rogers, *Gatley on Libel and Slander* 9th edn. (London, Sweet & Maxwell, 1998) at 23.

[35] *South Hetton Coal Co.* v. *N-E News* [1894] 1 QB 133.

[36] *Lewis* v. *Daily Telegraph Ltd.* [1964] AC 234 at 262, *per* Lord Reid.

tort in this context. First, to be defamatory a statement must
constitute 'a personal imputation upon [the competitor], either
upon their character, or upon the mode in which their business
is carried on'.[37] Simply to disparage a rival trader's goods does
not give rise to an action for defamation. A passage from the
judgment of Lord Esher MR in *South Hetton Coal* v. *N-E News
Association*[38] is often used to illustrate this distinction:

> Suppose the plaintiff was a merchant who dealt in wine and it was
> stated that the wine which he had for sale of a particular vintage was
> not good wine; that might be so stated as only to import that the wine
> of the particular year was not good in whosoever hands it was, but not
> to imply any reflection on his conduct of his business. In that case the
> statement would be with regard to his goods only, and there would be
> no [defamation] although such as statement, if it were false and made
> maliciously, with intention to injure him, and it did injure him, might
> be made ths subject of an action [in injurious falsehood]. On the other
> hand, if the statement were so made as to import that his judgment in
> the selection of wine was bad, it might import a reflection on his con-
> duct in his business and show that he was an inefficient man of busi-
> ness. If so, it would be [defamatory]. In such a case a jury would have
> to say which sense the [statement] really bore; if they thought it related
> to the hoods only, they ought to find that it was not [defamatory]; but,
> if they thought that it related to the conduct of the man's business,
> they ought to find that it was [defamatory].

Second, the 'one meaning' rule applies to actions for defamation. In fact the rule was originally formulated in this context.[39]
Ironically, however, the rule may be of less importance to
actions for defamation than it is to actions for injurious falsehood. This is because juries are still normally available in
defamation trials and, when a statement is capable of bearing
several meanings, a judge must leave it to the jury to decide
which of them is to count as the 'one' meaning.[40] As the editors

[37] *Griffiths* v. *Benn* (1911) 27 TLR 346 at 350, *per* Cozens-Hardy MR.

[38] [1894] 1 QB 133 at 139.

[39] *Slim* v. *Daily Telegraph Ltd.* [1968] 2 QB 157 at 171–72 *per* Diplock LJ,
Charleston v. *News Group Ltd.* [1955] 2 AC 65 at 71, *per* Lord Bridge.

[40] *Hart* v. *Wall* (1877) 2 CPD 146 at 149, *per* Lord Coleridge CJ; *Cassidy* v.
Daily Mirror [1929] 2 KB 331 at 339, *per* Scrutton LJ.

of *Gatley on Libel and Slander* point out, 'since juries do not reveal their reasoning it may well be that some of them in fact find for the plaintiff on the same basis on which the case is left to them, namely that *some* people *might* rationally have understood the words in a defamatory sense, while others not'.[41]

Third, 'in the great majority of cases statements such as "A is better at . . . than B" will be so obviously expression of opinion within the scope of fair comment that no action will be brought.'[42] It may be that a comparative advertisement implies that the advertiser is 'better' at conducting his business than a competitor. Provided that this opinion is based upon true facts, the advertiser will be protected from an action in defamation even though it is prejudiced, exaggerated or obstinate.[43] As the Faulks Committee on Defamation put it: '[t]he adjective "Fair" in the phrase "Fair Comment" is seriously misleading having regard to the actual nature of the defence, which in reality protects *unfair* comments'.[44]

Fourth, just as in the context of injurious falsehood, the courts are reluctant to grant interlocutory injunctions against a defendant who intends to raise a defence of justification.[45]

In light of these limitations upon the application of the tort, defamation may be a more limited weapon against comparative advertising than it might initially appear.

---

[41] P. Milmo and W. V. H. Rogers, *Gatley on Libel and Slander* 9th edn. (London, Sweet & Maxwell, 1998) at 88.

[42] *Ibid.*, at 30.

[43] *Merivale* v. *Carson* (1887) 20 QBD 275 at 280, *per* Lord Esher MR. For an outline of the defence of fair comment see P. F. Carter-Ruck and H. N. A. Starte, *Carter-Ruck on Libel and Slander* 5th edn. (Butterworths, London, 1997), chap. 11.

[44] *Report of the Committee on Defamation*, Cmnd 5909 (1975).

[45] *Coulson* v. *Coulson* (1887) 3 TLR 846; *Bonnard* v. *Perryman* [1891] 2 Ch. 269 at 283, *per* Bowen and Lopes LJJ.

3. Statute

(a) Civil and Criminal Actions

Statute has created a web of civil and criminal actions to regulate the content of advertising. Rarely, these give consumers direct rights of action against the advertiser. For example, a consumer who enters into a contract with an advertiser on the basis of a misrepresentation may have an action for damages under the Misrepresentation Act 1967. More commonly, the civil and criminal actions that regulate advertising are enforced by one of four regulatory agencies.

First, each metropolitan borough and county or regional council has a Trading Standards Department. These departments have responsibility for overseeing the operation of about 70 Acts of Parliament, 800 regulations, 47 codes of practice and thousands of standards, many of which impact upon advertising practice. In particular, sections 1 and 14 of the Trade Descriptions Act 1968 prohibit false or misleading statements about goods and services and section 20 of the Consumer Protection Act 1987 prohibits misleading price indications. These sections can give rise to criminal prosecutions brought by the relevant local authority, although they cannot give rise to an action for breach of statutory duty brought by an individual.[46]

Second, the activity of the Trading Standards Departments is supplemented by the work of the Office of Fair Trading. Under regulation 4 of the Control of Misleading Advertisements Regulations 1988, enacted to implement Directive 84/450/EEC[47] ('the Misleading Advertising Directive'), the Director General of Fair Trading can receive complaints about misleading advertising. However, the jurisdiction of the Director General is only supplementary and he is unlikely to act unless the relevant Trading Standards Department or the ASA has first been approached. The Director General will ask an advertiser whom he believes to have breached the regulations to give an

[46] *H. P. Bulmer Ltd.* v. *Bollinger SA* [1978] RPC 79 at 110, *per* Buckley LJ.
[47] [1984] OJ L250/17.

undertaking that the deception will not be repeated. If the undertaking is either not given or subsequently not honoured, the Director General has standing to bring an action in the High Court seeking an injunction to prevent the advertiser from continuing with the advertisement.

Third, neither the Trading Standards Departments, the ASA, nor the Director General of Fair Trading has jurisdiction over advertisements played on commercial television or radio stations. In relation to this type of advertising, the Broadcasting Act 1990[48] imposes a statutory duty upon the Independent Television Commission ('ITC') and the Radio Authority ('RA') to draw up, and regularly to review, codes of practice. The ITC Code of Advertising Standards and Practice ('ITCC') and the Radio Authority Advertising and Sponsorship Code ('RAC') impose an obligation upon a television or radio broadcast licensee to ensure that any advertising its station carries complies with the relevant code.[49] The ITC and the RA can enforce the codes in a number of ways. They can, for example, order the withdrawal of an advertisement or the issue of an apology, impose a fine or even revoke a broadcasting licence.[50] The ITC and RA do not give pre-broadcast advice on the compliance of an advertisement, but recommend the services of two approved organisations, the Broadcast Advertising Clearance Centre and the Radio Advertising Clearance Centre. The ITC and RA do, however, give licensees advice on the interpretation of the relevant codes.

The basic principles underpinning the ITCC and RAC reflect those of the AC and CSP. Both codes require that advertising be 'legal, decent, honest and truthful'.[51] Both codes confirm the legitimacy of comparative advertising 'in the interest of vigorous

[48] Broadcasting Act 1990, ss. 9(1) and 93(1).

[49] Independent Television Commission, *The ITC Code of Advertising Standards and Practice* (Autumn 1998) at iii and Radio Authority, *Advertising and Sponsorship Code* (March 1997) at 2. See App. I.

[50] Broadcasting Act 1990, ss. 9(6), 9(7), 40, 41, 42, 93(6), 93(7), 109, 110 and 111.

[51] ITCC at 1 and RAC at 2.

competition and public information'.[52] Both codes contain specific provisions regulating comparative advertising that are equivalent to those contained in the AC. Comparative advertising may not be misleading or give the advertiser 'artifical advantage'. Comparisons must be based on 'fairly selected facts which can be substantiated'.[53] The ITCC expands this requirement to explain that comparisons must be of like with like and that 'generalised superiority claims must not be made on the basis of selective comparisons'.[54] Both codes provide that price comparisons must comply with the requirements of the Consumer Protection Act 1987 (Section III) against misleading price claims.[55] Finally, both codes provide that advertisements must not unfairly attack or discredit a competitor, his products or services.[56] The notes to the RAC claim that '[w]hilst it is acceptable of an advertiser whose product has a demonstrable advantage over a competitor to point this out, care must be taken to ensure that the competitor product is not depicted as generally unsatisfactory or inferior'.[57] The possible meaning of this puzzling comment is further discussed below, when the concept of 'denigration' is explored in the context of Article 3a(1)(e) of the Comparative Advertising Directive.[58]

(b) Trade Mark and Comparative Advertising

The extent to which a competitor's registered trade mark may be used in comparative advertising largely determines the legality of comparative advertising in which a competitor's product is explicitly identified. For this reason such advertising was almost unknown in the United Kingdom while the Trade Marks Act 1938 remained in force. The Trade Marks Act 1994 has significantly liberalised the law in relation to the use of trade marks

[52] ITCC rule 26 and RAC rule 14.
[53] ITCC rule 26 and RAC rule 14.
[54] ITCC rule 26.
[55] ITCC rule 25 and RAC rule 13.
[56] ITCC rule 27 and RAC rule 15.
[57] RAC at 9.
[58] See below at 80.

in comparative advertising, however, and explicit comparative advertising is becoming more common.

(i) Trade Marks Act 1938 section 4(1)

Section 4(l) of the Trade Marks Act 1938 listed the acts that amounted to infringement of a registered mark. A registered trade mark could be infringed by affixing the mark, or one nearly resembling it, to goods so as to suggest that they originated with the trade mark owner. A Part A mark—a mark which was 'adapted to distinguish', rather than merely 'capable of distinguishing' the trade mark owner's goods[59]—could also be infringed by 'importing a reference'.[60] Section 4(3)(b) provided an exception to liability for importing a reference where the reference was to indicate the compatibility of spare parts or accessories. Potential liability for importing a reference was obviously a great restraint on comparative advertising in which a competitor's product was explicitly identified.

The inclusion of liability for importing a reference in section 4 was the result of the decision of the House of Lords in *Irving's Yeast-Vite Ltd.* v. *F. A. Horsenail*[61] and the subsequent report of the Goschen Committee. In the *Yeast-Vite* decision, the House of Lords had decided that liability for infringement under the Trade Marks Act 1905 could only be found where there had been use of mark to indicate a connection between the party using the mark and particular goods. Thus an advertisement which read 'Yeast tablets—a substitute for Yeast-Vite' was not an infringement of the 'Yeast-Vite' mark. However, the Goschen Committee[62] argued that the *Yeast-Vite* decision was unsatisfactory as it enabled an advertiser to exploit the goodwill associated with a competitor's mark. The committee claimed that even when there was no risk of confusion, the trade mark

[59] Trade Marks Act 1938 ss. 9(2) and 10(1).

[60] *Ibid.*, s. 4(1)(b). On this provision see A. Ohly, 'Die vergleichende Werbung im britischen Recht' *GRUR Int.* 1993, 730 at 731ff.

[61] (1934) 51 RPC 110.

[62] *Report of the Departmental Committee on the Law and Practice Relating to Trade Marks* (London, HMSO, 1934), Cmnd. 4568 at point 184.

owner had to be protected against parasitic advertising. Without further analysis of the issue, the report went on to suggest draft legislation that was included in the Trade Marks (Amendment) Act 1937 and then again in the Trade Marks Act 1938.

Two years after the new law had been adopted, the Court of Appeal had to determine its operation in relation to comparative advertising in *Bismag Ltd.* v. *Amblins (Chemists) Ltd.*[63] In this case, the plaintiff was the owner of the 'bisurated' mark for magnesia tablets. The defendant advertised his product, 'bismuthated' magnesia tablets, in a list in which they were compared with 'bisurated' magnesia tablets. The advertisement claimed that the preparations were essentially the same, but that the defendant's product was cheaper. The court decided by a majority that, despite its unclear wording, section 4(1)(b) prohibited any use of a competitor's trade mark that was intended to identify the trade mark owner's goods. Some doubt was cast upon this decision by several members of the House of Lords in *Aristoc Ld.* v. *Rysta Ld.*,[64] but it was subsequently repeatedly affirmed.[65]

Three limitations upon the potentially rather strict operation of section 4(1)(b) were, however, to be imposed by the courts. First, in *M. Ravok (Weatherwear) Ltd.* v. *National Trade Press Ltd.*[66] it was held that section 4(1)(b) only applied where there had been both 'use' of the trade mark and use in the course of trade in goods for which the mark had been registered. Thus the inclusion of the mark in a trade directory, consumer survey or similar publication could not constitute infringement. This exception did not apply to comparative advertising, however, because use of a competitor's trade mark in comparative advertising almost always constituted use in the course of trade in

---

[63] (1940) 57 RPC 209.

[64] (1945) 62 RPC 65 at 79, 82 and 85.

[65] See, for example, *British Northrop Ltd.* v. *Texteam Blackburn Ltd.* [1974] RPC 75; *News Group Newspapers Ltd.* v. *Mirror Group Newspapers (1986) Ltd.* [1989] FSR 126; and *Chanel Ltd.* v. *Triton Packaging Ltd.* [1993] RPC 32.

[66] [1955] 1 All ER 621.

competing goods. Second, use of the trade mark had also to be use 'in a trade mark sense'[67]: the mark had to be used to indicate a connection between the registered proprietor and his goods. Thus, in one case in which a trade mark registered for audio recordings was used as the title to a song on a competing recording, there was some question whether the use constituted importing a reference.[68] In *Mars GB Ltd.* v. *Cadbury Ltd.*[69] the use of the expression 'Treat Size' to describe confectionery did not infringe the mark 'TREETS' registered for the same class of goods. However, again this limitation did not save comparative advertising that used a competitor's mark from infringement as importing a reference. In a comparative advertisement the mark is being used precisely to indicate a connection between the mark and its proprietor. Third, in *Pompadour Laboratories* v. *Frazer*[70] it was held that the use of a mark could not constitute importing a reference if it was merely used as a part of the trade mark owner's company name.[71] In one case the use of the trade mark as a part of a company's name on a swing tag for clothing was held not to be use of the trade mark for the purposes of an action for revocation, even though the part of the name that constituted the trade mark was 'in bigger, bolder and more prominent type than the rest of the' name and even though the name as a whole was arranged in such a way that it could be read continuously neither clockwise nor anti-clockwise.[72] Thus, while 'Pepsi is better than Coca-Cola' would have constituted importing a reference, it seems that 'Pepsi is better than the

---

[67] *Bismag Ld.* v. *Amblins (Chemists) Ld.* (1940) 57 RPC 209 at 234, *per* Sir Wilfrid Greene MR.

[68] *News Group Newspapers Ltd.* v. *The Rocket Record Co. Ltd.* [1981] FSR 89 at 99–101, *per* Slade J.

[69] [1987] RPC 387.

[70] [1966] RPC 7.

[71] *Autodrome Trade Mark* [1969] RPC 564 at 573; *Harrods Ltd.* v. *Schwartz-Sackin & Co. Ltd.* [1986] FSR 490; *News Group Newspapers Ltd.* v. *Mirror Group Newspapers (1986) Ltd.* [1989] FSR 126; and *Mattel Inc.* v. *Tonka Corporation* [1992] FSR 28.

[72] *Orient Express Trade Mark* [1996] RPC 25.

drink manufactured by the Coca-Cola Company Ltd' would not have.[73]

(ii) Trade Marks Act 1994 section 10(6)

That these three exceptions were the only exceptions to liability for importing a reference under the Trade Marks Act 1938 shows just how dramatic a liberalisation of the law in relation to comparative advertising came with section 10(6) of the Trade Marks Act 1994, the United Kingdom legislation implementing Directive 89/104/EEC ('the Trade Marks Directive'). This liberalisation has been even further carried forward with the interpretation that the section has so far received in the courts.

Section 10(1) of the Trade Marks Act 1994 provides that it is an infringement of a registered mark to use it in relation to goods identical to those for which the trade mark is registered. 'Use in relation to goods' includes use in advertising. There is some question whether this section is limited by requirements that the trade mark be 'used',[74] and used in a trade mark sense.[75] But whether or not these limitations apply, most comparative advertising using a competitor's mark would *prima facie* infringe that mark under section 10(1).

The effect of section 10(1) is, however, mitigated by section 10(6).[76] Section 10(6) is derived neither from European Union, nor from international, law. It reads:

> Nothing in the preceding provisions of this section shall be construed as preventing the use of a registered trade mark by any person for the purpose of identifying goods or services as those of the proprietor or a licensee.

[73] See *Duracell International Ltd.* v. *Ever-Ready Ltd.* [1989] FSR 71 at 80–3 and the form of the injunction issued in *Compaq Computer Corporation* v. *Dell Computer Corporation* [1992] FSR 93 at 109.

[74] *Trebor Bassett Limited* v. *The Football Association* [1997] FSR 211.

[75] See *Bravado Merchandising Services Ltd.* v. *Mainstream Publishing (Edinburgh) Ltd.* [1996] FSR 205; *British Sugar Plc* v. *James Robertson & Sons Ltd.* [1996] RPC 281; *Philips Electronics BV* v. *Remington Consumer Products* [1998] RPC 283; and *British Telecommunications Plc* v. *One in a Million Ltd.* [1999] FSR 1.

[76] Section 11(2) of the Trade Marks Act 1994 may also operate to save some comparative advertisments. See below at 55.

But any such use otherwise than in accordance with honest practices in industrial and commercial matters shall be treated as infringing the registered trade mark if the use without due cause takes unfair
advantage of, or is detrimental to, the distinctive character or repute
of the trade mark.

The effect of the section has been determined by two decisions of the High Court, *Barclays Bank Plc* v. *RBS Advanta*[77]
and *Vodafone Group Plc* v. *Orange Personal Communications
Services Ltd.*[78] These decisions were summarised, and a gloss
upon them added, in *British Telecommunications Plc* v. *A T & T
Communications (UK) Ltd.*[79] in a passage which has subsequently been approved.[80] The summary constitutes the first
nine of 13 points made in *British Telecommunications Plc* v.
A T & T Communications (UK) Ltd. and the gloss constitutes a
further four:

(1) The primary objective of s 10(6) . . . is to permit comparative
advertising . . .

(2) As long as the use of a competitor's mark is honest, there is
nothing wrong in telling the public of the relative merits of competing goods or services and using registered trade marks to identify
them . . .

(3) The onus is on the registered proprietor to show that the factors
indicated in the proviso to s 10(6) exist . . .

(4) There will be no trade mark infringement unless the use of the
registered mark is not in accordance with honest practices . . .

(5) The test is objective: would a reasonable reader be likely to say,
upon being given the full facts, that the advertisement is not honest?
. . .

(6) Statutory or industry agreed codes of conduct are not a helpful
guide as to whether an advertisement is honest for the purpose of
s 10(6). Honesty has to be gauged against what is reasonably to be
expected by the relevant public of advertisements for the goods or
services in issue . . .

---

[77] [1996] RPC 307 at 313. See App. I.

[78] [1997] FSR 34. See App. I.

[79] Ch. D, 18 Dec. 1996, Mr Crystal QC, unreported. See App. I.

[80] *Cable & Wireless Plc* v. *British Telecommunications Plc* [1998] FSR 383. See
App. I.

(7) It should be borne in mind that the general public are used to the ways of advertisers and expects hyperbole . . .

(8) The 1994 Act does not impose on the courts an obligation to try and enforce through the back door of trade mark legislation a more puritanical standard than the general public would expect from advertising copy . . .

(9) An advertisement which is significantly misleading is not honest for the purposes of s10(6) . . .

(10) The advertisement must be considered as a whole . . .

(11) As the purpose of the 1994 Act is positively to permit comparative advertising, the court should not hold words used in the advertisement to be seriously misleading for the purposes unless on a fair reading of them in their context and against the background of the advertisement as a whole they can really be said to justify that description . . .

(12) A minute textual examination is not something upon which the reasonable reader of an advertisement would embark . . .

(13) The court should therefore not encourage a microscopic approach to the construction of a comparative advertisement on a motion for interlocutory relief.

In _Cable & Wireless Plc_ v. _British Telecommunications Plc_[81] Jacob J further refined the notion of honesty for the purposes of the proviso. Jacob J was concerned with the situation in which a claim had been carefully researched by an advertiser before publication but subsequently proved untrue. In this situation Jacob J held that, although the test of honesty was objective and a misleading claim would not normally be an honest one, the advertiser would not be liable for trade mark infringement unless he persisted with the claim after he knew that it was false. If this approach to the requirement of honesty is accepted, points 5 and 9 of the summary offered in _British Telecommunications Plc_ v. _A T & T Communications (UK) Ltd._[82] might then be replaced with the test of 'whether a reasonable trader could honestly have made the statements [the advertiser] made based upon the information that he had'.[83]

[81] _Ibid._
[82] Ch. D, 18 Dec. 1996, Mr Crystal QC, unreported.
[83] _Cable & Wireless Plc_ v. _British Telecommunications Plc_ [1998] FSR 383 at

It is clear that in reading section 10(6) the courts have been keen to liberalise the law in relation to comparative advertising. First, they have collapsed the proviso to the protection offered under the section into a requirement of 'honesty'. Second, they have elided honesty and truthfulness. It is true that both Laddie J in *Barclays Bank Plc* v. *RBS Advanta*[84] and Jacob J in *Vodafone Group Plc* v. *Orange Personal Communications Services Ltd.*[85] speak of a misleading advertisement as merely an 'example' of one that is not honest, but no other type of dishonesty is discussed in the cases. Indeed, Jacob J sums up the proviso to section 10(6) by saying, '[i]f the slogan is misleading there will be infringement'.[86] It is difficult to imagine a situation in which the courts, in their current frame of mind, would regard an advertisement which is not misleading[87] as neverthless dishonest and therefore not protected by section 10(6).

This is indeed a cavalier reading of the section. The proviso to section 10(6) is arguably concerned not only with behaviour that constitutes misrepresentation, but also with behaviour that constitutes 'dilution' of the mark. Dilution consists in harm to the mark which occurs either (i) because it is repeatedly used by others in a way that causes it to lose its distinctiveness as associated with the trade mark owner and his goods (this is normally use that involves taking unfair advantage of the reputation of the trade mark), or (ii) because it becomes in some way 'tarnished' by its use in an inappropriate context (this is a type of denigration of the mark). However, as suggested at the outset of this study, all comparative advertising is somewhat prone to take unfair advantage of a competitor's goodwill, and hence his mark,

---

391, *per* Jacob J. The issue of which approach to honesty is to be followed was left open in the only subsequent decision to address the issue, *Emaco Ltd.* v. *Dyson Appliances Ltd.*, Ch. D, 26 Jan. 1999, Parker J, unreported. See App. I.

[84] [1996] RPC 307 at 315.

[85] [1997] FSR 34 at 39.

[86] *Ibid.*, at 40.

[87] Or at least not published by a trader who had inadequate grounds to believe its truthfulness. See *Cable & Wireless Plc* v. *British Telecommunications Plc* [1998] FSR 383 at 390–1, *per* Jacob J.

or to denigrate them. Claims of equivalence might unfairly appropriate goodwill. Critical claims might constitute denigration. The task of deciding which types of comparative advertising fall foul of these standards and which do not is a difficult one that is considered more fully below.[88] But, however difficult, it is not a task that can simply be ignored by claiming that the words 'takes unfair advantage of, or is detrimental to, the distinctive character or repute of the trade mark' in section 10(6) add nothing to the requirement of honesty. It will be interesting, therefore, to see how the United Kingdom courts respond to the comparative advertising directive in which notions of 'denigration' and 'taking unfair advantage' figure so prominently.

4. Conclusion

From the preceding sections it can be seen that comparative advertising is a highly regulated activity in the United Kingdom even without considering the impact of the Comparative Advertising Directive. This is important to emphasise because many Continental writers have, not surprisingly, confused the law of the United Kingdom with that of the United States and have imagined that the legal systems of both countries have a similarly permissive attitude towards comparative advertising. In reading this survey of the United Kingdom regulatory systems, many readers will be surprised to find standards against misleading comparative advertising, and even comparative advertising that is denigrating or takes unfair advantage of a competitor's reputation, that reflect similar concerns to those underpinning the pre-Directive regulatory systems of countries such as Germany. The United Kingdom approach to comparative advertising has certainly been more permissive than the German approach, but not as permissive as many have made out.

This does not mean, however, that the United Kingdom regulatory systems have adopted a coherent or defensible approach

[88] See below at 76 ff.

to the problems of misleading comparative advertising and comparative advertising that denigrates or takes unfair advantage of a competitor's reputation. The principal difficulty with the current situation in the United Kingdom is that the sources of law regulating comparative advertising, and the agencies to enforce it, are so various that the situation remains unclear for both consumers and traders. Moreover those standards themselves are often cast in extremely vague terms.

That this uncertainty has not created great problems for traders may be attributed to two things. First, the restrictive effect of the Trade Marks Act 1938, together with wariness of the negative effects of comparative advertising,[89] has meant that comparative advertising in which a competitor is explicitly identified has been extremely rare in the United Kingdom. Such advertising is, however, becoming more common as a result of the liberalisation of trade mark law represented by section 10(6) of the Trade Marks Act 1994. Second, although comparative advertising in which the competitor is only implicitly identified has been very frequent, it is so much a part of the advertising landscape that it has rarely led to complaint. This will not necessarily be the case, however, once the Directive is implemented. The Comparative Advertising Directive has an enormous potential to impact upon this rather fragile balance of uncertain standards and apparently agreed practice.

[89] For a summary of the literature see T. E. Barry, 'Comparative Advertising: What Have We Learned in Two Decades?' [1993] *Journal of Advertising Research* 19.

3
Comparative Advertising in Germany

At least initially, the German law on comparative advertising seems less complex than its United Kingdom counterpart because it is contained in one single piece of legislation, the *Gesetz gegen den unlauteren Wettbewerb*[1] ('UWG'). The UWG is the legal basis of the German law of unfair competition, a specific branch of tort law. The legal regulation of comparative advertising falls within different provisions of the UWG. The most important provision for the regulation of comparative advertising is §1 of the UWG, the general tort of unfair competition, which will be considered in more detail below. In addition, §14 of the UWG, which resembles the general provisions against defamation in §824 of the *Bürgerliches Gesetzbuch*[2] ('BGB') and §186 of the *Strafgesetzbuch*[3] ('StGB'), provides for the protection against defamation of a trader, his goods or services. Unlike British law, the UWG also contains a private law tort of misleading advertising in §3. This provision has been particularly effective against misleading advertising because it is available both to individual competitors and also to trade and consumer organisations.[4]

This regulation of comparative advertising in the UWG has traditionally been seen as comprehensive. In principle, the general private law torts might also apply to comparative advertising.[5] Unlike the UWG, their ambit is not restricted to acts made

[1] Act against Unfair Competition.
[2] Civil Code.
[3] Criminal Code.
[4] UWG §13 II.
[5] §§823–826 BGB.

for the purpose of competition. However, comparative advertising will almost always satisfy this requirement, and so the provisions of the BGB do not provide for additional relief in situations not covered by the UWG. The protection against defamation afforded by §§824, 823 II[6] and 823 I BGB is not broader than that given by §14 UWG. The German equivalents to the common law tort of passing off are found in trade mark law which, for reasons discussed in the following paragraph, has traditionally been no bar to comparative advertising, and in unfair competition law.[7] Similarly, criminal law does not play any role in the control of comparative advertising. In particular, §3 of the UWG grants only a civil right of action against misleading advertising. §4 UWG, which provides for criminal sanctions against certain types of misleading advertising, is rarely applied in practice.

Finally, trade mark law has traditionally had little role to play in the regulation of comparative advertising, although this may change as a result of the reforms effected by the trade marks directive. The old German *Warenzeichengesetz*[8] required a mark to be used in a 'trade mark sense' for the use to constitute infringement. However the concept of 'trade mark use' was narrower than the concept for which the same term was used in United Kingdom law. A potential infringer had to be using the mark to indicate a connection in the course of trade between the mark and *his own* goods.[9] In the explanatory memorandum to

[6] §823 II of the BGB functions in a way comparable to the common law tort of breach of statutory duty. The section applies when the defendant has violated a statutory duty and when this duty is intended to protect the plaintiff. Protection against defamation is granted by §823 II of the BGB in connection with §§185–187 of the StGB.

[7] Only in exceptional circumstances will a misrepresentation about the origin of goods or services constitute misleading advertising under §3 of the UWG (unless such a misrepresentation relates to a geographical indication). However such a representation may be caught by the general tort of unfair competition (§1 of the UWG).

[8] Trade Marks Act (1968).

[9] *Bohnergerät* BGH GRUR 1958, 343 at 344. See A. Baumbach and W. Hefermehl, *Warenzeichenrecht* 12th edn. (Munich, Beck, 1985) at §15, para. 22ff and 42 and R. Ingerl and C. Rohnke, *Markengesetz* (Munich, Beck, 1998) at §14 para. 89.

the trade marks legislation implementing the Trade Marks Directive, the *Markengesetz*, the government expressed the view that this condition still applied and that comparative advertising was therefore outside the ambit of trade mark law.[10] Whether this is in fact the case is discussed below when the exclusivity of the Comparative Advertising Directive is considered.[11] At any rate, the drafters of the *Markengesetz* did not consider it necessary to provide for a specific exception to infringement comparable to section 10(6) of the Trade Marks Act 1994. Hitherto there have been no reported cases and hardly any literature on the application of the *Markengesetz* to comparative advertising.[12]

1. The History of §1 UWG

The law of unfair competition has an interesting history. In the mid-nineteenth century some regional courts were prepared to grant protection against unfair competition. In doing so they relied upon §1382 of the French civil code which applied in some western parts of Germany and provides that anyone who causes another damage is liable in damages. However the Reichsgericht, the highest court in Germany between 1879 and 1945, ruled that no such protection could be granted.[13] The court argued that, by introducing intellectual property legislation, the legislature had clearly shown that it did not intend to grant any further rights. This position was widely criticised,[14] and the legislature responded to that criticism by passing the first UWG in 1896.

The first UWG contained specific provisions such as those now contained in §3 and §14, but no general tort of unfair competition. This was widely seen as a deficiency. Kohler compared

---

[10] *Bundestagsdrucksache* Nr 12/6581 of 14 Jan. 1994 at §14, para. 7.

[11] See below at 54.

[12] For references to the recent literature see below at 00.

[13] RGZ 3, 67; 18, 93; 20, 71.

[14] J. Kohler, *Der unlautere Wettbewerb* (Berlin, Rothschild, 1914) at 57ff and A. Baumbach, *Kommentar zum Wettbewerbsrecht* (Berlin, Liebmann, 1929) at 123.

unfair competition to a Proteus which adopts a thousand forms to bypass specific rules.[15] After the BGB entered into force in 1900, the Reichsgericht restrained some acts of unfair competition on the basis of §826, which provides protection against the deliberate causation of harm in a way in which offends '*die guten Sitten*'.[16] However, the requirement that the harm be deliberately caused proved a limitation on the applicability of §826. Finally, in 1909 the legislature intervened again. The UWG was restructured and a general tort of unfair competition was introduced as §1 of the new Act. This provision has not been changed since. It runs:

> §1 *Wer im geschäftlichen Verkehr zu Zwecken des Wettbewerbs Handlungen vornimmt, die gegen die guten Sitten verstoßen, kann auf Unterlassung und Schadensersatz in Anspruch genommen werden.*[17]

In debates leading to the passing of this legislation it was disputed whether the use of the vague concept of '*gute Sitten*' was appropriate.[18] Some speakers argued that this sweeping provision would give too much discretion to the judiciary. The majority, however, was convinced that honesty in the market place could only be achieved if the law contained a flexible provision which could not easily be circumvented.

At first sight, §1 of the UWG does seem difficult to apply. Around 1900 a certain code of honest practices may have existed among traders, but with the growing complexity of economic relations and an ever-diminishing consensus about matters of morality the quest for standards of honesty seems to be futile. It may therefore seem surprising that nobody in Germany

[15] J. Kohler, *Das Recht des Markenschutzes* (Würzburg, Stahel'sche Universitätsbuchhandlung, 1884) at 60.

[16] 'Honest practices'.

[17] 'Any person who, in the course of trade and for purposes of competition, commits acts contrary to honest practices may be enjoined from continuing in those acts and held liable in damages.' See App II.

[18] On the parliamentary debates about unfair competition of 1909 see A. Ohly, *Richterrecht und Generalklausel im Recht des unlauteren Wettbewerbs—ein Methodenvergleich des englischen und des deutschen Rechts* (Cologne, Carl Heymanns, 1997) at 202ff.

seriously advocates the abolition of the tort of unfair competition.[19] The reason for this striking unanimity is probably a methodological one. Statute-based legal systems and common law systems are often seen as polar extremes. §1 of the UWG is a good example of how the differences between the systems are often exaggerated.[20] Within the broad framework provided by statute the courts have developed an extensive case law. Neither lawyers presenting their cases, nor courts in their judgments, argue about notions of fairness. Instead they apply precedent in a way strongly reminiscent of common law practice.[21] Cases are applied or distinguished, and over time general principles emerge. Thus, under the umbrella of §1 there is today a number of categories of unfair practice which can be restrained by the courts. These categories cover various types of unfair conduct including taking unfair advantage of a competitor's goodwill and denigration.

2. The Application of §1 UWG to Comparative Advertising

Unfair comparative advertising constitutes a particular category of proscription under §1 of the UWG.[22] The relevant cases go

[19] The Bundesverfassungsgericht held in BVerfGE 32, 311 at 317 that §1 of the UWG was constitutional. The uncertainty of the wording had to be tolerated, because the many forms of possible unfair competition demanded a flexible provision. The court also pointed out that the uncertainty was diminished by the large number of judgments in which the superior courts had applied the section.

[20] See H. Kötz, 'Taking Civil Codes Less Seriously' (1987) 50 *MLR* 1.

[21] See A. Ohly, *Richterrecht und Generalklausel im Recht des unlauteren Wettbewerbs—ein Methodenvergleich des englischen und des deutschen Rechts* (Cologne, Carl Heymanns, 1991) at 253ff and F. K. Beier, 'The Law of Unfair Competition in the European Community—Its Development and Present Status' [1985] *EIPR* 284 at 291.

[22] On comparative advertising in German law before the Directive see generally: J. Meyer, *Die kritisierende vergleichende Werbung* (Regensburg, Roderer, 1991); H. Köhler and H. Piper, *Gesetz gegen den unlauteren Wettbewerb* (Munich, Beck, 1995) at §1 para. 129ff; Z. Gülbay, *Vergleichende Werbung, Subsidiarität und Europa* (Berlin, Verlag, 1997); B. Hartlage, *Vergleichende Werbung in*

back to the early 1930s. In its *Hellegold* decision of 1931,[23] the Reichsgericht held that comparative advertising would normally be contrary to honest business practices. The court advanced two arguments. First, no trader had to suffer being used as a competitor's promotional tool. Second, nobody could be a judge in his own cause. In subsequent decisions the court recognised four exceptions to this rule.[24] First, comparisons were allowed if they referred to different methods of manufacture or different systems of distribution rather than to particular products (a '*Systemvergleich*').[25] Second, comparative advertising was considered legal if it was the only way to inform consumers about a technological advance (a '*Fortschrittsvergleich*').[26] Third, a trader was allowed to answer when a customer explicitly asked for a comparison (an '*Auskunftsvergleich*').[27] Fourth, comparative advertising was permitted as a means of self-defence (an '*Abwehrvergleich*').[28]

After 1945, the Bundesgerichtshof, the highest court in modern Germany, retained the general prohibition while gradually extending the exceptions. By 1961 the law had reached the stage where the different exceptions could be generalised.[29] From

England und Deutschland (Munich, VVF, 1997); A. Baumbach and W. Hefermehl, *Wettbewerbsrecht* 20th edn. (Munich, Beck, 1998) at §1 para. 329ff; W. Gloy and D. Bruhn, 'Die Zulässigkeit von Preisvergleichen nach der Richtlinie 97/55/EG—Kehrtwende oder Kontinuität?' *GRUR* 1988, 226 at 227ff; U. Doepner and F. Hufnagel, 'German Courts Implement the EU Directive 97/55/EC—A Fundamental Shift in the Law on Comparative Advertising?' (1999) 88 *TMR* 1.

[23] RG GRUR 1931, 1299.

[24] For an overview see H. Droste, 'Das Verbot der bezugnehmenden Werbung und die Ausnahmefälle' *GRUR* 1951, 140 at 142ff and B. Hartlage, *Vergleichende Werbung in England und Deutschland* (Munich, VVF, 1997) at 19ff.

[25] *Gesenkhammer*, RG GRUR 1933, 256 at 257; *Dauerdose*, BGH GRUR 1952, 416 at 417.

[26] *Floating Power*, RG 1937, 941 at 945, *Bohnergerät*, BGH 1958, 343 at 344.

[27] *Buchgemeinschaft*, RG MuW 1927/28, 345; *Backhilfsmittel*, BGH GRUR 1967, 308 at 310.

[28] *Holzimprägnierungsmittel*, RG GRUR 1936, 813 at 816; *Bünder Glas* BGH GRUR 1957, 23 at 24.

[29] *Betonzusatzmittel*, BGH GRUR 1962, 45 at 48.

then on, comparative advertising was not considered unfair if the advertiser had a reasonable cause for the comparison and if the comparison did not exceed the limits of what was necessary to reach this aim.[30] When deciding whether a 'reasonable cause' existed or whether a comparison was 'necessary' the courts continued to refer to individual precedents. As the need to provide consumers with useful information became increasingly accepted as a 'reasonable cause', some writers doubted whether the prohibition of comparative advertising could still be considered as the rule or whether it had actually become the exception.[31] However, for two reasons the better view seems to be that comparisons were still *prima facie* regarded as unfair until 1998. First, the advertiser had to plead that he had a sufficient cause.[32] Second, in practice both the Bundesgerichtshof and the appeal courts applied the reasonable cause exception in a rather restrictive way. Increasingly, academic writers began to challenge this practice and advocated liberalisation.[33]

While the first Reichsgericht decisions did not distinguish between different types of comparative advertising, Nerreter[34]

---

[30] *Tauchkühler*, BGH GRUR 1970, 422 at 423; *Vorsatz-Fensterflügel*, BGH GRUR 1986, 618 at 620; and *Generikum-Preisvergleich*, BGH GRUR 1989, 688 at 689.

[31] See R. Sack, *GRUR* 1987, 51 and A. Baumbach and W. Hefermehl, *Wettbewrebsrecht* 20th edn., (Munich, Beck, 1998) at §1 para. 335.

[32] There is some dispute about the question whether the Directive changes the onus of proof. While the Oberlandesgericht Frankfurt has held that the old rule still applies (Pharma Recht 1998, 322 at 324), most writers argue that under the Directive the plaintiff must show that a particular comparison is prohibited: see W. Gloy and D. Bruhn, 'Die Zulässigkeit von Preisvergleichen nach der Richtlinie 97/55/EG—Kehrtwende oder Kontinuität?' *GRUR* 1998, 226 at 238 and C. Plassmann, 'Vergeichende Werbung im Gemeinsamen Markt' *GRUR* 1996, 377 at 381.

[33] See M. Kloepfer and G. Michael, 'Vergeichende Werbung und Verfassung' *GRUR* 1991, 170; J. Meyer, *Die kritisierende vergleichende Werbung* (Regensburg, Roderer, 1991) at 123ff; G. Schricker, 'Zur Werberechtspolitik der EG—Liberalisierung und Restriktion im Widerstreit' *GRUR* 1992, *Int.* 347 at 352; V. Emmerich, *Recht des unlauteren Wettbewerbs* (Munich, Beck, 1995) at 118ff.

[34] P. Nerreter, 'Vergeichende Reklame' *GRUR* 1993, 8.

and later on Droste[35] argued in favour of drawing a distinction between critical claims, claims of equivalence and personal references to a competitor (such as 'A is German while B is a foreigner').[36] This approach proved influential. In its more recent decisions the Bundesgerichtshof restricted the term 'comparative advertising' to critical claims.[37] Only these were subjected to the reasonable cause test. Claims of equivalence, on the other hand, were categorised as cases of taking unfair advantage of a competitor's goodwill ('*Rufausbeutung*').[38] This latter category of case also dealt with the use of well-known marks on goods different from those for which they were registered before this area became encompassed by the new trade marks legislation.[39] Whereas critical comparisons were sometimes considered legal, claims of equivalence were usually prohibited.[40] The Bundesgerichtshof regarded all attempts to exploit a competitor's reputation with utmost suspicion. This attitude led to decisions which even restricted references to another trader's mark or product where these references would have provided consumers with necessary information. Some decisions regarding claims of therapeutical equivalence in drug advertisements provide striking examples. Although the generic drugs in question could be freely distributed because patent protection for the brand products had elapsed, the Bundesgerichtshof nevertheless regarded

[35] H. Droste, 'Das Verbot der bezugnehmenden Werbung und die Ausnahmefälle' *GRUR* 1951, 140.

[36] A critical account of the implications of this distinction is given by A. Peschel, *Die anlehnende vergleichende Werbung im deutschen und französischen Wettbewerbs- und Markenrecht* (Cologne, Carl Heymanns, 1996) at 113 and 123ff.

[37] *Bioäquivalenz-Werbung*, BGHZ 107, 136 at 138.

[38] See A. Baumbach and W. Hefermehl, *Wettbewerbsrecht* 20th edn. (Munich, Beck, 1998) at §1, para. 541ff and H. Köhler and H. Piper, *Gesetz gegen den unlauteren Wettbewerb* (Munich, Beck, 1995) at §1, para. 307ff.

[39] See now §9 I No 3 and §14 II No 3 of the *Markengesetz* which correspond to ss. 5(3) and 10(3) of the Trade Marks Act 1994. These sections implement Articles 4(3) and 5(2) of the Trade Marks Directive.

[40] See A. Peschel, *Die anlehnende vergleichende Werbung im deutschen und französischen Wettbewerbs- und Markenrecht* (Cologne, Carl Heymanns, 1996) at 129ff and H. Köhler and H. Piper, *Gesetz gegen den unlauteren Wettbewerb* (Munich, Beck, 1995) at §1, para. 310.

claims of chemical identity as an unfair exploitation of the brand owner's reputation.[41]

When the European Commission introduced its first draft directive on comparative advertising in 1991[42] and its second draft in 1994,[43] the reaction of German academics and practitioners was far from unanimous. Some welcomed the drafts as a long-awaited liberalisation, whereas others argued in favour of the more restrictive practice adopted by the Bundesgerichtshof. The latter position was also taken by the German government. During the negotiations about the various drafts Germany maintained a fundamental reservation against the proposal and voted against the Directive in 1997. However, the first comments on the Directive[44] accept its purpose while criticising some provisions which are widely seen as unjustified by German authors.

3. The Judicial Implementation of the Directive

In February 1998, when there was still considerable debate in the German legal literature about the interpretation of the Directive and about possible means of implementation, the Bundesgerichtshof handed down a surprising decision.[45] The court used the first case it had to decide after the Directive had entered into force to announce that it would apply the Directive

[41] *Bioäquivalenz-Werbung*, BGHZ 107, 136 at 139; *Therapeutische Äquivalenz* GRUR 1992, 625 at 627.

[42] See App. III.

[43] See *ibid.*

[44] C. Plassmann, 'Vergeichende Werbung im Gemeinsamen Markt' *GRUR* 1996, 377; W. Tilmann, 'Richtlinie vergleichende Werbung' *GRUR* 1997, 790; and W. Gloy and D. Bruhn, 'Die Zulässigkeit von Preivergleichen nach der Richtlinie 97/55/EG—Kehrtwende oder Kontinuität?' *GRUR* 1998, 226.

[45] *Testpreis-Angebot*, BGH GRUR 1998, 824. See App. II. See the comments by S. Leible and O. Sosnitza, 'Richtlinienkonforme Auslegung vor Ablauf der Umsetzungsfrist und vergleichende Werbung' *NJW* 1998, 2507; A. Ohly *GRUR* 1998, 828, T. Wambach *MDR* 1988, 1238; B. Menke, 'Die vergleichende Werbung in Deutschland nach der Richtlinie 97/55/EG und der BGH-Entscheidung *Testpreis-Angebot*', WRP 1998, 811 at 813; and F. Henning-Bodewig, 'Vergleichende Werbung—Liberalisierung des deutschen Rechts?' *GRUR Int.* 1999, 385 at 389.

immediately, even before the legislature had acted. The court felt authorised to do so by the wide wording of §1 UWG. Before the Directive, the decision about whether comparative advertising constituted unfair competition within the meaning of §1 was decided by the courts. Now the Bundesgerichtshof held that the power to decide this issue still remained with the courts, since it was technically a matter of statutory interpretation. The court pointed out that after the end of the implementation period it would be obliged by general principles of European Community law to construe §1 UWG in the light of the Directive. Before this date there was no such obligation, but as long as no specific statutory provisions to the contrary existed it was better to interpret §1 UWG in conformity with European law rather that to continue a line of cases which was in conflict with the Directive. The court also considered it to be a practical advantage of this interpretation that decisions on the correct interpretation of §1 in light of the Directive could immediately be brought to the European Court of Justice.

The case itself, which is usually referred to as the *Testpreis-Angebot* case, concerned a comparison of tennis racquets. An advertisement compared two methods of production. While recommending the racquets distributed by the defendant the advertisement referred to the production method used by some competitors by saying '*Billige Composite Rackets muten wir Ihnen nicht zu*'.[46] The Bundesgerichtshof decided that this advertisement fell within the scope of the Directive as it identified all competitors that manufactured and sold composite racquets. The court went on to hold that the comparison was not allowed under Article 3a, because the sweeping statement claiming the inferiority of composite racquets was a denigration within the meaning of Article 3a(1)(e) of the Directive.

This judgment raises two questions, one concerning the implementation of the Directive in Germany, the other one concerning the interpretation of the Directive. First, there is some dispute among legal authors whether the legislature still has to

---

[46] 'We would not seriously expect you to buy cheap composite racquets'.

act to implement the Directive or whether this 'judicial implementation' is sufficient. Second, the conclusions reached by the
court on the questions of interpretation have been criticised by
legal authors in Germany. Each of these issues is addressed
below.[47] However, in practice there is no doubt that the law of
comparative advertising has already changed and that the pre-
Directive cases are now only of very limited precedential value.

Meanwhile the *Testpreis-Angebot* case has been confirmed by
the Bundesgerichtshof on two occasions. The first of these judgments, *Preisvergleichsliste II*,[48] concerned a list distributed by a
co-operative buying association which compared prices of joinery products. The plaintiff argued that this list was neither complete nor objective and that it discriminated against certain
producers. The Bundesgerichtshof held that the list had to meet
the requirements listed in Article 3a of the Directive, in particular the list was required objectively to compare material, relevant, representative and verifiable features of the products in
question. Whether this requirement was met by the defendants
depended on evidence which had not been heard at first
instance. The case was therefore referred back to the Düsseldorf
Oberlandesgericht. In the second case, *Vergleichen Sie*,[49] the
defendant sold costume jewellery by means of a pyramid-selling
system. The defendant sent letters to potential new sales representatives which claimed that the products sold by the defendant
were high-quality designer jewellery and invited the recipients of
these letters to compare the jewellery sold by the defendant with
the products offered in the catalogue of a well-known competitor. The Bundesgerichtshof considered this letter permissible
under the Directive. The defendant compared 'goods meeting
the same needs or intended for the same purpose' as required
by Article 3a(1)(b). The comparison was also verifiable since
everyone who received the letter had the opportunity to obtain
the plaintiff's catalogue. Finally, the latter neither denigrated the
plaintiff nor took unfair advantage of its reputation.

[47] See below at 80–81 and 87–89.
[48] BGH GRUR 1999, 69 See App. II.
[49] BGH GRUR Int. 1999, 453 See App. II.

These decisions have already had an impact on German advertising practice. Comparative advertising used to be virtually unknown in Germany. This reluctance to engage in comparative advertising is, however, beginning to wane.[50] In the telecommunications sector, where the abolition of German Telecom's monopoly resulted in fierce competition, there has been a comparative advertising battle between German Telecom and another supplier of telecommunication services. Recently, Burger King was enjoined from publishing an advertisement which claimed that a test had revealed a majority of those tested to prefer hamburgers produced by Burger King to those produced by McDonalds.[51] 'Media-Markt', a well-known discount supplier of electronic equipment, has started an advertising campaign which parodies comparative advertising. Prices for electronic equipment at 'Media Markt' outlets are compared with those offered by fictional dentists, policewomen and others not engaged in electronics retailing. While not constituting comparative advertising itself, this advertising campaign has already become famous for its slogan: '*Wer nicht vergleicht, ist blöd*'.[52]

---

[50] Further examples are given by U. Doepner and F. Hufnagel, 'German Courts Implement the EU Directive 97/55/EC—A Fundamental Shift in the Law on Comparative Advertising?' (1999) 88 *TMR* 1 at 11ff.

[51] LG Köln, No 81 O 185/98, judgment of 29 Jan. 1999, unreported. See App. II.

[52] 'You're foolish if you don't compare'.

4

The History, Scope and Exclusivity of the Directive

1. History of the Directive[1]

Recital 3 of the Directive notes that the regulation of comparative advertising still differs widely between the European Union Member States. The recital claims that these differences may constitute an obstacle to the free movement of goods and services and distort competition within the common market. Although the Commission seems to have held this view for some decades, plans to harmonise the law against unfair advertising have proved difficult to realise. In 1976 the Commission presented a draft directive on misleading and unfair advertising[2] which contained, *inter alia*, a provision on comparative advertising.[3] However, in subsequent years it became clear that no agreement could be reached on the questions of unfair advertising.

The project was narrowed in scope, and in 1984 the Misleading Advertising Directive entered into force.[4] In the United Kingdom the omission of any reference to unfair advertising was celebrated as 'an almost total victory for the long campaign waged by the United Kingdom',[5] whereas German commentators expressed their disappointment that the new

---

[1] Where relevant, references to the 1991, 1994, 1996 and 1997 versions of the Comparative Advertising Directive use such Article numbers as would appear in the Misleading Advertising Directive as amended by the relevant draft.

[2] OJ 1978 C 70/4.

[3] *Ibid.*, Article 4.

[4] OJ 1984 L250/17.

[5] (1984) 7 *Consumer Law Today* 1.

Directive had not gone far enough.[6] After 1984, the Commission singled out another aspect of advertising regulation and prsented a draft directive on comparative advertising in 1991.[7]

The explanatory memorandum to the 1991 draft[8] gave three reasons for harmonising and liberalising the law in relation to comparative advertising. First, the memorandum noted that cross-border advertising was increasing and would continue to do so after the establishment of the single market.[9] Second, the memorandum placed considerable importance on the way in which comparative advertising can serve the consumer's need for information. In the single market consumers will be confronted with foreign goods the size, packaging or quality of which will seem unfamiliar. Under these circumstances comparative advertising is a useful source of information which can enhance rational consumer choice.[10] Third, the memorandum emphasised that comparative advertising can stimulate competition, especially because it enables newcomers to challenge leading brands.[11] Set against these reasons for harmonising and liberalising comparative advertising are passages in the memorandum stressing that strict limits on comparative advertising are necessary to prevent consumer deception and, it is claimed, distortion of the market.[12] The definition of comparative advertising given in the 1991 draft differs only marginally from that in Article 2(2a) of the Directive. The most important of the criteria in Article 3a of the Directive are also already present.

---

[6] See K. Keilholz, 'Die mißlungene Harmonisierung des Verbots der irreführenden Werbung in der EG und ihre Konsequenzen für die deutsche Rechtsprechung' *GRUR Int.* 1987, 390.

[7] OJ 1991 C180/14 and OJ 1994 C136/4.

[8] COM(91)147 final—SYN 343 See App. III.

[9] *Ibid.*, at paras. 3.2 and 3.8.

[10] *Ibid.*, at paras. 3.5 and 3.6.

[11] *Ibid.*, at paras 3.7 and 3.8. This claim may be thought rather surprising, given that the Trade Marks Directive, which grants extensive protection to well-known marks and arguably entrenches their market position, was devised at the same time.

[12] *Ibid.*, at para. 4.1.

The 1991 draft was not to be implemented by the Member States. At the outset of this study it was emphasised that the Commission's choice to harmonise comparative advertising is not one that will be explored. However, it is important to stress that the growth of cross-border advertising does not, of itself, justify regulation, particularly in so culturally sensitive an area as advertising. The position adopted at the outset of this study was that the cultural costs of uniformity are justified by the extent to which differing regimes increase costs for firms and hamper the creation of a truly single market. But subsidiarity is an important principle of European law, and it was partly on the grounds of subsidiarity that the 1991 draft was rejected. The 1991 draft was first rejected by various Member States, among them Germany, where some commentators defended the German prohibition of comparative advertising[13] and others criticised the draft for its unclear language.[14] Then, at the Edinburgh summit of 1992, the Member States agreed on a package of draft directives that were to be postponed because their consistency with the principle of subsidiarity was doubted.[15]

The rejection of the draft and subsequent negotiations led to the presentation of a further draft directive in 1994. Ironically, this draft, far from leaving the regulation of comparative advertising to the Member States, was even more detailed in its prescriptions. The draft explicitly stated that comparative advertising was permissible *only* if the criteria set forth in Article 3a were met.[16] Further, advertising which is directed against a competitor personally was prohibited.[17]

[13] See O. von Gamm, 'Vorschlag der EG-Kommission für eine Richtlinie des Rates über vergleichende Werbung und zur Änderung der Richtlinie 84/450/EWG über irrefürende Werbung' *WRP* 1992, 143 and R. Funke, 'Das deutsche Wettbewerbsrecht im europäischen Binnenmarkt' *WRP* 1991, 550.

[14] See G. Schricker, 'Zur Werberechtspolitik der EG—Liberalisierung und Restriktion in Widerstreit' *GRUR Int.* 1992, 347 at 352ff and the opinion of the Deutsche Vereinigung für gewerblichen Rechtsschutz und Urheberrecht *GRUR* 1992, 370.

[15] COM(94)151 final—COD 343, Introduction.

[16] OJ 1994 C136/4, Article 3a(1).

[17] *Ibid.*, Article 3a(1)(d).

This trend towards ever more detailed prescription continued until, by the time of the adoption of the Directive in 1997, the criteria for permissible comparative advertising had grown from the three contained in the 1991 draft of Article 3a to the seven contained in the 1997 draft. These seven were arguably expansions of the concepts underlying the original three, although Article 3a(f) and (h), the rules that goods with different indications of origin must not be compared and that no advertising may present goods as imitations of other goods, demonstrates how closely comparative advertising was to be regulated. These provisions were included at the very last minute, following a French proposal.[18]

2. Scope of the Directive

In line with Recital 6, the definition of comparative advertising offered in the Directive is extremely broad and is likely to give rise to several difficulties of interpretation. These relate to the concepts of 'advertising' and of a 'competitor' and to the mode and content of the reference to a competitor, his goods or services, required for advertising to constitute 'comparative' advertising.

(a) 'Advertising'

The concept of 'advertising' was defined in Article 2(1) of the 1984 Directive, according to which 'advertising' means 'the making of a representation in any form . . . to promote the supply of goods or services'. At first sight the term 'advertising' seems narrower than the term 'representation'. Whereas 'advertising' could arguably be limited to representations made to the public generally or to some section of the public, a representation can also be made to a single person. Indeed, under §3 of the UWG, which uses the word 'representation' rather than 'advertising', representations made by a shopkeeper to a prospective

---

[18] See *Committee of Permanent Representatives to the Council, Report of 27 October 1995*, Doc 11112/95 CONSOM 71 at 5 n. 6.

purchaser are considered to be misleading advertising.[19] If this is also the position adopted by the Directive, then its effects could be very far-reaching indeed. The teenage salesperson who seeks to persuade a customer in a store that one pair of jeans is 'cooler' than another may have engaged in comparative advertising which neither is 'objective' nor compares 'verifiable' features of the goods, and is therefore prohibited.[20]

(b) 'Competitor'

In order to constitute comparative advertising, an advertisement must identify 'a competitor or goods or services offered by a competitor'. This raises the interesting question whether advertisements placed by retailers comparing the products of different manufacturers can constitute comparative advertising. Of course, in one sense, retailers and manufacturers are not in competition at all. Yet to exclude this type of advertising from the scope of the Directive would be to create an obvious means of circumventing its requirements in those countries in which comparative advertising would otherwise be legal, and unnecessarily to restrict this type of advertising in those countries in which it would not be. It is suggested that the term 'competitor' in the Article should be read to mean a competitor of the trader whose goods or services it is sought to promote, rather than a competitor of the advertiser himself. This reading of the Article is in line with the approach of the Bundesgerichtshof in *Preisvergleichsliste II* in which a purchasing co-operative for joinery products published a list of various manufacturers' prices

---

[19] See A. Baumbach and W. Hefermehl, *Wettbewerbsrecht* 20th edn. (Munich, Beck, 1998) at §3, para. 18; H. Helm in W. Gloy (ed.), *Handbuch des Wettbewerbsrechts* 2nd edn. (Munich, Beck, 1997) at §20, para. 20. The Bundesgerichtshof has held that for the purposes of §3 the sound of chickens in a radio advertisement constituted a representation which suggested that fresh eggs were used for the preparation of pasta (*Hühnergegacker*, BGH GRUR 1961, 544). Gestures may also count as representations, see RG GRUR 1939, 801 at 805.

[20] Provided, of course, that the argument of this book regarding the exclusivity of the Directive is accepted (see below at 51ff) and provided that the Directive has the effect of prohibiting 'image' comparisons (see below at 69ff).

and was held, contrary to the finding of the Oberlandesgericht Düsseldorf, to have engaged in comparative advertising.[21]

(c) The Mode of the Comparative Reference

In relation to the mode of the comparison, Article 2(2a) makes it clear that the Directive covers both explicit and implied references to a competitor or his goods or services. This raises two important issues.

First, there may be some difficulty in determining what constitutes an implied reference in the context of oligopolistic markets. Advertisers are fond of using comparative and superlative language without express reference. Expressions such as 'a better class of car' and 'the best hot dogs' are commonplace in advertising puffery. In many cases these puffs cannot be construed as a reference to any particular competitor. 'Simply the best restaurant in London' is hardly comparative advertising.[22] In other cases such puffs do constitute references to the goods or services of a competitor. In the case *Lyne* v. *Nicholls*,[23] the claims that the circulation of a local newspaper was '20 to 1 of any other weekly paper' in the district, and that the paper had the 'largest guaranteed circulation in the mining and china clay district in Mid Cornwall', were taken to be representations regarding the circulation of the only other paper in the district.[24] The difference between these two cases is that in the first there are simply too many potential objects of the comparative or superlative phrase for any particular competitor to identify it as a reference to his goods or services. In the second case the reference could easily be implied because there was only one competitor to which the comparison could be applied. Yet situations of oligopoly will arguably fall between these two categories. In a German case, a television advertisement showing young people

[21] BGH GRUR 1999, 69.

[22] In its report, a commission appointed by the German Ministry of Justice points out that it is doubtful whether this case is covered by the Directive: see *GRUR* 1997, 201 at 207.

[23] (1906) 23 TLR 86.

[24] *Ibid.*, at 88.

who compared Pepsi Cola and several unidentified cola drinks was held to imply a reference to Coca-Cola.[25] Under other circumstances it may be difficult to determine whether the number of potential objects of a comparative or superlative reference is sufficiently limited for any one of them to claim to be identified in the advertisement.

Second, it is unclear whether a reference to all producers who use a certain method of manufacture can be considered as an implicit reference to a particular competitor. Recently, the Bundesgerichtshof had to consider an advertisement which compared different types of tennis racquets.[26] No individual competitor was mentioned, but the advertisement warned its readers not to buy '*billige Composite Rackets*',[27] thereby referring to all manufacturers of this class of product. As outlined above,[28] a '*Systemvergleich*' did not count as comparative advertising under §1 of the UWG and was therefore permissible under the pre-Directive German law. Surprisingly, the Bundesgerichtshof, without even mentioning this doctrine, held that this advertisement came within the definition of Article 2(2a).[29] While it is true that statements of the sort made in this advertisement do indeed identify goods offered by a competitor—provided the public knows who uses which method of production—and therefore seem to be covered by Article 2(2a), it can be doubted whether the strict criteria provided by Article 3a are appropriate in this situation. A comparison of two classes of

[25] *Cola-Test*, BGH GRUR 1987, 49 at 50.

[26] *Testpreis-Angebot*, BGH GRUR 1998, 824.

[27] 'Cheap composite racquets'.

[28] See above at 34.

[29] For this reason, the *Testpreis-Angebot*, BGH GRUR 1998, 824 judgment is also criticised by M. Eck and K. Ikas, 'Neue Grenzen vergleichender Werbung' *WRP* 1999, 251 at 254 and by S. Leible and O. Sosnitza, 'Richtlinienkonforme Auslegung vor Ablauf der Umsetzungsfrist und vergleichende Werbung' *NJW* 1998, 2507 at 2508. However Eck and Ikas (*ibid.*) and F. Henning-Bodewig, 'Vergleichende Werbung—Liberalisierung des deutschen Rechts?' *GRUR* 1999, 385 at 391 assume that, because of additional facts of the case which were not addressed in the judgment, individual competitors were identifiable in an unusually apparent way.

goods appears to be particularly informative for consumers, while less damaging to the goodwill of any particular trader than a specific comparison drawn between his own goods and those of a competitor.

(d) The Content of the Comparative Reference

In relation to the content of the reference to a competitor that must be made for an advertisement to constitute comparative advertising, two issues again arise. First, it is surprising that Article 2(2a) does not require the reference to be comparative at all. The section seems to be built upon a concept not dissimilar to that of importing a reference under section 4(1)(b) of the Trade Marks Act 1938.[30] Imagine that the manufacturer of toy construction bricks advertises its product as 'compatible with the market leader' or that the manufacturer of car parts advertises its parts as appropriate for a 'Ford Mondeo' and the manufacturer and Ford are competitors in the market for car parts.[31] Each of these advertisements would identify a competitor or the goods offered by a competitor, but it would be difficult to call either comparative advertising on any natural reading of the term. Indeed, if Article 2(2a) were read broadly, the Directive could be taken to cover any traditional case of passing off in which the plaintiff and defendant were competitors.[32]

It is unlikely, however, that the section will be given this effect. The purpose of the Directive must surely be to regulate not all references to a competitor, his goods or services, but simply references which are in some way *comparative*: that is, references that involve a critical claim or a claim of equivalence. Even on this interpretation, incidentally, the scope of the Directive appears broad from a German perspective. As outlined above,

[30] See above at 19ff.

[31] This was a use of a trade mark which was in fact preserved from infringement as importing a reference by the Trade Marks Act 1938 s. 4(3), but see *British Northrop Ltd.* v. *Texteam Blackburn Ltd.* [1974] RPC 57.

[32] See G. Schricker, 'Zur Werberechtspolitik der EG—Liberalisierung und Restriktion im Widerstreit' *GRUR Int.* 1997, 347 at 352.

German law usually restricted the category of comparative advertising to that involving critical claims.[33]

A second issue relating to the content of the reference required for advertising to constitute comparative advertising is whether a reference to a competitor himself rather than to his goods or services is covered by the Directive. United Kingdom and German law have differed on the extent to which references to a competitor are allowed in advertising. Even during the period in which importing a reference to a mark constituted trade mark infringement in the United Kingdom, a mark could still be used where it constituted a part of a competitor's name and the use was of the competitor's name and not his mark.[34] References to a competitor personally have only been restrained in as much as they constitute defamation. In German law, references to a competitor were generally prohibited. Some commentators take the view that personal references may be justified under exceptional circumstances, but are unclear about when such circumstances may arise.[35] The position under the Directive is less clear.

In the Directive, Article 2(2a) covers references to a competitor, as well as references to his goods or services, while under Article 3a(1)(b) comparative advertising is only permitted when it compares 'goods or services meeting the same needs or intended for the same purpose'. References to the personal attributes of a competitor are not explicitly mentioned in this provision. This apparent inconsistency may mean one of three things.

First, it may mean that advertising referring to the personal attributes of a competitor is always illegal. Such an approach

[33] See above at 36.

[34] *Pompadour Laboratories Ltd.* v. *Stanley Frazer* [1965] RPC 7; *Harrods Ltd.* v. *Schwartz-Sackin & Co. Ltd.* [1986] FSR 490; *Duracell International Inc.* v. *Ever Ready Ltd.* [1989] FSR 71; *News Group Newspapers Ltd.* v. *The Mirror Group Newspapers (1986) Ltd.* [1989] FSR 126; *Mattel Inc.* v. *Tonka Corporation* [1992] FSR 28; *PC Direct Ltd.* v. *Best Buy Ltd.* [1997] 2 NZLR 723; *Orient Express Trade Mark* [1996] RPC 25.

[35] See A. Baumbach and W. Hefermehl, *Wettbewerbsrecht* 20th edn. (Munich, Beck, 1998) at §1, para. 431.

might find some support in the 1994 draft of the Directive, in which such references were explicitly prohibited.[36] However, it is suggested that a blanket prohibition of references to competitors in advertising would be an unfortunate effect of ambiguous wording in the Directive. As one New Zealand judge has pointed out, such a prohibition would have an unnecessarily restrictive effect on freedom of speech.[37] It would also be incompatible with the goal of the Directive, outlined below, in assisting rational consumer choice. There will be circumstances in which it is important that consumers should have information about a trader that a competitor may communicate without either denigration or unfairly taking advantage of the trader's reputation. Imagine, for example, that a trader has engaged in nationalistic advertising, but that the trader is the local subsidiary of an overseas company and profits from the trader's local operation are all sent overseas. It might be appropriate, and assist rational consumer choice, for a locally based competitor to point out the contradiction between the trader's nationalistic advertising and the realities of its business identity.

Second, it may be that references in advertising to the personal attributes of a competitor are not covered by the Directive at all. Such an approach has the support of some German commentators.[38] However, it does not seem to give Article 2(2a) its intended effect. Moreover, Article 3a(1)(e) seems to envisage that permitted comparative advertising may refer to the 'circumstances of a competitor'.

Third, the best approach to the apparent consistency of Articles 2(2a) and 3a(1)(b) seems to be to classify references to the personal attributes of a competitor as references to a com-

[36] OJ 1994 C136/4, Article 3a(1)(d).

[37] *PC Direct Ltd.* v. *Best Buy Ltd.* [1997] 2 NZLR 723 at 730 and 733.

[38] This interpretation is adopted by W. Tilmann, 'Richtlinie vergleichende Werbung' *GRUR* 1997, 790 at 795 and C. Plassmann, 'Vergleichende Werbung im Gemeinsamen Markt' *GRUR* 1996, 377 at 379. B. Menke, 'Die Vergleichende Werbung in Deutschland nach der Richtlinie 97/55/EG und der BGH-Entscheidung *Testpreis-Angebot' WRP* 1998, 811 at 813, argues that this prohibition still applies under the Directive.

petitor's 'services' for the purposes of Article 3a(1)(b). Article 3a(1)(b), while not doing so explicitly, would then permit references to a competitor's personal attributes, but only as long as such references met all the other criteria of permitted comparative advertising.

3. Exclusivity of the Directive

While it is unclear whether the Directive covers every type of comparative advertising in which a competitor is identified, it is even less clear whether it aims at a comprehensive regulation of comparative advertising or whether it leaves room for other legislation. Two issues arise: (a) whether Member States are free to provide for more liberal rules regarding comparative advertising, and (b) whether comparative advertising which is permitted by the Directive may nevertheless be prohibited under national trade mark or copyright law.

(a) Pre-emption of More Liberal Regimes

According to Article 3a, comparative advertising 'shall be permitted' when the criteria set out in subsections (a) to (h) are satisfied. This begs the question whether all comparative advertisements that do not meet these requirements are illegal as a matter of European law or whether the Member States can still provide for more liberal standards.

Unlike Article 3a of the 1994 draft, which provided that '[c]omparative advertising [would] *only* be permitted, when'[39] the relevant conditions were met, the final version of Article 3a does not answer this question explicitly.[40] When, however, some

---

[39] OJ 1994, C136/4, Article 3a(1).

[40] This question is disputed among German authors; for pre-emption see C. Plassmann, 'Vergleichende Werbung im Gemeinsamen Markt' *GRUR* 1996, 377 at 381; W. Tilmann, 'Richtlinie vergleichende Werbung' *GRUR* 1997, 790 at 790; B. Menke, 'Die vergleichende Werbung in Deutschland nach der Richtlinie 97/55/EG und der BGH-Entscheidung *Testpreis-Angebot*' *WRP* 1998, 811 at 818; W. Gloy and D. Bruhn, 'Die Zulässigkeit von Preisvergleichen nach der Richtlinie 97/55/EG—Kehrtwende oder Kontinuität?' *GRUR* 1998, 226 at

other provisions of the Directive and the recitals are taken into account, it seems that this omission was not supposed to have any effect. According to Article 4(1), Member States are obliged to provide for adequate and effective means to ensure 'the compliance with the provisions on comparative advertising'. These means must include the possibility of taking legal action 'against such advertising' or bringing 'such advertising before an administrative authority competent either to decide on complaints or to initiate appropriate legal proceedings'. Article 4(2) explicitly refers to 'unpermitted comparative advertising'. According to recital 11, 'the conditions of comparative advertising should be cumulative and respected in their entirety'. Recitals 7, 8, 9 and 15 also seem to rest on the assumption that all types of comparative advertising not permitted by Article 3a are prohibited. This interpretation of the Directive was accepted in the decision in *IPC Magazines Ltd.* v. *MGN Ltd.*[41] in which it was held that the Directive required Member States to legislate against unpermitted comparative advertising.

(b) Pre-emption of Trade Mark and Copyright Law

A second issue relating to the exclusivity of the Directive is whether comparative advertising that is permitted by the Directive may nevertheless be restrained by intellectual property law, in particular trade mark or copyright.

At first glance it may be thought that no issue of pre-emption arises in relation to trade mark law, because the national trade mark acts of all European Union Member States were passed to implement the Trade Marks Directive.[42] However, this isssue is in fact rather complex and depends upon the national legislation

239; and F. Henning-Bodewig, 'Vergleichende Werbung—Liberalisierung des deutschen Rechts?' *GRUR Int.* 1999, 385 at 391; for subsidiarity see R. Sack, 'Die Bedeutung der EG-Richtlinie 84/450/EWG und 97/55/EG über irreführende und vergleichende Werbung für das deutsche Wettbewerbsrecht' *GRUR Int.* 1998, 263; J. McCormick, 'The Future of Comparative Advertising' [1998] *EIPR* 41 at 42 points out the problem but does not give a definite answer.

[41] [1998] FSR 431.

[42] OJ 1989 L40/1 (hereafter 'the Trade Marks Directive').

implementing the Trade Marks Directive and its interpretation in the courts.[43]

The Trade Marks Directive provides in Article 5(1) for infringement by the use of a 'sign which is identical with [a] trade mark in relation to goods or services which are identical with those for which the trade mark is registered', a provision which is given effect in section 10(1) of the Trade Marks Act 1994 and §14 II No 1 of the *Markengesetz*. Comparative advertising in which a competitor's mark is used must, at least *prima facie*, constitute an infringement on this basis.

Surprisingly, this possibility is simply denied in the recitals to the Comparative Advertising Directive. Recital 15 to the Directive provides that:

> such use of another's trade mark, trade name or other distinguishing marks does not breach this exclusive right [i.e., that granted in Article 5 of the Trade Marks Directive] in cases where it complies with the conditions laid down by this Directive, the intended target being solely to distinguish between them and thus to highlight differences objectively;

This recital seems to imply that the use of a trade mark which neither causes consumer confusion nor constitutes dilution of the mark cannot constitute infringement of the Trade Marks Directive. Yet Article 5(1) is not dependent upon proof of either confusion or dilution. It merely requires use of a sign identical to the mark. This apparent conflict between the Trade Marks and Comparative Advertising Directives cannot simply be resolved by reference to recital 15.

This conflict will, however, be of different importance in the United Kingdom and Germany. In the United Kingdom, it is likely that a comparative advertisement that makes use of a competitor's trade mark but complies with the Comparative Advertising Directive would be saved by section 10(6) of the Trade Marks Act 1994,[44] the effect of which was outlined

---

[43] See the comparative overview by A. Kur, 'Die vergleichende Werbung in Europa: kurz vor dem Pyrrhus-Sieg?' in M. Levin (ed.), *Vennebog til Mogens Koktvedgaard* (Stockholm, Nerenius & Santérus Förlag, 1993) at 449ff.

[44] And perhaps also by section 11(2) of the Trade Marks Act 1994. See below at 100.

above.[45] In such a case there would be no direct conflict between national trade mark law and the provisions of the Directive. Indeed, the only potential for such conflict is that, given the very generous interpretation that section 10(6) is currently receiving in the courts,[46] it is conceivable that a comparative advertisement might satisfy the requirements of section 10(6) and yet fall foul of the Directive.

In Germany the position is rather more complex. It will be recalled that the German understanding of use as a trade mark under the *Warenzeichengesetz* meant that few comparative advertisements could have constituted infringements. This is because a potential infringer had to be using the mark to indicate a connection in the course of trade between the mark and *his own* goods.[47] Opinion is divided on whether this requirement also applies to actions for infringement under the *Markengesetz*.[48] However, after the European Court of Justice's decision in *BMW* v. *Deenik*[49] it seems doubtful whether the old German concept of 'trade mark use' can be upheld under the Trade Marks Directive. In the light of this judgment, the better view seems to be that the use of a mark in comparative advertising can constitute trade mark infringement under §14 II No 1 of the *Markengesetz*. Since the *Markengesetz* does not contain an exception similar to that provided by section 10(6) of the Trade Marks Act 1994, it is not clear how comparative advertisements permitted by the Comparative Advertising Directive can escape trade mark infringement. Some writers argue that the use of a mark in comparative advertising should be considered as indicating the kind or the quality of a product.[50] Such use, as long

---

[45] See above at 22ff.

[46] Ibid.

[47] See above at 30.

[48] An overview of both opinions is given by K. H. Fezer, *Markenrecht* (Munich, Beck, 1997) at §14, para. 29ff and R. Ingerl and C. Rohnke, *Markengesetz* (Munich, Beck, 1998) at §14, para. 50ff.

[49] Case C–63/97, [1999] 1 CMLR 1099 at 1110.

[50] See K. Fezer, *Markenrecht* (Munich, Beck, 1997) at §14, para. 496 and J. Starck, 'Markenmäßiger Gebrauch—Besondere Voraussetzung für die Annahme einer Markenverletzung?' *GRUR* 1996, 688 at 691.

as it is in accordance with honest practices, is permissible under Article 5(5) of the Trade Marks Directive, given effect in §23 No 2 of the *Markengesetz* and section 11(2) of the Trade Marks Act 1994. This approach has received strong, albeit *obiter,* support in the United Kingdom in the decision of Jacob J in *British Sugar Plc* v. *James Robertson & Sons Ltd.*[51] Others think that the principle of exhaustion applies, because the advertisement refers to products marketed by the trade mark owner.[52]

The relationship of the Directive to copyright law is even less clear. Imagine that a trade mark consists of a drawing or other artistic work which is the subject of copyright protection.[53] May a trader prevent the use of this mark, not by relying upon the Comparative Advertising Directive, or even trade mark law, but by relying upon the law of copyright? This issue was exemplified in *IPC Magazines Ltd.* v. *MGN Ltd.*[54] In this case a newspaper seeking to promote a colour supplement directed at women produced a television advertisement. The advertisement included (i) a reproduction of the front cover of a well known women's magazine with a black band and the price 59p superimposed upon it and (ii) a reproduction of the front cover of the newspaper's colour supplement with a black band and the word 'free' superimposed upon it. The women's magazine claimed infringement of its copyright in the magazine's logo or masthead, the layout of its front cover and particular photographs. Richard McCombe QC found for the plaintiffs on the copyright issues and the defendants raised, *inter alia*, a defence based on the Comparative Advertising Directive. They argued that, (i) although the Directive was not yet in force, its purpose was to permit comparative advertising so as to encourage the free movement of goods, (ii) national laws which restricted such advertising ought therefore to be seen as *prima facie* infringing

[51] [1996] R.P.C. 281 at 298–299

[52] See A. Kur, 'Die Harmonisierung der europäischen Markengesetze, Resultate—offene Fragen—Harmonisierungslücken' *GRUR* 1997, 241 at 250.

[53] This section assumes that the use of such a drawing or other artistic work would not normally be rendered impermissible by the Comparative Advertising Directive itself. However see below at 83.

[54] [1998] FSR 431.

the provisions of the European Community Treaty regarding free movement of goods, and (iii) United Kingdom copyright law would have this effect if enforced in this case because both the newspaper and advertisement concerning it were distributed in the Republic of Ireland as well as the United Kingdom. This rather far-fetched argument was rejected in the case.

However, unfortunately, no suggestion was made as to how the issue might have been handled had the Directive already been in force. It seems odd that a directive which was apparently designed to amend the Misleading Advertising Directive should be given the effect of amending copyright law. However, fact situations similar to that considered in *IPC Magazines Ltd.* v. *MGN Ltd.* will often arise and it would be equally odd if plaintiffs were able to render nugatory the liberalisation of comparative advertising by relying upon their rights in copyright. In the case of *Parfums Christian Dior SA* v. *Evora BV* the European Court of Justice refused to allow the owner of copyright in an artistic work which was also a trade mark to assert more control over the use of the mark than the trade mark owner could have had in the same situation.[55] This was said to be because copyright was effectively being used as 'a form of control on marketing . . . and . . . commercial exploitation of copyright raises the same issues as that of any other industrial or commercial property'.[56] An analogous principle could be applied in the situation of comparative advertising. If copyright is used to prevent comparative advertising it is used as a control on marketing, and it might be argued that the regime for regulating marketing constituted by the Comparative Advertising Directive ought to prevail. It is to be regretted that this difficult policy issue was not more satisfactorily addressed by the drafters of the Directive. There is a real danger that courts with a less purposive tradition of statutory interpretation, such as those of the United Kingdom, will simply apply the copyright statute in all its rigour and thereby undermine the effect of the Directive.

---

[55] Case C–337/95 *Parfums Christian Dior SA* v. *Evora BV* [1998] RPC 166.
[56] *Ibid.*, at 197.

5

The Substance of the Directive

1. The Apparent Purpose of the Directive

It is the primary purpose of the Comparative Advertising Directive to protect consumers by permitting comparative advertising when, but only when, it serves the function of assisting rational consumer choice. The recitals and the history of the Directive make it clear that it is built upon a particular view of how the market best serves consumers and of the proper role of advertising. The Directive assumes that markets operate to serve consumers best when traders compete on the basis of the quality and price of their goods or services and consumers assess quality and price on the basis of objective information that is readily available to them. It assumes that the purpose of advertising is to assist rational consumer choice by communicating reliable factual information[1] about the quality and price of particular goods or services.[2] The paradigm of useful comparative

---

[1] Recital 5 even refers to a 'right to information' which was included in a list of five basic consumer rights in the first and the second EEC programmes for a consumer protection and information policy (OJ 1975 C92/1, and OJ 1981 C133/1). The Commission is, rather surprisingly, not alone in assuming that the principal economic function of advertising is to communicate information. See, for example, R. Posner, *Regulation of Advertising by the FTC* (Washington, DC, American Institute for Public Policy Research, 1973).

[2] See recitals 2 ('uniform conditions of the use of comparative advertising . . . will help demonstrate objectively the merits of the various comparable products') and 5 ('whereas comparative advertising, when it compares material, relevant, verifiable and representative features and is not misleading, may be a legitimate means of informing consumers of their advantage'); see also the explanatory memorandum to the 1991 draft (COM(91) 147 final—SYN 343 at paras. 3.5 and 3.6) where the function of comparative advertising in assisting rational consumer choice is highlighted. Providing consumers with accurate

advertising that informs the Directive resembles tables in consumer magazines such as *Which?* and *Test*.[3] The extent to which the Directive recognises that advertising might sometimes have the effect of creating, rather than informing, consumer demand and that consumer choice might sometimes be based upon image or status associations of goods is a moot point that is considered in more detail below.[4]

A second, and related, purpose of the Directive is made clear in Article 1. This purpose is to protect not only consumers, but also competitors. Even objective and reliable information about a competitor's product can damage his goodwill, and the Directive seeks to offer at least some protection against such damage. At this point it seems helpful to refer to the concept of proportionality. As a substantive legal principle, proportionality is primarily a principle of public law. It provides that the European Union must not interfere more than necessary with citizens' rights[5] or with the competence of the Member States.[6] However, as a logical structure, proportionality has also been used by the European Court of Justice in at least one private law context, that of the interpretation of Article 82 EC.[7] In relation

information is also the aim of Directive 98/6/EC concerning consumer protection in the indication of the prices of products offered to consumers, (OJ 1998 L80/27), which in recital 6 stresses the relation between price information and the ability of the consumer to 'make informed choices on the basis of simple comparisons'.

[3] *Which?* is a magazine published in the United Kingdom by the Consumers Association that gives comparative information on consumer products and services. *Test* is a magazine of the same type published by *Stiftung Warentest*, a private-law foundation established in 1964 by the German federal government as an institute for carrying out comparative product tests and surveys on services.

[4] See below at 74–6.

[5] See Cases C–41/79 *Testa* v. *Bundesanstalt für Arbeit* [1980] ECR 1979 at 1997–8 and C–331/88 *R.* v. *Minister for Agriculture, Fisheries and Food, ex parte Fedesa* [1990] ECR I–4023 at I–4063.

[6] Article 5(3) EC.

[7] See Cases C–27/76 *United Brands* v. *Commission* [1978] ECR 207 at 301, C–26/75 *General Motors* v. *Commission* [1975] ECR 1367 at 1378–9 and N. Koch in E. Grabitz and M. Hilf, *Kommentar zur Europäischen Union* (Munich, Beck, 1997) at §86, para. 43.

to comparative advertising, application of the concept might help to balance the interests of rival competitors and the consuming public. When comparative advertising is (i) capable of assisting rational consumer choice and (ii) not more damaging to a competitor's goodwill than necessary to assist rational consumer choice, the consumer interest in information tips the scales in favour of permitting the comparison. On this basis, two types of unpermitted comparative advertising can be distinguished. First, misleading comparative advertising and comparative advertising that does not relate objectively to relevant and verifiable features of the goods or services is disallowed as incapable of assisting rational consumer choice. Second, comparative advertising that denigrates a competitor's marks, products, services or activities or that takes unfair advantage of a competitor's reputation is disallowed, because it damages or exploits a competitor's goodwill more than neccesary to assist rational consumer choice. Each of these types of advertising should be considered in turn.

2. Comparative Advertising Incapable of Assisting Rational Consumer Choice

(a) Misleading Advertising

The prohibition of misleading comparative advertising in Article 3a(1)(a) is easy to justify. Misleading advertising is the antithesis of useful information. It can cause erroneous consumer decisions, thereby distorting the market. As misleading advertising is incapable of assisting rational consumer choice, it also affects the competitor's goodwill to a disproportionate extent. Thus both United Kingdom and German law include standards against misleading advertising, standards that were to some extent harmonised by the Misleading Advertising Directive of 1984.[8]

The difficulty in this area is not so much agreeing that misleading advertising is wrong, as agreeing what it means for advertising to be misleading. The courts of the United Kingdom

[8] OJ 1984 L250/17.

have usually been prepared to accord consumers a higher degree of scepticism than have their German counterparts. Unfortunately, Article 2 of the Misleading Advertising Directive did little to harmonise a standard for protection against misleading advertising as it did not define the concept of 'deception'.[9] The opportunity to remedy this deficiency was missed in the Comparative Advertising Directive and Article 2(2) remains unchanged.

This failure to define the concept of deception leads to a curious paradox in the Comparative Advertising Directive. While the Directive does little to define what it might mean to mislead consumers, it does seem to submit misleading comparative advertising to an undefined common European standard. This conundrum arises because Article 3a(1)(a) refers to Articles 2(2), 3 and 7(1). Article 2 obliges the Member States to provide a certain, though undefined, level of protection against misleading advertising. Article 7(1) provides that the Misleading Advertising Directive only set a minimum standard and that Member States can ensure more extensive protection. Confusingly, Article 7(2) then provides that '[p]aragraph 1 shall not apply to comparative advertising *as far as the comparison is concerned*'. Perhaps this was meant to exclude the issue of the standard of deception relevant to comparative advertising altogether.[10] This interpretation is, however, hard to reconcile with

[9] See G. Schricker, 'Law and Practice Relating to Misleading Advertising in the Member States of the EC' [1990] *IIC* 620; 'European Harmonization of Unfair Competition Law—A Futile Venture?' [1991] *IIC* 788; and K. Keilholz, 'Die mißlungene Harmonisierung des Verbots der irreführenden Werbung in der EG und ihre Konsequenzen für die deutsche Rechtsprechung' *GRUR Int.* 1987, 390.

[10] Presumably the drafters intended to ensure that the standards set in Article 3a(1) were maximum standards, i.e. that the Member States were precluded from providing more extensive protection against comparative advertising. This assumption is supported by a declaration made by the Commission in the Council meeting of 9 Nov. 1995: '*La Commission déclare qu'à son avis le renvoi à l'article 7 paragraphe 1 dans l'article 3bis paragraphe 1 a) se réfère uniquement aux éventuels élements trompeurs d'une publicité comparative*' (see W. Tilmann, 'Richtlinie vergleichende Werbung' *GRUR* 1997, 790 at 792). However, to have achieved this result, Article 7(2) might better have read: '[a]s far as

the actual wording of Article 7(2). The more natural reading of Article 7(2) is that Article 7(1), which exclusively concerns misleading advertising, applies only to part of a comparative advertisement, namely to everything but the comparison itself. If the courts give effect to this more natural reading and do not treat it as a drafting error, they will have to decide what constitutes the comparison itself.[11] Since Article 7(1) does not apply to it, Member States are not free to provide more extensive protection against deception and thus a 'European' standard of deception, whatever it may be, applies.

Such a muddle could have been avoided either by more effectively excluding any treatment of the standard for deception from the Comparative Advertising Directive altogether, or by clearly providing a common European standard for deception in all advertising, including comparative advertising. This second approach would obviously have been more satisfactory if harmonisation is to be achieved. Two issues would arise in agreeing a common standard against misleading advertising.

First, there has been some discussion whether the determination of deception is a factual or a normative problem. The approach adopted by the German courts (which frequently[12]

comparative advertising is concerned, paragraph (1) shall only apply to such parts of the comparison as are potentially misleading'.

[11] Every comparison consists of thee components: (a) a statement about object A ('Car A consumes 12 litres of petrol per 100 miles'), (b) a statement about object B ('Car B consumes 13 litres of petrol per 100 miles') and (c) a juxtaposition of the two under a common *'tertium comparationis'* ('Car A is more economical'). If all three components were exempted from Article 7(1), stricter national standards of deception would apply to statements of the type contained in components (a) and (b) if no comparative component (c) were added, but not if it were. To avoid this strange result, Article 7(2) should be read as applicable only to component (c). See also W. Tilmann, 'Richtlinie vergleichende Werbung' [1997] *GRUR* 790 at 792; B. Menke, 'Die vergleichende Werbung in Deustchland nach der Richtlinie 97/55/EG und der BGH-Entscheidung *Testpreis-Angebot*' [1998] *WRP* 811 at 820; and M. Eck and K. Ikas, 'Neue Grenzen vergleichender Werbung' [1999] *WRP* 251 at 257.

[12] The judge can only decide the issue without reference to an opinion poll when (i) the goods in question are consumer goods used in everyday life, (ii) the judge is himself a member of the relevant section of the consuming public, and

use opinion polls to determine the percentage of the consuming public that has been deceived[13]) is said to be factual, whereas the standard of the 'reasonably circumspect consumer' relied upon by the European Court of Justice in the *Mars* case[14] is said to be normative.[15] However, the position of the European Court is still far from clear. In its recent *Gut Springenheide* decision the court instructed the national court to 'take into account the presumed expectations which [the advertising] evokes in an average consumer who is reasonably well-informed and reasonably observant and circumspect'.[16] While this test clearly seems to be normative, the court goes on to add that 'community law does not preclude the possibility that, where the national court has particular difficulty in assessing the misleading nature of the

(iii) there are no additional factors that cast doubt on the ability of the judge to determine the issue: see H. J. Ohde in W. Gloy (ed.), *Handbuch des Wettbewerbsrechts* 2nd edn. (Munich, Beck, 1997) at §18, para. 2.

[13] On the use of opinion polls in German unfair competiton law see H. J. Ohde in W. Gloy (ed.), *Handbuch des Wettbewerbsrechts* 2nd edn. (Munich, Beck, 1997) at §18; R. Knaak, *Demoskopische Umfragen in der Praxis des Wettbewerbs- und Warenzeichenrechts* (Weinheim, VCH, 1986); and E. Noelle-Neumann and C. Schramm, 'Höhe der Verkehrsgeltung' *GRUR* 1966, 70.

[14] Case C–470/93 *Verein gegen Unwesen in Handel und Gewerbe Köln e.V.* v. *Mars GmbH* [1995] ECR I–1923 at 1944. See also the Opinion of Tesauro AG in Case C–373/90 *Complaint against X* [1992] ECR I–131 at 145 ('*Vigilantibus non dormientibus iura scurrerunt*') and the Opinion of Mischo AG in Case C–120/96 *Gut Springenheide GmbH* v. *Oberkreisdirektor des Kreises Steinfurt* [1992] ECR I–4657 at para. 55ff. On the consumer model adopted by the ECJ see K. H. Fezer, 'Das wettbewerbsrechtliche Irreführungsverbot als ein normatives Modell des verständigen Verbrauchers im Europäischen Unionsrecht' *WRP* 1995, 671; V. Deutsch, 'Der Einfluß des europäischen Rechts auf den Irreführungstatbestand des §3 UWG' *GRUR* 1996, 541; M. Dauses, 'Die Rechtsprechung des EuGH zum Verbraucherschutz und zur Werbefreiheit im Binnenmarkt' *EuZW* 1995, 425 at 429; and D. von Wild, *Der 'vernünftige Verbraucher' im Wettbewerbsrecht* (Munich, VVF, 1998) at 138ff.

[15] See W. B. Schünemann in R. Jacobs, W. F. Lindacher and O. Teplitzky (eds.), *Großkommentar zum UWG* (Berlin, de Gruyter, 1994), Introduction para. D258ff and K. H. Fezer, 'Das wettbewerbsrechtliche Irreführungsverbot als ein normatives Modell des verständigen Verbrauchers im Europäischen Unionsrecht' *WRP* 1995, 671 at 674ff.

[16] Case C–120/96 *Gut Springenheide GmbH* v. *Oberkreisdirektor des Kreises Steinfurt* [1998] ECR I–4657 at para. 31.

statement or description in question, it may have recourse, under the conditions laid down by its own national law, to a consumer research poll or an expert's report as guidance for its judgment'. As Reese observes, this attempt to reconcile contrary positions in a Solomonic way is less than convincing.[17]

Second, whether the consumer is conceived of factually or normatively, national attitudes differ in relation to the question of how many consumers need to have been misled for an advertisement to count as misleading. In German law a proportion of 10–15 per cent is sometimes regarded as sufficient.[18] In the United Kingdom, several different answers to this question have been aired, although the courts are more reluctant to protect small minorities of consumers than their German counterparts.[19] In the *Nissan* case the European Court of Justice held

[17] U. Reese, 'Das "6–Korn-Eier"—Urteil des EuGH—Leitentscheidung für ein Leitbild?' *WRP* 1998, 1035 at 1040.

[18] See *Kontinent Möbel*, GRUR 1979, 716 at 718 (10%), *Lübecker Marzipan*, GRUR 1981, 71 at 74 (13.7%). See, generally, W. F. Lindacher in R. Jacobs, W. F. Lindacher and O. Teplitzky (eds.), *Großkommentar zum UWG* (Berlin, de Gruyter, 1994) at §3, para. 98; H. Köhler and H. Piper, *Gesetz gegen den unlauteren Wettbewerb* (Munich, Beck, 1995) at §3, para. 99; and D. von Wild, *Der 'vernünftige Verbraucher' im Wettbewerbsrecht* (Munich, VVF, 1998) at 3ff and 18ff. The German position has been criticised by V. Emmerich, *Das Rechts des unlauteren Wettbewerbs* 4th edn. (Munich, Beck, 1995) at 235 and G. Schricker, 'Law and Practice Relating to Misleading Advertising in the Member States of the EC' [1990] *IIC* 620 at 630.

[19] On the one hand, some cases have suggested that the courts should protect even minorities of readers who might be misled. Under the Control of Misleading Advertisements Regulations 1988 it seems that the courts are inclined to protect even those who read advertisements with little scepticism (*Director General of Fair Trading* v. *Tobyward Ltd.* [1989] 2 All ER 266 at 270). Similarly, the courts have occasionally held that the action for passing off should protect even the ignorant and the unwary (*Singer Manufacturing Co.* v. *Loog* (1882) 8 App. Cas. 15 at 18, *per* Lord Selborne LC and *Taittinger* v. *Allbev Ltd.* [1994] 4 All ER 75). On the other hand, the courts will not protect the notorious 'moron in a hurry' (*Morning Star Co-operative Society Ltd.* v. *Express Newspapers Ltd.* [1979] FSR 113) and have said that the persons to consider in determining whether there has been misrepresentation for passing off are 'ordinary, sensible members of the public' (see C. Wadlow, *The Law of Passing Off* (London, Sweet & Maxwell, 1995) at 378–80 and the cases there cited). The courts have also made it clear that in applying injurious falsehood and s. 10(6)

that a 'significant' number of consumers must be misled.[20] A more paternalistic approach to determining when an advertisement is misleading has the advantage of protecting the most vulnerable of consumers. A less paternalistic approach has the advantage of protecting advertisers from responsibility for the ignorance of the public, though advertisers can be expected to know how the target audience will receive their message.

In relation to these two issues, it seems too crude both (i) to distinguish between a purely factual and a purely normative approach to the question of who should count as a consumer and (ii) to settle upon some arbitrary number of consumers that must have been misled for an advertisement to count as misleading. Any test for deception needs to involve a mixture of factual and normative elements, the respective weight of which can differ in various situations. The term 'significant', suggested by the European Court, seems to be a reasonable compromise for the purpose of harmonisation, because it is flexible enough to allow the courts to consider all relevant factors. 'Significance' should depend on a number of criteria such as (i) the number of consumers likely to be misled, (ii) the nature of the goods and services in question, (iii) the likely consequences to the minority having been misled and (iv) the ease with which the advertiser could have avoided misleading the respective part of the consuming public. This approach, while more complex than either the test of whether the 'reasonably circumspect consumer' would be misled or the test of whether a particular number of real consumers would be misled, seems capable of producing predictable results. It also seems to avoid the excesses of either

of the Trade Marks Act 1994 a certain amount of scepticism should be assumed in the ordinary member of the public (see above at 10 and 74).

[20] Case C–373/90 *Complaint against X* [1992] ECR I–131 at 159; see the comments by R. Sack, 'Die Bedeutung der EG-Richtlinie 84/450/EWG und 97/55/EG über irreführende und vergleichende Werbung für das deutsche Wettbewerbsrecht' *GRUR Int.* 1998, 263 and V. Deutsch, 'Der Einfluß des europäischen Rechts auf den Irreführungstatbestand des §3 UWG' *GRUR* 1996, 541 and 'Noch Einmal: Das Verbraucherleitbild des EuGH und das *Nissan—* Urteil' *GRUR* 1997, 44.

under-protecting consumers and competitors or casting an unreasonable burden of responsibility for the public's ignorance upon the advertiser.

Apart from the prohibition of misleading advertising, Article 3a(1)(d) prohibits comparative advertising that creates confusion. This raises the question whether this paragraph adds anything to paragraph (1)(a). Is there a difference between misleading advertising and advertising that creates confusion? The taxonomy of German law in this area may suggest an affirmative answer. In German law, advertising that creates confusion is traditionally outside the scope of §3 of the UWG, which prohibits misleading advertising.[21] The consequences of this distinction are mainly procedural. According to §13(2) of the UWG, violations of §3 are actionable at the suit of consumers' organisations and trade associations. This 'collective action' cannot be brought against the infringement of a registered or unregistered trade mark. Some authors reject this distinction and are in favour of also admitting collective action against advertising that creates confusion.[22] However, although the structure of German law may suggest a distinction between misleading advertising and advertising that creates confusion, that distinction seems to have no substantive merit.[23] Misleading advertising and advertising that creates confusion are almost identical with regard to protecting both consumers and competitors. Both misleading advertising and advertising that creates confusion can lead to wrong purchase decisions. Both misleading advertising and advertising that creates confusion can unfairly damage a competitor's goodwill. For the purpose of harmonisation, the Directive had to ensure that both types of advertising were

[21] See 'White Horse', BGH GRUR 1996, 267 at 270 and A. Baumbach and W. Hefermehl, Wettbewerbsrecht 20th edn. (Munich, Beck, 1998) at §3, paras. 261 and 263.

[22] See F. Henning-Bodewig and A. Kur, Marke und Verbraucher, Funktionen der Marke in der Marktwirtschaft (Weinheim, VCH, 1988–9) ii at 30ff.

[23] It is interesting that no similar distinction has been drawn in the interpretation of s. 52 of the Australian Trade Practices Act 1974 which prohibits misleading or deceptive conduct in trade or commerce.

equally prohibited, but a distinction between the two ought not to be developed as Article 3a comes to be interpreted.

Remarkably, Article 3a(1)(d) refers only to comparisons creating confusion[24] and not to comparisons that run the *risk* of creating such confusion. In European trade mark law,[25] a risk of confusion is sufficient to establish trade mark infringement. Similarly, Article 2(2) of the Directive defines advertising as misleading if it deceives consumers or if it *is likely* to deceive. Finally, the 1994 draft of the Directive explicitly referred to advertising that creates the risk of confusion.[26] It remains to be seen whether the European Court of Justice will consider only advertising that creates actual confusion as illegal or whether the risk of confusion will also be sufficient. The wording of Article 3(1)(d) suggests the former solution, while only the latter would be consistent with European trade mark law and with Article 2(2) of the Directive.

(b) Comparing Like with Like

Article 3a(1)(b) requires the comparison to be made between 'goods and services meeting the same needs or intended for the same purpose'. Advertisements that do not meet this criterion might be incapable of assisting rational consumer choice for one of two reasons.

First, a comparison between 'apples and oranges' could be seen as potentially misleading.[27] If so, then it could be asked

[24] The equivalent wording in the 1991 draft was criticised by some German authors: see G. Schricker, 'Zur Werberechtspolitik der EG—Liberalisierung und Restriktion im Widerstreit' *GRUR Int.* 1992, 347 at 353 and O. von Gamm, 'Vorschlag der EG-Kommission für eine Richtlinie des Rates über vergleichende Werbung und zur Änderung der Richtlinie 84/450/EWG über irreführende Werbung' *WRP* 1992, 143 at 146. See also C. Plassmann, 'Vergleichende Werbung im Gemeinsamen Markt' *GRUR* 1996, 377 at 380 and W. Tilmann, 'Richtlinie vergleichende Werbung' *GRUR* 1977, 790 at 796.

[25] See Article 5(1)(b) of the Trade Marks Directive implemented as s. 10(2) of the Trade Marks Act 1994 and §14 II No 2 of the *Markengesetz*.

[26] OJ 1994 C136/4, Article 3a(1)(d).

[27] This metaphor is used only guardedly. Apples and oranges may or may not be interchangeable products in a particular market. See below at 67–9 and B. Menke, 'Die vergleichende Werbung in Deutschland nach der Richtlinie

whether the general prohibition of misleading comparative advertising in Article 3a(1)(a) would not have been sufficient to prohibit it. In practice, there are likely to be many instances of advertisements not comparing like with like which are already covered by Article 3a(1)(a). Imagine, for example, that the prices of two insurance packages are compared, but the packages do not cover the same risks. This comparison will be likely to mislead consumers if the different coverage is not evident from the advertisement.

Second, comparisons of this kind could also be disallowed because they provide no information to the consumer that might be important for a rational purchase decision. This is the only justification for prohibiting comparisons between goods that are evidently different from one another. However, Article 3a(1)(b) does not require that the goods be identical, but only that they meet the same needs or be intended for the same purpose. This wording is reminiscent of the definition of the relevant product market under Article 82 EC which the European Court of Justice and the Commission make in accordance with the 'reasonable interchangeability test'.[28] The approaches of this test and that of Article 3a(1)(b) are similar in that neither refers to the physical, chemical and technical identity of products but to their substitutability from the viewpoint of the consumer.[29] This is not to say that the rules developed by the Court with regard to Article 82 EC could be readily applied to the Directive, because the functions of the two provisions are quite different. Whereas the task under Article 82 EC is to determine whether

97/55/EG und der BGH-Entscheidung *Testpreis-Angebot* *WRP* 1998, 811 at 822 and P. Spink and R. Petty, 'Comparative Advertising in the European Union' (1988) 47 *ICLQ* 855 at 865.

[28] OJ 1997 C372/5. See also N. Koch in E. Grabitz and M. Hilf, *Kommentar zur Europäischen Union* (Munich, Beck, 1997) at §86, para. 35 and C. W. Bellamy and G. Child, *Common Market Law of Competition* 4th edn. (London, Sweet & Maxwell, 1993) at para. 9–008ff. This comparison is also drawn, though without qualification, in P. Spink and R. Petty, 'Comparative Advertising in the European Union' (1988) 47 *ICLQ* 855 at 865.

[29] See N. Koch in E. Grabitz and M. Hilf, *Kommentar zur Europäischen Union* (Munich, Beck, 1997) at §86. para. 35.

an undertaking has a dominant position in a particular market, the legality of comparative advertising depends on its character as information. Under Article 82, the European Court of Justice tends to adopt a narrow definition of the relevant product markets.[30] Similarly narrow limits do not seem to be suitable for Article 3a. In 1972 the Bundesgerichtshof considered an advertisment that read: '*ONKO-Kaffee können Sie getrost statt Blumen verschenken*'.[31] Imagine that the advertisement had been for wine rather than coffee and had gone on to compare the price of a particular bottle of wine and the price of flower bouquets in a local store. Such a comparison ought arguably to be permissible because both wine and flowers can be given as gifts to a host and the comparison provides useful information to consumers. *Statt Blumen ONKO-Kaffee* itself raises an even more interesting problem, because, while coffee and flowers are not traditionally interchangeable as gifts, the clear intention of the advertiser is that they ought to become so. Once the substitutability of the two products has been suggested, comparative price information might arguably be useful in assisting rational consumer choice. If this can be accepted, then the words 'meeting the same needs or intended for the same purpose' in Article 3a(1)(b) ought to be interpreted very broadly indeed.

Whereas Article 3a(1)(b) prohibits the comparison of apples and oranges, Article 3a(1)(f) goes one step further by prohibiting the comparison of different types of apples. If products with a designation of origin are compared, the comparison must relate to products with the same designations. This provision, which follows a French model,[32] is hard to justify, because it quarantines certain products from most types of comparative

[30] See, for example, Cases C–53/92 *Hilti* v. *Commission* [1994] ECR I–667 and C–241/91P and C–242/91P *Radio Telefis Eireann & Independent Television Publications* v. *Commission* [1995] ECR I–743.

[31] *Statt Blumen ONKO-Kaffee*, BGH [1972] *GRUR* 553: 'Onko coffee makes just as good a gift as flowers'. The advertisement was held not to contravene §1 UWG.

[32] Article L 121–10 of the *Code de la consommation*. See T. Dreier and S. von Lewinski, 'Länderbericht Frankreich' in G. Schricker (ed.), *Recht der Werbung in Europa* (Baden-Baden, Nomos, 1995) at para. 113.

advertising. A comparison between a Bordeaux and an Australian Cabernet Sauvignon (or even a bouquet of flowers) provides consumers with useful information, especially because both products serve the same purpose. This information is therefore capable of assisting rational consumer choice, and Article 3a(1)(g) would have been sufficient to ensure that the comparison does not take unfair advantage of a competitor's reputation. This privilege afforded to a certain group of producers by Article 3(1)(a)(f) can only be explained on political grounds, because the provision sits oddly with the rest of the Directive.[33]

(c) Objectively Comparing Material, Relevant, Verifiable and Representative Features

A third type of comparative advertising which the Directive prohibits as incapable of assisting rational consumer choice is advertising which does not objectively compare 'one or more material, relevant, verifiable and representative features' of the relevant goods or services. This prohibition, which is contained in Article 3a(1)(c), is problematic in its interpretation, in its breadth of potential application and in its underlying policy. Each of these issues will be considered in turn.

(i) The Interpretation of Article 3a(1)(c)

Three difficulties of interpretation arise in relation to Article 3a(1)(c). First, it is difficult to know what the difference between 'material' and 'relevant' features of particular goods or services might be and what the requirement that they be 'representative' could add. The best view seems to be that at least the terms 'relevant' and 'material' are synonomous.[34]

---

[33] This provision has also been vigorously criticised by C. Plassmann, 'Vergleichende Werbung im Gemeinsamen Markt' *GRUR* 1996, 377 at 380 and W. Tilmann, 'Richtlinie vergleichende Werbung' *GRUR* 1997, 790 at 797.

[34] See C. Plassman, 'Vergleichende Werbung im Gemeinsamen Markt' *GRUR Int.* 1996, 377 at 379 and W. Gloy and D. Bruhn, 'Die Zulässigkeit von Preisvergleichen nach der Richtlinie 97/55/EG—Kehrtwende oder Kontinuität?' *GRUR* 1998, 226 at 236. For a contrary view see W. Tilmann, 'Richtlinie vergleichende Werbung' *GRUR Int.* 1997, 790 at 796.

Second, there has been some discussion in the German literature of whether, in the context in which the comparative representation is made not to consumers in general but to a particular consumer, the feature of the goods or services compared must be 'material', 'relevant' and 'representative' in objective terms or from the point of view of the consumer to whom the representation is made. This constitutes an attempt to import the '*Auskunftsvergleich*' exemption—the exemption concerning representations made in response to consumer requests for information[35]—into interpretation of the Directive.[36] The view that the exemption applies in the context of the Directive has the appeal that it respects the consumer's ability to determine the information that he needs in order to make an informed purchase in light of his own goals and priorities. However, to find the exemption in the text of the Directive requires a rather liberal reading of Article 3a(1)(c) and runs the risk that an exception to the application of the Article might develop in Germany which is unknown in the other Member States.

Third, the criterion of 'verifiability' raises the questions of what it means for a claim to be verifiable, by whom the relevant claim must be verifiable and to what standard of proof.

In relation to the issue of what it means for a claim to be verifiable, take the difficult case of comparative image advertising. Much advertising—particularly in markets characterised by little possible variation in product quality or price[37]—is designed simply to create positive associations regarding the image or status of goods or services. The economic and cultural value of such advertising has been fiercely contested.[38] But the importance of

[35] See above at 34.

[36] See C. Plassmann, 'Vergleichende Werbung im Gemeinsamen Markt' *GRUR* 1996, 377 at 379 and W. Tilmann, 'Richtlinie vergleichende Werbung' *GRUR* 1997, 790 at 796.

[37] For a description of this process and a catalogue of examples see R. Goldman and S. Papson, *Sign Wars: The Cluttered Language of Advertising* (New York, Guildford Press, 1996), chap. 1.

[38] For a summary of the economic debates see E. Mensch and A. Freeman, 'Efficiency and Image: Advertising as an Antitrust Issue' [1990] *Duke LJ*

this type of advertising and competition on the basis of image cannot be ignored. If an advertisement claims that a particular product is more 'trendy' than another product, then it is difficult to know whether it is making a verifiable claim. On the one hand it might be said that such a claim is an unverifiable statement of opinion. On the other hand, it might be that the claim, properly interpreted, is a verifiable claim of fact such as (i) that more consumers of the relevant age and type and in the relevant market hold the opinion that the competitor's product is less fashionable, or (ii) that the rival trader has presented his product as being one more associated with a 'classic' than a 'trendy' image. A recent decision of the Landgericht Köln, held that comparative taste tests of hamburgers and french fries showing that more of those tested preferred the products of Burger King to those of McDonald's were 'meaningless'.[39] However, the reasoning of this case is difficult to follow. There seems to be no clear reason why claims regarding consumer preference or the image that a rival trader projects for his product may not be verifiable claims of fact, capable of objective comparison. Further, the image of a product, whether measured by consumer perception or by the competitor's own promotional activities, may well be one of its material, relevant and representative features. Of course, it would even be possible for a trader to make a verifiable statement regarding his own opinion of the image of the two products,[40] but it would be difficult to classify such statements as capable of objective comparison. As will be outlined below, this issue of interpretation has enormous policy implications.[41]

---

321. For a strong critique of the cultural function of comparative image advertising see R. Goldman and S. Papson, *Sign Wars: The Cluttered Language of Advertising* (New York, Guildford Press, 1996).

[39] *McDonald's/Burger King*, LG Köln, No 81 O 185/98, 29 Jan. 1999, unreported. See App. II. See also P. Spink and R. Petty, 'Comparative Advertising in the European Union' (1998) 47 *ICLQ* 855 at 866.

[40] '[T]he state of a man's mind is as much a fact as the state of his digestion': *Edgington* v. *Fitzmaurice* (1885) 29 Ch. D 459 at 433, *per* Bowen LJ.

[41] See below at 74.

In relation to the issue of by whom the comparison must be verifiable, the Bundesrichtshof, in a decision handed down in 1996, held that each consumer should be able to verify the comparison.[42] This would reduce the need for expensive expert testimony in court, but seems unnecessarily to reduce the usefulness of permitted comparative advertising. Many comparisons can be verified only by persons who have the technical means to do so and comparative advertising should have the effect of discharging the consumer from the burden of verifying the information presented. It is this function of reducing consumer costs that is so central to the purpose of the Directive. A statement should therefore be regarded as verifiable if the advertiser can provide the respective information on request.[43] This position has now also been adopted by the Bundesgerichtshof, modifying its former view.[44]

In relation to the issue of the standard of proof to which the comparison must be verifiable, the Directive gives no guidance and courts will be likely to apply standards varying from case to case and from jurisdiction to jurisdiction. Uncertainty in this area is likely to lead to real disparities in the law of comparative advertising in Member States, an issue that echoes the need for a common European standard of deception.[45] The interpretation of Article 3a(1)(c) is obviously a matter regarding which significant questions have yet to be answered.

(ii) The Breadth of Article 3a(1)(c)

Yet however it is interpreted, the prohibition contained in Article 3a(1)(c) is potentially very sweeping in its effects. This

[42] *Preisvergleich II*, BGH GRUR 1996, 983 at 984ff.

[43] See C. Plassmann, 'Vergleichende Werbung im Gemeinsamen Markt' *GRUR* 1996, 377 at 379; W. Tilmann, 'Richtlinie vergleichende Werbung' *GRUR* 1997, 790 at 796; G. Schricker, 'Zur Werberechtspolitik der EG—Liberalisierung und Restriktion im Widerstreit' *GRUR Int.* 1992, 347 at 353; B. Menke, 'Die vergleichende Werbung in Deutschland nach der Richtlinie 97/55/EG und der BGH-Entscheidung *Testpreis-Angebot*' *WRP* 1998, 811 at 820; and F. Henning-Bodewig, 'Vergleichende Werbung—Liberalisierung des deutschen Rechts?' *GRUR Int.* 1997, 385 at 387.

[44] *Preisvergleichsliste II*, BGH GRUR 1999, 69.

[45] See above at 60ff.

is because Article 3a(1)(c) does not, on its face, contain any exceptions to the requirement that the comparison be of 'material, relevant, verifiable and representative features of [the] goods or services'. If no exceptions to these criteria can be read into the section, it has the surprising effect of rendering European law even stricter than existing German unfair competition law. Whereas in Germany comparisons made at the request of a consumer could refer to unrepresentative features,[46] Article 3a(1)(c) does not provide a similar exception. Likewise, under German law a trader was allowed to react to a competitor's unfair advertising campaign by publishing a comparison which would otherwise have been illegal, if it was in his legitimate interest to do so.[47] When the purported goal of the Directive was a liberalisation of European law on comparative advertising, it would be surprising if the Directive were, even in these respects, to render German unfair competition law more restrictive than it was. It is certainly conceivable that the German courts will find a way to save these well-established categories of permitted comparative advertising. This might be achieved by interpretation of the Directive (as, for example, in the approach to the '*Auskunftsvergleich*' exemption discussed above).[48] Alternatively, it might be achieved by reliance on the general defences of tort law.[49] For example, a comparison reacting to illegal comparative advertising published by a competitor might be permissible as self-defence.[50] However, either of these

[46] See *Bünder Glas*, BGH GRUR 1957, 23 at 24; *Vorsatz-Fensterflügel*, GRUR 1986, 618 at 620; A. Baumbach and W. Hefermehl, *Wettbewerbsrecht* 20th edn. (Munich, Beck, 1998) at §1, para. 374ff; and H. Köhler and H. Piper, *Gesetz gegen den unlauteren Wettbewerb* (Munich, Beck, 1995) at §1, para. 140ff.

[47] See *Betonzusatzmittel*, BGH GRUR 1962, 45 at 48; A. Baumbach and W. Hefermehl, *Wettbewerbsrecht* (20th edn., Munich, Beck, 1998) at §1, para. 369ff and H. Köhler and H. Piper, *Gesetz gegen den unlauteren Wettbewerb* (Beck, Munich, 1995) at §1, para. 137ff.

[48] See above at 34.

[49] In Germany, the law of unfair competition is a subcategory of tort law. See above at 29–30.

[50] This reasoning can be found in some judgments of the Reichsgericht, see *Leipziger Zeitungsstreit*, RG JW 1915, 913 at 915 and *Stahlbeton*, GRUR 1944, 34 at 35.

approaches would undermine the goal of the Directive in the harmonisation of the law of comparative advertising. The German courts, like those elsewhere in Europe, are therefore faced with the invidious choice of either giving this very sweeping prohibition full effect or undermining the goal of harmonisation.

(iii) The Policy of Article 3a(1)(c)

But perhaps more problematic than either the interpretation of Article 3a(1)(c), or even its potential breadth, is an issue concerning its underlying policy. Assuming that most image-based comparisons are unverifiable, the Article renders comparative image advertising essentially illegal. This is a policy choice that requires considerable justification.

It may be that the Directive adopts this approach to comparative image advertising because of its policy against misleading advertising, denigrating advertising and advertising that takes unfair advantage of a competitor's reputation. Assume that a statement regarding the image of a competitor's product is not a verifiable claim about consumer perception or the competitor's promotional activity. First, it is extremely difficult to present a competitor's market image accurately and therefore much comparative image advertising is likely to be misleading. Second, a critical claim regarding image is more likely to be denigrating than is a critical claim regarding accurate and important factual information about two products. Third, a claim of equivalence regarding image will almost certainly be taking advantage of the competitor's investment in creating that image. Given that such an advertisement will not also be communicating important factual information, it may be presumed that the advantage it takes of the competitor's investment is unfair. A prohibition on comparative image advertising may therefore be consistent with the overarching policy of the Directive.

However, these claims that comparative image advertising not involving verifiable claims of fact is likely to be misleading, denigrating or to take unfair advantage of a rival trader's reputation are highly contentious. As outlined below, the Directive's policy against advertising that constitutes denigration or taking unfair advantage of a competitor's reputation is itself contentious.[51] But even if that policy is accepted, it is not clear that comparative image advertising ought always on that basis to be prohibited.

First, image comparisons may involve statements of opinion that are neither verifiable nor, in that they do not constitute inaccurate claims of fact of the type outlined above, misleading. Take, for example, a series of advertisements in which the Pepsi Cola Company claimed that the Coca-Cola image of classic Americana was actually an image of 'snail-paced tedium'.[52] No-one in the relevant audience would have read this exaggerated claim as implying any statement of fact regarding issues such as the opinion of a majority of relevant consumers about Coca-Cola or the image that Coca-Cola had projected in its advertising. It was simply a joke made at the expense of the association with traditional 'Americana' that the Coca-Cola brand evokes. Read this way, it is hard to see how the advertisement could have been misleading.

Second, comparative image advertising need not be denigrating. Image comparisons may not claim that there is anything wrong with a competitor's image, but rather use that image to emphasise that the advertiser is trying to reach a different group of consumers. In the final section of this study an advertisement is discussed which involved the comparison of an English and two German types of car. The advertisement involved a play on image associations evoked by reference to the nationalities of the cars' manufacturers. There was no sense in which the image evoked for the German manufacturers was a derogatory one, and the gentle nationalism of the advertisement could hardly be seen as denigrating.

Third, comparative image advertising, even if it takes advantage of a rival trader's reputation, may not take *unfair* advantage of that reputation. Imagine, for example, that a particular trader

---

[51] See below at 77ff.

[52] R. Goldman and S. Papson, *Sign Wars: The Cluttered Language of Advertising* (New York, Guildford Press, 1996) at 32.

has been so successful in promoting an image for his product that it has come to be identified with that image in a particular market. It may be that, in order to enter that market, competitors must place their product in the consumer's mind by reference to the image benchmark set by the existing product. It is at best difficult to know whether comparative image advertising claiming that the advertiser's product has just as positive an image as the established product would be unfair in such circumstances. The extent to which image advertising creates barriers to entry has been fiercely contested[53] and a desire to reduce such barriers was a purported goal of at least the 1991 draft of the Directive.

It is clear, therefore, that many questions remain both about how Article 3a(1)(c) is likely to be interpreted and about the desirability of its underlying policy. It is suggested that the judges ought at least to keep the policy of the Directive against misleading advertising, denigrating advertising and advertising that takes unfair advantage of a trader's reputation in mind when applying this section and that they be reluctant to prohibit comparative image advertising that does not offend against that policy.

3. Comparisons that do More than is Necessary to Assist Rational Consumer Choice

As outlined above, comparative advertising may be capable of assisting rational consumer choice and yet still be prohibited by the Directive. This is advertising that either denigrates a competitor's goods or services or takes unfair advantage of a competitor's reputation in a way that exceeds what would be necessary to assist rational consumer choice.

This section attempts to make sense of the provisions of the Comparative Advertising Directive that prohibit denigration or taking unfair advantage of a competitor's reputation. It does so,

---

[53] See E. Mensch and A. Freeman, 'Efficiency and Image: Advertising as an Antitrust Issue', [1990] *Duke LJ* 321.

however, subject only to a very clear caveat. The caveat is that compliance with standards against denigration and taking unfair advantage ought not to have been made a mandatory condition for the permissibility of comparative advertising. One way in which at least some level of harmonisation might have been achieved without providing for mandatory compliance with these standards is discussed below.[54]

In order to understand why compliance with standards against denigration and taking unfair advantage ought not to have been made a mandatory condition for the permissibility of comparative advertising, it is important to recognise that these standards have received quite different levels of recognition in the legal systems of the European Union.

Thus, standards against denigration and taking unfair advantage have a respectable lineage in German law. §14 of the UWG provides for protection against denigration in competition. §1 of the UWG also provided for the protection of well-known trade marks against denigration, even before the *Markengesetz* of 1994. For example, under §1, the proprietor of the trade mark 'Mars' could restrain the parody of the slogan *'Mars macht mobil, bei Arbeit, Sport und Spiel'* as *'Mars macht mobil, bei Sex, Sport und Spiel'* on condom packets.[55] Unfair competition law also grants extensive protection from traders who take unfair advantage of a competitor's reputation. As outlined above, §1 of the UWG prohibits both explicit and implicit claims of equivalence.[56] In its judgments in *Rolls Royce*[57] and *Dimple*[58] the

---

[54] See below at 36.

[55] 'Mars makes you mobile, at work, sports and play'—*Markenverunglimpfung II*, BGH GRUR 1995, 57.

[56] *Bioäquivalenz-Werbung*, BGHZ 107, 136 at 138; *Konservenzeichen I*, GRUR 1966, 33 at 33; *Kräutermeister* [1981] GRUR 142 at 144. See also H. Köhler and H. Piper, *Gesetz gegen den unlauteren Wettbewerb* (Munich, Beck, 1995) at §1, para. 307ff; A. Baumbach and W. Hefermehl, *Wettbewerbsrecht* 20th edn. (Munich, Beck, 1998) at §1, para. 547ff; A. Peschel, *Die anlehnende vergleichende Werbung im deutschen und französischen Wettbewerbs- und Makenrecht* (Cologne, Carl Heymanns, 1996) at 113ff.

[57] BGHZ 86, 90 at 95.

[58] BGHZ 93, 96 at 98.

Bundesgerichtshof held that it constitutes unfair competition to exploit a competitor's goodwill by using his mark or by depicting his goods in advertising. The court has subsequently affirmed this principle and applied it in a variety of fact situations.[59] Of course most of these cases would probably now fall under §14 II No 3 of the *Markengesetz*. This section implements Article 5(2) of the Trade Marks Directive, an optional provision that, in certain circumstances, provides protection against the use of a sign which takes unfair advantage of, or is detrimental to, the distinctive character or repute of a registered trade mark. However the principle remains valid under §1 of the UWG.

By way of contrast, standards against denigration and taking unfair advantage of a competitor's reputation have been far less clearly recognised in United Kingdom law. Denigration was traditionally only actionable if it constituted injurious falsehood or defamation.[60] Taking unfair advantage of a competitor's reputation was traditionally only actionable if it operated by means of a misrepresentation under the action for passing off or caused consumer confusion as the infringement of a registered trade mark.[61] It is true that in some cases passing off has been found on the basis of only very attenuated misrepresentations, so that the actionable wrong has seemed more like taking unfair advantage of a trader's reputation.[62] It is true that the legislature of the United Kingdom chose to implement Article 5(2) of the Trade Marks Directive even though that provision was optional. It is further true that the AC, ITCC and RAC contain standards against denigration and that the AC also explicitly prohibits the exploitation of a competitor's goodwill.[63] However, the majority

[59] *Salomon*, BGH [1991] *GRUR* 465; *SL* [1991] *GRUR* 609; *McLaren* [1994] *GRUR* 732. See also A. Ohly, *Richterrecht und Generalklausel im Rechts des unlauteren Wettbewerbs—ein Methodenvergleich des englischen und des deutschen Rechts* (Cologne, Carl Heymanns, 1997) at 270ff.

[60] See above at 9.

[61] See above at 8.

[62] See, for example, *Taittinger* v. *Allbev* [1990] FSR 647, [1993] FSR 641 or *Chocosuisse* v. *Cadbury Limited* 15 Mar. 1999, CA, Lord Bingham CJ, Brooke and Chadwick LJJ.

[63] See above at 6–7 and 17–18.

of passing off decisions still insist on the need for proof of misrepresentation[64] and the interpretation of Article 5(2) as a provision against the dilution of trade mark was slow to take hold in the United Kingdom courts[65] and amongst some academic commentators.[66] Denigration and taking unfair advantage of a competitor's reputation are concepts that have yet to enjoy wide acceptance in United Kingdom law.

This divergence in the level of recognition that standards against denigration and taking unfair advantage have enjoyed in the different legal systems of Europe exists because of fundamental disagreements about the extent to which such standards can be defined, and about how they may impact on the operation of a free market and the principle of free speech. These are questions that do not appear to have been adequately addressed in the discussion leading up to the Comparative Advertising Directive. It is our submission that protection against denigration and taking unfair advantage ought not to have been introduced in advance of such discussion. It ought certainly not to have been introduced *en passant* as part of a directive aimed at liberalising comparative advertising. The broader issues of when denigration or taking unfair advantage of a competitor's reputation ought to be actionable are issues upon which there is still much work to be done.

---

[64] See, for example, *Hodgkinson & Corby Ltd.* v. *Wards Mobility Services Ltd.* [1995] FSR 169 at 175 where Jacob J claimed, perhaps somewhat hyperbolically, that '[a]t the heart of passing off lies deception or its likelihood, deception of the ultimate consumer in particular . . . Never has the tort shown even a slight tendency to stray beyond cases of deception. Were it to do so it would enter the field of honest competition, declared unlawful for some reason other than deceptiveness. Why there would be any such reason I cannot imagine.'

[65] See *BASF Plc* v. *CEP (UK) Plc* Knox J, Ch.D, 26 Oct. 1995, unreported, and *Baywatch Production Co. Inc.* v. *Home Video Channel* [1997] FSR 22. However compare *Marks & Spencer Plc* v. *One in a Million Ltd.* [1998] FSR 265 at 272–3; *Oasis Stores Ltd.'s Trade Mark Application* [1998] RPC 631 at 646–8; *Audi-Med Trade Mark* [1998] RPC 863 at 869–71; and *British Telecommunications Plc* v. *One in a Million Ltd.* [1999] FSR 1 at 25.

[66] See, for example, W. R. Cornish, *Intellectual Property* 3rd edn. (London: Sweet & Maxwell, 1996) at 624–5.

Accepting, however, that these standards have been included in the Comparative Advertising Directive, it remains to be determined whether they can be given shape in that context.

(a) Denigration

Article 3a(1)(e) prohibits advertising which discredits or denigrates the 'trade marks, trade names, other distinguishing marks, goods, services, activities or circumstances of a competitor'.

Even if it is accepted that a standard against denigration ought to have been included in the Comparative Advertising Directive, it is difficult to give Article 3a(1)(e) any content. This is because it is difficult to imagine an advertisement in which a comparison is made that (i) denigrates a competitor, his marks, his goods or services in a way that is disproportionate to the goal of assisting rational consumer choice, but (ii) relates to material, relevant, verifiable and representative features of the goods or services in a way that is not misleading, is objective and compares like with like.

One decision in which Article 3a(1)(e) has been considered is that of the Bundesgerichtshof in *Testpreis-Angebot*.[67] In this case the court held that the slogan '*Billige Composite Rackets muten wir Ihnen nicht zu*'[68] was denigratory and prohibited under Article 3a(1)(e). In doing so, the court suggested that any advertisement which claims that a competitor's product is inferior is denigratory.[69] By this the court may have intended that all claims that a competitor's product is inferior are derogatory. Alternatively, it may have been suggesting an approach similar to that represented in the United Kingdom by the practice note to rule 15 of the Radio Authority's *Advertising and Sponsorship Code*. It will be recalled that that section claims that a compet-

[67] BGH GRUR 1998, 824.

[68] 'We would not seriously expect you to buy cheap composite racquets'.

[69] B. Menke, 'Die vergleichende Werbung in Deutschland nach der Richtlinie 97/55/EG und der BGH-Entscheidung *Testpreis-Angebot*' *WRP* 1998, 811 at 816 and F. Henning-Bodewig, 'Vergleichende Werbung—Liberalisierung des deutschen Rechts?' *GRUR Int.* 1999, 385 at 393 agree with this conclusion.

ing product ought not to be 'depicted as generally unsatisfactory or inferior'.[70] By the term 'generally' it is presumably intended to describe advertisements that criticise a competitor's products or services without making reference to their specific features. This may have been what the defendant was doing in *Testpreis-Angebot* in simply referring to the composite racquets as '*Billige*'.[71]

However, neither of these approaches offers a satisfactory reading of Article 3a(1)(e). The first of these approaches ought to be rejected because every critical comparison necessarily claims that a rival product is either of an inferior quality or over-priced, a point that was recognised by the Bundesgerichtshof itself in the *Vergleichen Sie* case.[72] The interpretation therefore has the potential to render nugatory much of the liberalisation of comparative advertising intended by the framers of the Directive. The second of these approaches ought to be rejected because, by effectively requiring that an advertisement offer a comparison of 'one or more material, relevant, verifiable and representative features of' a competitor's goods or services, it adds nothing to the explicit requirements of Article 3a(1)(c).

A better approach to Article 3a(1)(e) is to apply it in situations in which an otherwise acceptable comparison is expressed in a manner that is denigrating, though not so exaggerated as to make the advertisement lacking in objectivity or misleading. Three such situations suggest themselves. First, the Article may apply where the language of a particular advertisement is colourful, though not exaggerated to the point of inaccuracy. Imagine, for example, that an advertisement claims that 'Drink A is twice as !?*!%*! sweet as drink B'. The claim regarding sugar content may itself be verifiable, but the use of an expletive might be said to denigrate the competitor's product. Second, the Article may apply where the advertisement illustrates an acceptable comparison with images that have an emotional impact that denigrates

---

[70] RAC at 9 See above at 18.

[71] 'Cheap' in a pejorative sense.

[72] GRUR Int. 1999, 453 at 455.

the competitor's product and is not proportionate to the probative value of the objective comparison that is being drawn. Imagine, for example, that an advertisement claims that one particular brand of child's car seat is safer than another. If such an advertisement were to illustrate this comparison with pictures of an undamaged and a mutilated crash dummy sitting in each of the chairs, it might be that these pictures would be held to denigrate the competitor's product, even though they might be part of an objective and truthful comparison of material, relevant, verifiable and representative features of the car seats.[73] Third, the Article may apply where a mark associated with a particular product is parodied, but the central claim of the advertisement otherwise meets the criteria of Article 3. Imagine, for example, that an advertisement claimed particular tyres were more shock-absorbent than those produced by Michelin and included a parody of the Michelin Man made, not from rubber tyres, but from Stone Age wheels. Such a parody may well fall foul of the requirement that comparisons be objective and not misleading contained in Article 3a(1)(a) and (c). But if it did not, on the basis that the Michelin tyres were in fact less shock-absorbent and that the public would be unlikely to be misled by the parody as to the extent to which they were less shock absorbent, Article 3a(1)(e) may nevertheless operate to prohibit the advertisement. Even if the central claim of the advertisement that the tyres were more shock absorbent than those made by Michelin otherwise met the criteria of Article 3a(1), the parody might denigrate the Michelin Man. Other than in these specific situations, it will be difficult to find examples of comparative advertisements that might satisfy Article 3a(1)(a)–(d),(f) and (g) and yet fall foul of Article 3a(1)(e).

(b) Taking Unfair Advantage

Article 3a(1)(g) prohibits comparative advertising which takes 'unfair advantage of the reputation of a trade mark, trade name

[73] AC rule 20.2 provides: '[t]he only acceptable use of another business's broken or defaced products in advertisements is in the illustration of comparative tests, and the source, nature and results of these should be clear'.

or other distinguishing marks of a competitor or of the designation of origin of competing products'. The effect of this Article is strengthened by Article 3a(1)(h) which prohibits comparative advertising that presents 'goods or services as imitation or replicas of goods or services bearing a protected trade mark or trade name'. Like Article 3a(1)(e), Article 3a(1)(g) is of potentially limited operation and it is not easy to give the Article content. Article 3a(1)(h) is an even more puzzling and anomalous addition to Article 3a(1)(g).

Consider first the operation of Article 3a(1)(g). It will be recalled that Article 3a(1)(c) may have the effect of virtually prohibiting advertising involving comparisons of image rather than factual information. If it does, then it is difficult to see when a permissible comparative advertisement—one that relates to verifiable, material, relevant and representative features of the goods or services and compares them in a way that is objective and not misleading—could be said to take unfair advantage of a competitor's reputation. Just two situations in which Article 3a(1)(g) may be operative suggest themselves.

First, corresponding to the context in which an otherwise permissible critical comparison is expressed in a manner that renders it denigratory, there may be situations in which an otherwise permissible comparison is expressed in a way that unnecessarily takes advantage of a competitor's goodwill. The Association pour la Protection de la Propriété Internationale (AIPPI) has suggested that the use of logos and picture marks in a comparison is apt to take unfair advantage of a competitor's goodwill whenever the same comparison could be made using a trade name.[74] It is suggested, however, that the use of logos and picture marks to identify a competitor ought presumptively to be fair if this is how the competitor normally chooses to be identified in the market place. The goal of promoting consumer information justifies the use of images by which consumers will most easily identify a competitor.

A second situation in which Article 3a(1)(g) may be operative

[74] See F. Henning-Bodewig, 'Vergleichende Werbung—Liberalisierung des deutschen Rechts?' *GRUR Int.* 1999, 385 at 393.

is that in which a factual comparison is drawn between two products in a context in which consumer choice is usually based upon image associations rather than objective, verifiable and material criteria. In particular, the Article may prohibit claims concerning the equivalence of some generic and luxury goods. Take, as an example, a *table de concordance* pointing to the chemical equivalence of certain generic and branded perfumes. The relevance of Article 3a(1)(g) to this situation depends upon three assumptions. Assume first that the manufacture of such perfumes is legal, although whether this is the case will vary between the jurisdictions of the European Union.[75] Assume, too, that the advertisement is not caught by Article 3a(1)(h), although it is likely that Article 3a(1)(h) would be operative in this context. Finally, assume that the chemical formula of a perfume is a material, relevant and representative feature of the perfume, although it is possible that this is not the case, given that few consumers are likely to base purchase decisions on chemical formulae. In the situation in which these three assumptions held, a court could nevertheless hold that a trader advertising his perfume as chemically identical to a well-known fragrance was, in fact, unfairly exploiting the reputation of the well-known brand. This is because the purpose of the advertisement would not be to inform consumers that the two products could perform the same function, nor even really to inform them about a relevant, material and representative feature of the goods. It would be to assist them in appropriating the cachet of luxury goods without paying the premium that association with a luxury image suggests. This might be held unfairly to appropriate the reputation of the competing perfume's brand. Importantly, this argument would not be successful against *tables de concordance* comparing generic and branded products where something

[75] For example, whereas English law does not provide for protection against imitation outside the limits of intellectual property legislation and the common law tort of passing off, §1 UWG can be relied on to prevent imitation under certain circumstances. For an overview see P. J. Kaufmann, *Passing Off and Misappropriation*, (Munich, VCH, 1986); A. Kamperman Sanders, *Unfair Competition Law* (Oxford, Clarendon Press, 1997) and M. J. Spence, 'Passing Off and the Misappropriation of Valuable Intangibles' (1996) *LQR* 472.

other than the image of the goods is central to rational consumer choice, for example, *tables de concordance* comparing generic and branded drugs. Thus Article 3a(1)(g) seems written with the very particular situation of luxury goods in mind.

Given this apparently limited purpose of Article 3a(1)(g), the operation of Article 3a(1)(h) presents something of a puzzle. Article 3a(1)(h), which is modelled upon French law,[76] prohibits all representations of particular goods or services as replicas of branded products or services. It is to be assumed that Article 3a(1)(h), in referring to 'protected' trade marks or names, includes both registered and common law trade marks. This Article was presumably intended to give the holders of intellectual property rights a secondary line of attack against traders in counterfeit goods. However, the Article could add little to Article 3a(1)(g) in such a context and may have the unfortunate effect in other contexts of prohibiting the communication of information that is clearly important to rational consumer purchase decisions. Take, for example, the *table de concordance* that compares not perfumes but generic and branded drugs. Information about chemical composition is indisputably important to decisions about drug purchase, because it relates centrally to the function that the product is designed to serve. To communicate information about chemical equivalence in this context is not to take unfair advantage of a competitor's reputation; it is to provide vital information to consumers and to encourage fair competition on the basis of price. Making such information as widely available as possible is compatible with the goal of the patent system that, once a patent upon a particular drug has lapsed, competition in the production of the drug should be encouraged. Such competition in both the production and advertising of drugs will often have the effect of keeping drug prices low, resulting in lower community healthcare costs. However, in that *tables de concordance* could be interpreted as

[76] Article L. 121–9 of the *Code de la consommation.* On the legality of *tables de concordance* under French law see A. Peschel, *Die anlehnende vergleichende Werbung im deutschen und französischen Wettbewerbs- und Markenrecht* (Cologne, Carl Heymanns, 1996) at 79ff.

presenting generic products as 'imitations' or 'replicas' of branded products, it may be that Article 3a(1)(h) will prohibit tables dealing with medicines just as much as tables dealing with perfumes. This must be an anomalous effect of the Article, given the goal of the Directive to allow comparative advertising that assist rational consumer choice. It is suggested that the courts should read this Article as restrictively as possible, and certainly to read it with the overarching policy of the Directive always in mind.

6
The Implementation of the Directive

The issue of the most appropriate implementation of the Comparative Advertising Directive is far from straightforward. In large part, it touches upon the issue of the scope of the Directive considered above. It may be that the implementation of the Directive requires careful revision of national trade mark and even copyright law. Unfortunately, however, the Directive itself offers almost no guidance on these issues.

In the United Kingdom, the most likely form of implementation will be as an amendment to the Control of Misleading Advertisements Regulations 1988.[1] The enforcement of the provisions of the Directive will then ultimately be the responsibility of the Director General of Fair Trading, although under those regulations his jurisdiction is only supplementary and the Director General is unlikely to act unless the relevant Trading Standards Department or the Advertising Standards Authority has first been approached. It is currently unlikely that the trade marks legislation will be amended, and the amendment of copyright law has not even been discussed.[2]

In Germany, outside the specific questions of trade mark and copyright, the form of implementation for the Directive is currently a matter of considerable debate.[3] This issue arises because its style of drafting is difficult to reconcile with the style of the

---

[1] This was confirmed by the Department of Trade and Industry in a circular to interested parties dated 28 July 1999.

[2] *Ibid.*

[3] For an overview see B. Menke, 'Die vergleichende Werbung in Deutschland nach der Richtlinie 97/55/EG und der BGH-Entscheidung *Testpreis-Angebot*' [1998] *WRP* 811 at 817.

UWG. First, the provisions of the UWG are short. §1 of the UWG, which has so far been the statutory basis for the regulation of comparative advertising, consists of 25 words, whereas the text of the Directive is almost longer than the UWG itself. Second, the UWG uses general language while the Directive regulates comparative advertising in great detail. Third, the UWG contains only prohibitions and assumes that every act which is not prohibited is legal. The central provision of the Directive is, however, permissive.

Notwithstanding these differences of style, there are many who have argued that the Directive should be implemented by inserting it more or less verbatim into the UWG. It is argued that only this solution could ensure legal certainty and enable Germany to fulfil its obligations under the law of the European Union.[4]

Others, however, have argued that no legislative action is necessary.[5] Their position has been strengthened by the decision of the Bundesgerichtshof in *Testpreis-Angebot*,[6] now confirmed in *Preisvergleichsliste II*[7] and *Vergleichen Sie*.[8] These decisions, which are described above,[9] may render a change of the UWG superfluous. While it is true that there is no doctrine of *stare decisis* in German law, which means that lower courts are free to depart from a decision made by the Bundesgerichtshof, all courts are obliged to interpret national statutes in conformity with European Union directives as a matter of European law. This obligation may be sufficient to ensure that the Directive will be respected by all courts in the country.

[4] See C. Plassmann, 'Vergleichende Werbung im Gemeinsamen Markt' *GRUR Int.* 1996, 377 at 382 and W. Tilmann, 'Richtlinie vergleichende Werbung' *GRUR Int.* 1997, 790 at 791.

[5] See R. Sack, 'Die Bedeutung der EG-Richtlinie 84/450/EWG und 97/55/EG über irreführende und vergleichende Werbung für das deutsche Wettbewerbsrecht' *GRUR Int.* 1998, 263 at 272 and B. Menke, 'Die vergleichende Werbung in Deutschland nach der Richtlinie 97/55/EG und der BGH-Entscheidung *Testpreis-Angebot*' *WRP* 1998, 811 at 818.

[6] BGH GRUR 1998, 824.

[7] BGH GRUR 1999, 69. See App II.

[8] GRUR Int. 1999, 453. See App II.

[9] See above at 37ff.

However, there is also a case for a halfway solution.[10] A provision consisting of three paragraphs could be introduced into the UWG. The first paragraph could define comparative advertising in accordance with Article 2(2a) of the Directive (perhaps adding that the reference must be of a comparative nature). The second paragraph could provide that comparative advertising would not normally constitute unfair competition, but that it could exceptionally do so. The third paragraph could provide that the provision was to be interpreted in accordance with the Directive. This solution would respect the style of the UWG while ensuring that the Directive would be applied by all German courts. It seems to provide an appropriate means of both respecting the techniques of German unfair competition law and providing for Germany to meet its European law obligations.

---

[10] See also F. Henning-Bodewig, 'Vergleichende Werbung—Liberalisierung des deutschen Rechts?' *GRUR Int.* 1999, 385 at 394.

7

The Way Forward

In this study we have proposed a model for interpretation of the Comparative Advertising Directive that both makes sense of its opaque and sometimes confused language and is as faithful as possible to its apparent goals. However, our model does not render the application of the Directive straightforward and just in every situation.

Consider the following case. The programme of the 1992 BBC Royal Albert Hall 'Proms' concert series, the final concert of which is a famous musical celebration of British nationalism, included an advertisement for the car 'Jaguar'. The advertisement featured a picture of a Jaguar car on a German motorway and a sign pointing to Munich, the home of BMW, and to Stuttgart, the home of Mercedes-Benz. The caption read: 'Why a Jaguar?' I asked. 'Because', he said, 'I've always preferred Elgar to Wagner'. Imagine that either BMW or Daimler-Benz were to bring an action against Jaguar to prevent illegal comparative advertising. First, it would need to be established that this was a comparative advertisement, that is that it 'explicitly or by implication identifie[d] a competitor'. Although no competitor was mentioned explicitly, the implicit reference to German manufacturers of prestige saloon cars is obvious. BMW and Mercedes-Benz are known as the leading German producers in this market. This reference is underlined by the sign pointing to the cities where the companies are based. Second, it would have to be determined whether the comparative reference in the advertisement was to the competitors themselves or to their goods or services. If the reference were to the competitors themselves, and to their German nationality, the advertisement would either not be regulated by the Directive or, more probably, be rendered illegal on that basis alone.[1] Third, it would have to be determined whether the advertisement constituted *permitted* comparative advertising. The advertisement could not be found illegal on the basis that it was misleading or denigrating, or took unfair advantage of a rival trader's reputation. There was clearly no false claim of fact made expressly or impliedly in the advertisement. Its gentle nationalism could hardly be said to have been denigrating. After all, Wagner is a composer of at least equal stature to Elgar. Finally, Jaguar did not need to exploit the reputation of BMW and Mercedes to establish itself as a prestige mark. The cars were all clearly recognised as market substitutes. The advertisement may be rendered illegal, however, because the comparative statement, as an unattributed statement of opinion, probably constitutes an unverifiable and subjective comparison.

That so harmless and amusing an advertisement as this one might be rendered illegal by the Comparative Advertising Directive highlights two important difficulties with the application of the Directive.

First, the focus of the Directive on assisting rational consumer choice and its consequent prohibition of comparative image advertising may prove an unnecessary restriction upon freedom of speech. We take it as axiomatic that, in the absence of compelling reasons to curb it, even commercial speech should be free. This proposition has repeatedly been affirmed by the European Court of Human Rights under Article 10 of the European Convention on Human Rights.[2] Justification for curbing the freedom of commercial speech may, or may not, be found in balancing the rights of traders or in protecting the interests of consumers. But commercial speech which neither is misleading nor denigrating, nor takes unfair advantage of a rival trader's reputation, must presumptively be free. The tendency of the Directive to accumulate provisions designed to further the

[1] See above at 49.

[2] See Case 3/1988/147/201 *Markt Intern Verlag GmbH und Klaus Beermann* v. *Germany* para. 26; Case 8/1993/403/481 *Casado Coca* v. *Spain* para. 35ff; Case 59/1997/843/1049 *Hertel* v. *Switzerland* para. 31, 46ff.

same ends (for example, that advertising must be verifiable as well as simply not misleading, or that it must compare goods of the same designation of origin rather than simply goods intended for the same purpose) has the unfortunate consequence of sometimes curbing free speech when no strong competing interest is at stake. Even the pre-Directive German law, expressed as it was in general clauses, gave the judges greater room to manœuvre in the development of appropriate exceptions to the regulation of comparative advertising.

Second, there is a real danger that possible differences of interpretation across the community will thwart the goal of harmonisation in relation to comparative advertising. As will have been evident in the preceding sections of this study, comparative advertising is not a topic amenable to discrete regulation on the basis of standards that have wide acceptance across the European Union. The regulation of comparative advertising necessarily touches upon several extremely contentious, and fundamental, issues in the law of unfair competition, issues such as the extent to which traders ought to be protected from denigration or from the effects of others taking advantage of their goodwill. The harmonisation of comparative advertising law was from the outset destined to be a difficult task.

But the European Union did not approach the harmonisation of comparative advertising in a way that reflected an awareness of its complexity. It was always open to the Union to provide, as it did in the Misleading Advertising Directive, for a set of standards that would guarantee some level of common regulation across Europe, while allowing Member States to adopt quite different positions in relation to issues concerning which no common European standard has emerged and the Member States have quite divergent national traditions. This approach could, of course, have been effected by providing that the Directive was pre-emptive only of certain national laws prohibiting comparative advertising and not an exclusive code for the regulation of the subject.[3] Alternatively, it was open to the

---

[3] See above at 51ff.

Union to leave the regulation of comparative advertising until the fundamental issues upon which its regulation depends, but upon which there is yet to be specific agreement at a European level, have themselves been harmonised. This might have been particularly appropriate, given the principle of subsidiarity and the extent to which the practice of advertising is highly dependent upon local culture. Instead, the Union adopted the approach of exhaustively regulating comparative advertising, relying *en passant* upon standards that have yet to be agreed.

It is our belief that this approach to the regulation of comparative advertising is not only wrong in principle, in that it forces through harmonisation on questions about which there is yet to be substantial discussion, let alone agreement, at the European level, but that it will also mean that the Directive is less effective in achieving harmonisation than it might otherwise have been. The terminology employed in the Directive is often vague. Sometimes this is justified by the difficulty of setting precise standards against unfair competition, such as the difficulty of providing tests to distinguish critical and denigrating references to a competitor. All too often it is simply the result of poor drafting, such as in the provisions concerning the scope of the Directive. The harmonising effect of the Directive depends to a large extent on whether it is read sympathetically by judges in the national courts. It is at least arguable that a German and a United Kingdom judge, each approaching the Directive from the perspective of his or her different legal tradition, could read the vague language of this text in ways that might imply little change in the law of either country.

Consider how German and United Kingdom judges are likely to respond to the case of the Jaguar advertisement offered above. The German judge, used to the general prohibition of comparative advertising that has been prevailing in Germany for the last 70 years, is perhaps more prone to accept that the Directive would render the advertisement illegal. He may even disagree with the suggestion that the advertisement is harmless and see it as disparaging and unfair. A United Kingdom judge, by contrast, will resent a prohibition of this advertisement, which would seem to him an unnecessary interference with the advertiser's right to free speech. He will thus look for ways to avoid the application of the Directive to this case.

We have tried to develop a model which fits the interpretation of Article 3a to the apparent policy underlying the Directive. It is our hope that this model will help to overcome some of the difficulties caused by the wording of this piece of European legislation. Our model cannot, however, bridge the gap that still exists between United Kingdom and German attitudes about the the appropriate level of protection for a trader's goodwill. Much of the work remaining before the legal regulation of comparative advertising is really harmonised will have to be done by the European Court of Justice, which will have to apply the Directive in full awareness of its complexities. A number of precedents clustering around open-textured provisions such as 'denigration' or 'unfair advantage' will help to create a common understanding among European judges and lawyers. The development of this European case law should, however, be accompanied by further comparative research about what is fair and unfair in competition. In particular, both the Commission and the legal academic community need to turn their attention to the difficult central problem of the appropriate level of protection for a trader's goodwill.

APPENDIX I—United Kingdom Materials

1. Advertising Code*

Comparisons

19.1 Comparisons can be explicit or implied and can relate to advertisers' own products or to those of their competitors; they are permitted in the interests of vigorous competition and public information.

19.2 Comparisons should be clear and fair. The elements of any comparison should not be selected in a way that gives the advertisers an artifical advantage.

. . .

Denigration

20.1 Advertisers should not unfairly attack or discredit other businesses or their products.

20.2 The only acceptable use of another business's broken or defaced products in advertisements is in the illustration of comparative tests, and the source, nature and results of these should be clear.

Exploitation of Goodwill

21.1 Advertisers should not make unfair use of the goodwill attached to the trade mark, name, brand, or the advertising campaign of any other organisation.

* A full set of the British Codes of Advertising and Sales Promotion is available free from The Committee of Advertising Practice website (www.cap.org.uk) or by telephoning 020 7580 5555. The CAP Copy Advice Team on 020 7580 4100 are on hand to give best, free and commercially confidential copy advice to anyone involved in copy clearance.

2. The ITC Code of Advertising Standards and Practice

Prices and Price Claims

25 Advertisements indicating price, price comparisons or price reductions must comply with all relevant statutory requirements including those contained in the Consumer Protection Act 1987 . . .

Comparisons

26 Advertisements containing comparisons with other advertisers, or other products or services, are permissible in the interests of vigorous competition and public information provided they comply with the terms of this rule and rule 27.

(a) All comparisons must respect the principles of fair competition and must be so designed that there is no likelihood of the consumer being misled as a result of the comparison, either about the product or service advertised or that with which it is compared.

(b) The subject matter of a comparison must not be chosen in such a way as to confer an artificial advantage upon the advertiser.

(c) Points of comparison must be based on facts which can be substantiated and must not be unfairly selected.

In particular:

(i) the basis of comparison must be the same for all the products or services being compared and must be clearly established in the advertisement so that it can be seen that like is being compared with like;

(ii) generalised superiority claims must not be made on the basis of selective comparisons.

Denigration

27 Advertisements must not unfairly attack or discredit other products or services, advertisers or advertisements expressly or by implication.

3. Radio Authority Advertising and Sponsorship Code

Rule 13—Price Claims

Advertisements indicating price comparisons or reductions must comply with all relevant requirements of the Consumer Protection Act 1987 (Section III) and Regulations made under it.

Practice Notes

Actual and comparative prices quoted must be accurate at the time of broadcast and must not mislead. Claims of 'lowest prices' must be supported by evidence from the retailer that none of his competitors sell the advertised product or service at a lower price. Claims of 'unbeatable prices' or 'you can't buy cheaper' must be supported by evidence from the retailer that his prices are as low as his competitors' . . .

Rule 14—Comparisons

Advertisements containing comparisons with other advertisers, or other products, are permissible in the interest of vigorous competition and public information provided that:

(a) the principles of fair competition are respected and the comparisons used are not likely to mislead the listener about either product;
(b) points of comparison are based on fairly selected facts which can be substantiated;
(c) comparisons chosen do not given an advertiser an artificial advantage over his competitor;
(d) they comply with Rule 15.

Rule 15—Denigration

Advertisements must not unfairly attack or discredit other products, advertisers or advertisments directly or by implication.

Practice Note

Advertisers must not discredit competitors or their products by describing them in a derogatory way or in a denigratory tone of voice. This is particularly important in comparative advertising. Whilst it is acceptable for an advertiser whose product has a demonstrable advantage over a competitor to point this out, care must be taken to ensure that the competitor product is not depicted as generally unsatisfactory or inferior.

4. Trade Marks Act 1994, section 10(6)

10. Infringement of registered trade mark

(1) A person infringes a registered trade mark if he uses in the course of trade a sign which is identical with the trade mark in relation to goods or services which are identical with those for which it is registered.

(2) A person infringes a registered trade mark if he uses in the course of trade a sign where because—

(a) the sign is identical with the trade mark and is used in relation to goods or services similar to those for which the trade mark is registered, or

(b) the sign is similar to the trade mark and is used in relation to goods or services identical with or similar to those for which the trade mark is registered, there exists a likelihood of confusion on the part of the public, which includes the likelihood of association with the trade mark.

(3) A person infringes a registered trade mark if he uses in the course of trade a sign which—

(a) is identical with or similar to the trade mark, and

(b) is used in relation to goods or services which are not similar to those for which the trade mark is registered,

where the trade mark has a reputation in the United Kingdom and the use of the sign, being without due cause, takes unfair advantage of, or is detrimental to, the distinctive character or the repute of the trade mark.

(4) For the purposes of this section a person uses a sign if, in particular, he—

(a) affixes it to goods or the packaging thereof,
(b) offers or exposes goods for sale, puts them on the market or stocks them for those purposes under the sign, or offers or supplies services under the sign;
(c) imports or exports goods under the sign; or
(d) uses the sign on business papers or in advertising.

(5) A person who applies a registered trade mark to material intended to be used for labelling or packaging goods, as a business paper, or for advertising goods or services, shall be treated as a party to any use of the material which infringes the registered trade mark if when he applied the mark he knew or had reason to believe that the application of the mark was not duly authorised by the proprietor or a licensee.

(6) Nothing in preceding provisions of this section shall be construed as preventing the use of a registered trade mark by any person for the purpose of identifying goods or services as those of the proprietor or a licensee.

But any such use otherwise than in accordance with honest practices in industrial or commercial matters shall be treated as infringing the registered trade mark if the use without due cause takes unfair advantage of, or is detrimental to, the distinctive character or repute of the trade mark.

5. Barclays Bank PLC v RBS Advanta (Chancery Division, 26 January 1996, Laddie J, [1996] RPC 307)

Facts:

The plaintiff was the largest supplier of VISA credit card services in the country. The defendant was a joint venture incorporated in Scotland which planned to launch a competing credit card. The advertising literature that the defendant intended to use to launch this credit card consisted of (i) a leaflet outlining 15 claimed advantages to the new card in 'bullet points' and (ii) a brochure that included two tables comparing features of the new card with those of various established cards. The two tables referred to the plaintiff's card by means of its registered trade mark. The leaflet and brochure together constituted one advertisement. The plaintiff brought an action for an interlocutory injunction to restrain the distribution of the defendant's advertisement.

Held:

[*Laddie J set out section 10(6) of the Trade Marks Act 1994 and continued:*]

Both Mr Young QC who appeared before me on behalf of the plaintiff and Mr Silverleaf who appeared for the defendant were united in criticising the drafting of this provision. It is a mess. The first half of the subsection allows comparative advertising. Its meaning is clear. However the second half, beginning with the words 'But any such use . . .' is a qualifying proviso and its meaning is far from clear.

The origin of the wording in section 10(6)

Section 10(6) is not derived directly either from the EEC Trade Mark Directive 89/104/EEC ('the directive') or from the Paris Convention, neither of which expressly exempts comparative advertising from infringement. The result is that the first half of section 10(6) is home-grown. However the first half of the proviso can be traced back to Article 10bis(2) of the Paris Convention, dealing with unfair competition and from there to Article 6(1) of the directive. The latter has been adopted, with minor and, for present purposes, irrelevant changes in wording as section 11(2) of the Act which is as follows:

'A registered trade mark is not infringed by—
  (a) the use by a person of his own name or address,
  (b) the use of indications concerning the kind, quality, quantity, intended purpose, value, geographical origin, the time of production of goods or rendering of services, or other characteristics of goods or services or
  (c) the use of the trade mark where it is necessary to indicate the intended purpose of a product or service (in particular, as accessories or spare parts).

provided the use is *in accordance with honest practices in industrial or commercial matters.*' (emphasis added)

The same language is also to be found in Article 5(2) of the directive and, from there, in Schedule 1 paragraph 3(2) of the Act in relation to collective marks.

The language used in the second part of the proviso is to be found in Articles 4(3), 4(4) and 5(2) of the directive and in section 10(3) of the Act which provides:

'A person infringes a registered trade mark if he uses in the course of trade a sign which—
  (a) is identical with or similar to the trade mark, and
  (b) is used in relation to goods or services which are not similar to those for which the trade mark is registered,

where the trade mark has a reputation in the United Kingdom and the use of the sign, *being without due cause, takes unfair advantage of or is detrimental to, the distinctive character or repute of the trade mark.*' (emphasis added)

. . .

It is difficult to formulate any construction of the proviso to section 10(6) which affords every word in it a distinct function and which also is consistent with sections 10(3) and 11(2). In my view it is necessary to face up to the difficulties of draughting and to consider section 10(6) alone without deciding whether precisely the same construction of the wording used is appropriate for the other sub-sections.

Construction of Section 10(6)

As a general proposition, it seems to me that . . . the primary objective of section 10(6) is to allow comparative advertising. As long as the use of the competitor's mark is 'honest', then there is nothing wrong with telling the public of the relative merits of competing goods or services and using registered trade marks to identify them. The proviso should not be construed in a way which effectively prohibits all comparative advertising.

First, Mr Silverleaf argued that if it is to be brought into operation, the onus is on the registered proprietor to show that the factors indicated in the proviso exist. I did not understand Mr Young to dispute this and, in my view, Mr Silverleaf is right.

Secondly, there will be no infringement unless the use of the registered mark is not in accordance with honest practices. Both counsel agreed, rightly in my view, that this test is objective. This part of the proviso simply means that if the use is considered honest by members of a reasonable audience, it will not infringe. The fact that the advertising pokes fun at the proprietor's goods or services and emphasises the benefits of the defendant's is a normal incidence of comparative advertising. Its aim will be to divert customers from the proprietor. No reasonable observer would expect one trader to point to all the advantages of its competitor's business and failure to do so does not per se take the advertising outside what reasonable people would regard as 'honest'. Thus mere trade puffery, even if uncomfortable to the registered proprietor, does not bring the advertising within the scope of trade mark infringement. Much advertising copy is recognised by the public as hyperbole. The Act does not impose on the courts an obligation to try to enforce, through the back door of trade mark legislation, a more puritanical standard. If, on the other hand, a reasonable reader is likely to say, on being given the full facts, that the advertisement is not honest, for example because it is significantly misleading, then the protection from trade mark infringement is removed.

Mr Young suggested, at least in relation to section 11(2)(b), that if the registered mark is used in a trade mark sense in the comparative advertising it cannot be honest. I do not agree. Whether the mark is being used in that way has nothing to do with whether that use is honest. In any event the first half of section 10(6) exempts from infringement use of registered trade marks for the purpose of identifying goods or services as those of the proprietor or a licensee. Such use will almost invariably be used in a trade mark sense. If Mr Young's submission as to the scope of the proviso in section 11(2)(b) is correct, and applicable to the section 10(6) defence, then that defence would cease to exist, since the immunity given by the first half of the sub-section would be removed by the equal but opposite effect of the proviso. This cannot be right.

Thirdly, to come within the proviso the use must be otherwise than in accordance with honest practices in 'industrial and commercial matters'. It was suggested during the motion that this means that the court should look to statutory or industry-agreed codes of conduct to determine whether the advertisement is honest. That approach resulted in this case in much of the evidence on this motion being directed to the issue of whether the defendant's advertising met the specific requirements of the [Consumer Credit Act 1974 and the Consumer Credit (Advertisements) Regulations 1989]. If this approach to the proviso is correct, it would follow that in some trades where there are very detailed and restrictive codes of practice in relation to advertising, it would be easier to breach the code and therefore harder to avoid infringement of registered trade mark. I do not believe that this is the correct way to assess honesty for the purposes of section 10(6).

No doubt the nature of the products or services will affect the degree of hyperbole acceptable. What is tolerable in advertisements for second-hand cars may well not be thought honest if used to encourage the use of powerful medicines. The nature of the goods or services may therefore affect the reasonable perception of what advertising is honest. But it is quite another thing to say that statutory or industry imposed codes of advertising conduct define honesty for the purposes of section 10(6) of the 1994 Act. Although most such codes are concerned to ensure probity, they frequently cover other matters as well. Breach of such a code therefore does not necessarily mean that the advertisement is other than honest. It follows that the provisions of the 1974 Act and 1989 Regulations are of little direct relevance to the issue of trade mark infringement. Honesty has to be gauged against what is reasonably to be expected by the relevant public of advertisements for the goods or services in issue.

Fourthly, it seems to me that the final words of the proviso

> 'if the use without due cause takes unfair advantage of, or is detrimental to, the distinctive character or repute of the trade mark'

in most cases adds nothing of significance to the first part of the proviso. An advertisement which makes use of a registered mark in a way which is not honest will almost always take unfair advantage of it and vice versa. At the most these final words emphasise that the use of the mark must take advantage of it or be detrimental to it. In other words the use must either give some advantage to the defendant or inflict some harm on the character or repute of the registered mark which is above the level of *de minimis*.

The strength of the parties' cases on infringement

. . .

The nub of the plaintiff's complaint is that the contents of the leaflet are not honest. As Mr Young explained it, the leaflet indicated the 15 'bullet points' which were being put forward by the defendant as showing that its credit card was better than the plaintiff's. He accepted that the plaintiff could not complain if the defendant merely said that its credit card was better. However he said that in this case the defendant had descended to detail—to be precise, 15 details—and these were not accurate since they did not compare like with like. In particular he relied on paragraph 15 of the affidavit of Mr Macfarlane sworn on behalf of the plaintiff which complains that the defendant's literature makes no mention of other ancillary benefits which the plaintiff offers its cardholders and which the defendant does not have, such as a 24 hour service relating to emergencies on the road and an overseas emergency service. He also relied on paragraph 14 of Mr Lewis' affidavit [for the defendant] which contains the following:

'[The plaintiff's] additional benefits are not free but are, in effect, paid for by a least part of the higher interest rates charged by Barclays. RBS Advanta does not currently offer the ancillary services, which is part of the reason why RBS Advanta is able to offer lower interest rates. In my experience in the field of credit card services, many customers are attracted by lower interest rates and the absence of annual fees. The ancillary benefits are of limited importance when selecting a credit card. I believe that only a small percentage of Barclaycard customers are likely to use any of the ancillary services in any year. This is backed up by my experience at American Express . . .'

This, said Mr Young, amounts to an admission that the defendant is offering a lesser service than the plaintiff and therefore to refer to the defendant's lower rates without pointing out the other advantages of using the plaintiff's card is misleading and not honest. Furthermore he said that there was no dispute between the parties that of the 15 points identified in the defendant's leaflet, 6 or 7 were common to Barclaycard as well. For example the plaintiff's card is also accepted wherever you see a VISA sign (claim 6) and can be used to obtain cash from any ATM displaying the VISA sign (claim 8). It followed that it was not honest to say that the defendant's card was better all round than the plaintiff's.

In my view the plaintiff's case on this issue is very weak. It has the onus of showing that the defendant's use of the BARCLAYCARD mark in its advertising is not honest. It appears to me that it is most unlikely that any reasonable reader would take that view. On the contrary, read fairly, the advertisements convey the message that the package of 15 features, taken as a whole, is believed by the defendant to offer the customer a better deal. It seems most unlikely that a reasonable reader, and

particularly one to whom this advertisement is being directed—
that is to say one who is being tempted to change from an existing VISA card—would be mislead into thinking that the 15
features in the defendant's leaflet are, individually, only available
to users of the defendant's credit card. For example it is a matter of common knowledge that all VISA cards are accepted
wherever a VISA sign is displayed and can be used to draw cash
from VISA ATM machines. Furthermore the advertisement
does not say, and I think it is unlikely that a reasonable reader
would take it to mean, that there are no features of the plaintiff's
service which are better than the defendant's. The advertisement
merely picks out the features taken together which are being
promoted as making the defendant's product a good package.

. . .

Injunction refused.

6. *Vodafone Group PLC* v. *Orange Personal Communications Services Ltd.* (Chancery Division, 10 July 1996, Jacob J [1997] FSR 34)

Facts:

The plaintiff and defendant were operating in a highly competitive market for mobile telephone services. The defendant issued
an advertisement claiming that 'On average, Orange users save
£20 every month'. This saving was said to be in comparison
with the equivalent tariffs offered by the plaintiff and another
telecommunications company. The plaintiff brought an action
for malicious falsehood and trade mark infringement.

Held:

[Jacob J set out the facts of the case and continued:]

The law as to malicious falsehood

'There is no dispute as to this. To succeed Vodafone must show
that:

(1) the words complained of were false;

(2) they were published maliciously; and

(3) they were calculated to cause the plaintiff pecuniary damage.

The meaning of the words concerned is the first matter to be considered, for their truth or falsity is to be tested against that meaning. The meaning is for the court to determine when a judge sits without a jury. Evidence of the meaning to others is inadmissible. The question:

> is not one of construction in the legal sense. The ordinary man does not live in an ivory tower and he is not inhibited by the rules of construction. So he can and does read between the lines in the light of his general knowledge and experience of worldly affairs . . . What the ordinary man would infer without special knowledge has generally been called the natural and ordinary meaning of the words. But that expression is rather misleading in that it conceals the fact that there are two elements in it. Sometimes it is not necessary to go beyond the words themselves, as where the plaintiff has been called a thief or a murderer. But more often the sting is not so much in the words themselves as in what the ordinary man will infer from them, and that is also regarded as part of their natural and ordinary meaning, *per* Lord Reid in *Lewis* v. *The Daily Telegraph (sub nom. Rubber Improvement Ltd.. v. Daily Telegraph Ltd.* [1964] AC 234 at 258.).

That case was one of libel but the principle must be the same for malicious falsehood: for the question both in libel and malicious falsehood is 'what is the meaning to the ordinary man?'

The legal construct of the ordinary man—'Joe Soap', 'Joe Punter' and 'Joe Public' as he was variously called during the case—may in reality take a given set of words in different ways. Different people may react in different ways to a statement—and in particular may draw different 'stings' from it. But it is settled, as was accepted by both sides, that I must look for the single natural and ordinary meaning. In *Charleston* v. *News Group Newspapers Ltd.* [1995] 2 All ER 313 Lord Bridge (with whom the other members of the House agreed) referred at 317 to 'two principles which are basic to the law of libel':

The first is that, where no legal innuendo is alleged to arise from extrinsic circumstances known to some readers, the 'natural and ordinary meaning' to be ascribed to the words of an allegedly defamatory publication is the meaning, including any inferential meaning, which the words would convey to the mind of the ordinary, reasonable, fair-minded reader. This proposition is too well established to require citation of authority. The second principle, which is perhaps a corollary of the first, is that, although a combination of words may in fact convey different meanings to the minds of different readers, the jury in a libel action, applying the criterion which the first principle dictates, is required to determine the single meaning which the publication conveyed to the notional reasonable reader and to base its verdict and any award of damages on the assumption that this was the one sense in which all readers would have understood it. . . .

As a comparative stranger to this branch of the law I find the 'one meaning rule' strange, particularly for malicious falsehood. Without authority, I should have thought it would be enough to satisfy the criterion of falsity for the plaintiff to prove that the defendant made a statement which was false to a substantial number of people. That, for instance, is the position in passing off (a tort also concerned with false representations): for that tort it is enough to show that the representation fools some of the people, even if not most of them.

The reason for the libel rule in part relates to the entitlement of jury trial for libel (as Diplock LJ explained in [*Slim* v. *Daily Telegraph Ltd.* [1968] 1 All ER 497 at 504–6]). Save in exceptional circumstances the right to jury trial remains for libel and slander (see section 69(1) of the Supreme Court Act 1981) but there is no such right in relation to malicious falsehood. So it by no means follows that that historical reason for the rule in libel should apply to malicious falsehood. Another reason for the rule relates to the function of a jury in awarding damages for defamation: unless one has settled on a particular meaning one cannot judge the extent of the defamation. But in malicious falsehood damages are rather different: they are essentially compensatory for pecuniary loss as for most other torts. So again it does not seem necessarily to follow that the libel rule should apply to the tort. However, as I say, the parties were agreed that I should proceed on the basis that I am a notional jury identifying the single meaning of the words complained of. That is what I will do, and, as will be seen, in this case the point is academic.

But I must add a general comment. This is a case about advertising. The public are used to the ways of advertisers and expect a certain amount of hyperbole. In particular the public are used to advertisers claiming the good points of a product and ignoring others, advertisements claiming that you can 'save ££££ . . .' are common, carrying with them the notion that 'savings' are related to amount of spend, and the public are reasonably used to comparisons—'knocking copy' as it is called in the advertising world. This is important in considering what the ordinary meaning may be. The test is whether a reasonable man would take the claim being made as one made seriously, *De Beers Abrasive Products Ltd.* v. *International General Electric Co. of New York Ltd.* [1975] 1 WLR 972: the more precise the claim the more it is likely to be so taken—the more general or fuzzy the less so.

The law as to registered trade marks

Prior to the coming into force of the Trade Marks Act 1994 comparative advertising using a registered trade mark of a competitor was, subject to minor exceptions involving use of a company name, forbidden by section 4(1) of the Trade Marks Act 1938. But in an increasingly pro-competitive environment there was virtually a moratorium on enforcement of section 4(1) rights in a number of trades—for instance comparative advertising in the field of motor cars was very common for a number of years before the 1938 Act was repealed.

The 1994 Act now positively permits fair comparative advertising by section 10(6). . . . In this case it is common ground that there is no infringement unless the use of Vodafone in the comparison falls within the qualification of section 10(6). This qualification was considered by Laddie J in *Barclays Bank Plc* v. *RBS Advanta* [1996] RPC 307. He held that it is for the plaintiff to show that the use falls within the qualification and that the test of honesty is objective (ie would a reasonable reader be likely to say, upon being given the full facts, that the advertisement is not honest?). Laddie J gave as an example the case where the advertisement is 'significantly misleading'. In trade marks, as Mr Mellor rightly submitted, there is no 'one meaning rule'. If a comparison is significantly misleading on an objective basis to a substantial proportion of the reasonable audience, it is not an 'honest practice' within the section.

The provision contains a further qualification—'that the use without due cause takes unfair advantage of, or is detrimental to, the distinctive character or repute of the mark'. Here Orange say that even if the slogan is misleading it does nothing to the distinctive character of the mark Vodafone. I think this is false. The slogan clearly takes advantage of the distinctive character or repute of the mark: it would be meaningless if no-one had heard of Vodafone. And, on the hypotheses that the slogan is misleading, that would be an unfair advantage. I agree with Laddie J that these words 'in most cases add nothing of significance to the first part of the proviso' (*Barclays Bank Plc* v *RBS Advanta* [1996] RPC 307 at 316). If the slogan is misleading there will be infringement.

The background factual position

[*Jacob J outlined the state of the market in the mobile telephone industry and continued:*]

The meaning of the slogan

It is against that general background, particularly the low entry cost advertisements of Vodafone and Cellnet providers, that the ordinary man would come to read the Orange advertisement, launched on October 23, 1995. What would he make of it? I have little doubt that he would understand it to mean just what it says. It is saying that, on average, if Orange users had been on Vodafone or Cellnet, they would have had to pay £20 more a month. The ordinary reader would have no idea whether his actual or proposed usage would save him £20 a month. It is not a promise to him. Indeed if he was a potential or actual low user spending only £20 or so a month, he would not expect it to apply to him. He would be aware that the average would be affected by those people who seem to do nothing else but be on their mobiles. More generally I also think he would get the idea that the running costs on Orange were below those on Vodafone. That is indeed the message he was intended to get as appears from the WCRS creative brief. WCRS were Orange's advertising agency and the principal player there was a Mr Harris. The brief describes the 'proposition' (adspeak for ultimate message) as 'Orange costs less per month'.

Now Vodafone say that there is another message, another 'sting'. This is that on average Vodafone users would save £20 per month if they had instead been on Orange. This is the converse of what the advertisement actually says. It depends on an assumption that usage on Orange and Vodafone (or Cellnet) would be the same, irrespective of the costs. I do not see why the ordinary reasonable man who thought about the slogan would so think for a moment. He would realise that in general the more expensive the tariff the less would be the amount of use. Getting the message that Orange was on average cheaper would lead him to expect that Vodafone was used less on average. As Mr Lowe (who performed some of the numerical work which led up to the claim being made) observed in a memo of October 10: 'They [i.e. Cellnet and Vodafone users] will not use as much Answerphone as it is so much more expensive'.

I should mention a point about 'average'. Vodafone say it is inherently deceptive because the user profile is 'skewed', with most users making relatively little use of their phones and only a few making heavy usage. So the few bring the 'average' up. That by no means makes the slogan mean anything other than the 'average' which I have no doubt would mean the arithmetic average to the ordinary user. I think the evidence about 'modes' and 'medians' to be beside the point, either on meaning or falsity.

Thus in my opinion the 'single meaning' for the purposes of malicious falsehood is that if the users on Orange had been on Vodafone or Cellnet making the same usage as they made on

Orange, on arithmetic average they would have had to pay £20 more a month. If and to the extent that he thought about Ibi ['itemised billing and insurance'], I think the ordinary man would expect the comparison to be on a like for like basis. I should add that I think he would expect this figure to be inclusive of VAT. He would know that some business users can reclaim it, but in the absence of a separate VAT figure being mentioned his general experience would lead him to expect the figures to be VAT inclusive.

Having settled on the single meaning for malicious falsehood, I must also consider whether a substantial proportion of the addressees of the advertisement (virtually the entire adult population) would come to a different meaning. I do this for the purposes of trade mark infringement. Vodafone say that at least their users, faced with this advertisement would come to a different meaning, that on average, if there was a transfer to Orange, £20 a month would be saved. I am by no means convinced they would. I think they would say to themselves—'well it may be cheaper and I would welcome that because I could use my phone more'. I do not think it is established on the advertisement itself that there is a substantial body of the public who would expect usage to be the same irrespective of price. In economists' language the price (and accordingly usage) of the telephone is elastic and the public would expect that.

I am confirmed in my opinion by what happened. As I say Orange (through Mr Harris of the agency and Mr Gardner, Head of Marketing Services for Hutchison Telecom and its subsidiaries, including Orange) made presentations to a number of service providers who were also service providers of Vodafone and Cellnet. They explained how the claim was made—by notionally transferring Orange users to Vodafone or Cellnet equivalent tariffs. No-one suggested that this would be read the other way. No-one suggested that if it was so read it would mislead. On the contrary the service providers (who in due course became Orange service providers too), having had the basis of the claim explained and justified, were willing to make it themselves. If the ordinary meaning were as Vodafone suggest, then all these providers were themselves prepared to make a claim which they must have known was false. This is powerful evidence indeed against the Vodafone meaning. Then there is the reaction of the public itself. There were no complaints by anyone about the advertisement. This is less powerful evidence: an individual would not be able to assess whether the claim was true or false, it being a claim only about the 'average'. An individual would not know whether he was an average user (whatever that might mean) or indeed whether the overall average spoken of in the advertisement applied to such a user. Much more significant is the reaction of Cellnet. They were just as much victims of the slogan as Vodafone. There is no evidence of any complaint by them at all. I was told by Mr Baldwin, QC for Orange, that they inquired how the figures were derived and when told no more was heard.

[*Jacob J then reviewed the evidence of a witness from the Broadcasting Advertising Clearance Centre who had cleared the advertisement for publication, finding that it did not support Vodafone's reading of the advertisement. He continued:*]

In coming to my conclusion on meaning I do not overlook two points made by Vodafone. One relates to what was said to people who followed up the television advertisement. A telephone number was given so those interested could make further inquiries and be sent literature. I have a sample of that literature which goes into some detail as to how the savings are made (by a combination of per second billing, less peak hours, bundled minutes, cheaper answerphone and lower peak rates). No extra complaint is made about that literature. But for a fortnight some callers were told (only if they inquired in a particular way) that 'an average Cellnet or Vodafone customer can save around £20 per month just by moving over to Orange'. Mr Hartley [QC for Vodafone] submitted that this just shows how the actual statement and its reverse are one and the same thing to the ordinary man. Someone at Orange had themselves made the transposition. There is some force in this, but, to my mind, not enough for me to conclude that the ordinary or substantial meaning is as he contends. There is too much to outweigh it. . . .

Comparative Advertising

Malice

[*Jacob J rejected the plaintiff's allegation of malice and continued:*]

Falsity?

Vodafone say the whole comparison was inherently flawed and so false, virtually irrespective of meaning. Alternatively they say the claim was false on Orange's meaning, ie that on average Orange users would not save £20 per month if they transferred their usage to Vodafone. And they say it was false on the alleged Vodafone meaning, ie that on average if Vodafone users transferred to Orange and kept their usage the same they would not save £20 a month.

Orange say the comparison was both fair and true on their meaning (which I have held to be the correct meaning). Orange go further and take the war into the enemy camp by saying that in practice the message was true even on Vodafone's meaning.

Inherently flawed?

Vodafone begin by saying the statement was made to a market in which consumers were confused. There is some evidence which supports this in a general sort of way. It is not surprising, given all the cheap but varying offers which were about, and the unattractive fact that people were offering 'one year contracts' which in practice could only be terminated by three months' notice at the end of the year. But I do not think this sort of confusion is relevant. People would understand the advertisement to be referring to monthly, ie running, costs and it is not shown there was any confusion about that—on the contrary Orange's qualitative research had shown that people were concerned about this.

Next Vodafone submit that with several different tariffs it is impossible to make a fair comparison across the board. And in particular it was unfair to mix up low ('personal') and high ('business') tariffs. I do not see why. The whole statement is about an average. Readers would clearly recognise that different tariffs were included. At an earlier point it was suggested that in fact there were no comparable tariffs, but this suggestion failed

116

to survive the cross-examination of Vodafone's Mr Carl who agreed that in the vast majority of cases he could establish equivalents between tariffs. Moreover Vodafone themselves in an advertisement by way of riposte to Orange did compare their Lowcall with Vodafone's Talk 15. In that connection I do not think that Mr Ward's (of Vodafone) response—that it was the marketing people—much of an answer.

Further it is said it was unfair for Orange to leave out some Vodafone tariffs—the only pleaded one being a tariff called Metroworld. Orange left this out because it was felt they had no equivalent. Metroworld was an unusual tariff. The user could nominate a 'home' area within which calls were particularly cheap. Outside that area calls were expensive. I think there is nothing in this point for two reasons: first the advertisement makes it clear that the comparison is for equivalent tariffs, and, even more significantly, it was agreed by the experts that including Metroworld would make very little difference to the figures. It formed a small part of Vodafone's overall base and was dying. The fact that it formed a larger part of the digital Vodafone base is, I think, immaterial.

It is also said that the comparison makes no allowance for the fact that some large business users of Vodafone would benefit from a discount. That is true, but the comparison is with tariffs. This was not a pleaded point and was not shown to be significant.

The next point related to answerphone charges. These were taken into account and indeed formed a significant part of the £20 figure. It was said that no account was taken of the fact that some Vodafone users paid a £4.50 a month charge for reduced usage costs. Again this was not shown to affect the overall £20 figure if taken into account.

The final points suggesting that the whole comparison was unfair relate to VAT and start up costs. As I have indicated I do not think there is anything in either of these: it was perfectly fair to include VAT all round with the knowledge that some users could claim it back and start up costs are simply not monthly running costs.

False on Orange's meaning?

For this Vodafone relied on the evidence of an accountant, a Mr Falk. However he had made a number of assumptions which had to be corrected and in the end his figures required such correction that the figure went up above £20 per month. The figures are in Mr Davie's report, . . . essentially accepted as correct by Mr Falk. . . .

I should mention Ibi. Vodafone say it was unfair for these to be included in the calculation because many of their users do not take it, or only take one or the other. Moreover they say that strictly speaking 'tariff' means just the cost of the phone calls, Ibi being an additional extra and, even if taken, not a tariff as such. Orange say that their comparison was on a like for like basis. And so since they provide Ibi inclusive, that is the fair comparison. I think that is right. But in any event they did not need to include Ibi to reach the £20 figure at all and did not do so in their BACC submission. (They did include it in another part of the submission where they were trying to show that every user would save, but, whilst that seems to have been a BACC requirement, no doubt out of an abundance of caution, I do not think it relevant to the claim as actually made. Nor was there anything sinister about including it for this purpose but not for the main comparison as suggested by Mr Hartley.)

False on Vodafone's meaning?

Vodafone set out to prove that, if their users had been on Orange instead and had kept their usage the same, the saving would not have amounted on average to £20 per month. The exercise was done by taking just three service providers (Hutchison, Talkland and Unique Air). Mr Carl then worked out what the customers of those providers would, on average (and an arithmetical average was used) have saved. He came to an overall figure of £15.53. That figure without criticism shows that in reality Orange was cheaper to run than Vodafone and I can hardly think that the sting of the advertisement (according to Vodafone) would have been much less if it had referred to

£15 per month. The 'breakthrough' figure for Orange was at one point seen to be £10.

However Mr Carl's figures were attacked. He did not include Ibi which prevented the comparison from being on a like for like basis. He did not even include those Vodafone users who actually had and were paying for Ibi. Also he only added VAT for Talk 15 (the low users' tariff). The justification for this is that large users may well have been able to reclaim VAT. For the reasons I have given I do not think that is fair. The comparison was with running costs, irrespective of whether VAT could be reclaimed, or indeed irrespective of whether the whole cost of running the system could be claimed off pre-tax profits. Mr Carl also made an error about the cost of calls from Orange phones to other mobiles.

On this point Mr Davie also did some work. He showed that a sample (taken from those who completed Orange consumer questionnaires for a particular month) who had changed from Vodafone had indeed saved more than £20 per month. They were relatively high users but the exercise does provide some support for the proposition that the statement is true even on Vodafone's meaning.

It follows that the claim in malicious falsehood fails. The advertisement was not misleading and malice is not established.

It also follows that the claim in trade mark infringement also fails. To avoid any misunderstanding, nothing I say in this judgment applies to the present day position on the prices of the parties concerned.

Judgment accordingly.'

7. British Telecommunications PLC v. AT & T Communications (UK) Ltd., (Chancery Division, 18 December 1996, M. Crystal QC Unreported)

Facts:

The plaintiff provides telephone services to members of the public in the United Kingdom. In June 1996 the defendant launched its United Kingdom domestic telephone services. The launch of this service was accompanied by a comparative advertising campaign which the plaintiff contended was, in certain identified respects, false or seriously misleading. These proceedings were for an interlocutory injunction based on the claim of infringement of trade mark in the publication of three documents: (i) a brochure, (ii) a 'welcome pack' and (iii) a leaflet headed 'Summer Madness'.

Held

[*Mr Crystal QC set out the facts, the history of the proceedings, section 10(1) and (6) of the Trade Marks Act 1994 and continued:*]

The principles

Section 10(6) of the 1994 Act has been considered by Laddie J in *Barclays Bank plc* v. *RBS Advanta* [1996] RPC 307, 15 Tr L 262 ('*Advanta*') and by Jacob J in *Vodafone Group plc* v. *Orange Personal Communications Services Ltd.* [1997] FSR 34, [1997] EMLR 84 ('*Vodafone*'). So far as material for present purposes, those decisions appear to me to provide authority for the following propositions:

(1) The primary objective of s 10(6) of the 1996 Act is to permit comparative advertising (see *Advanta* at pages 311–213 and 315 of the former report and *Vodafone* at pages 4–5 of the transcript of the judgment);

(2) As long as the use of a competitor's mark is honest, there is nothing wrong in telling the public of the relative merits of competing goods or services and using registered trade marks to identify them (see *Advanta* at page 315, *Vodafone* at page 4);

(3) The onus is on the registered proprietor to show that the factors indicated in the proviso to s 10(6) exists (see *Advanta* at 315, *Vodafone* at page 4);

(4) There will be no trade mark infringement unless the use of the registered mark is not in accordance with honest practices (see *Advanta* at 315);

(5) The test is objective: would a reasonable reader be likely to say, upon being given the full facts, that the advertisement is not honest? (See *Advanta* at 315, *Vodafone* at page 4);

(6) Statutory or industry agreed codes of conduct are not a helpful guide as to whether an advertisement is honest for the purposes of s 10(6). Honesty has to be gauged against what is reasonably to be expected by the relevant public of advertisements for the goods or services in issue (see *Advanta* at 316);

(7) It should be borne in mind that the general public are used to the ways of advertisers and expects hyperbole (see *Advanta* at page 315, cf *Vodafone* at pages 3–4);

(8) The 1994 Act does not impose on the courts an obligation to try and enforce through the back door of trade mark legislation a more puritanical standard than the general public would expect from advertising copy (see *Advanta* at 315, *Vodafone* at page 4);

(9) An advertisement which is significantly misleading is not honest for the purposes of s 10(6) (see *Advanta* at 316, *Vodafone* at 4–5).

I venture with diffidence to make a number of additional observations.

(10) The advertisement must be considered as a whole (cf *Advanta* at pages 316–18);

(11) As a purpose of the 1994 Act is positively to permit comparative advertising, the court should not hold words used in the advertisement to be seriously misleading for interlocutory purposes unless on a fair reading of them in their context and against the background of the advertisement as a whole they can really be said to justify that description;

(12) A minute textual examination is not something upon which the reasonable reader of an advertisement would embark;

(13) The court should therefore not encourage a microscopic

approach to the construction of a comparative advertisement on a motion for interlocutory relief.

With these matters in mind, I turn to the advertising literature in question.

The A T & T brochure

This brochure is sent by A T & T to potential customers who communicate with A T & T by telephone or in writing. . . .

Mr Platts-Mills, QC, for British Telecom, complains of the following assertions in the brochure:

(1) You'll get cheaper rates on your international and long distance calls from home;

(2) When is it cost effective to use the A T & T calling service? For practically all non-local calls and especially for international calls;

(3) One little number . . . great big savings on your international and long distance calls.'

Mr Platts-Mills, who subjected the brochure to protracted examination, submits that there is an arguable case that these assertions are seriously misleading either:

(1) because a call by call comparison between A T & T and British Telecom rates for national and international calls does not demonstrate that practically all A T & T calls are in fact cheaper than British Telecom's calls; and/or

(2) because a call by call comparison between British Telecom and A T & T is in any event entirely inappropriate because of the companies' differential pricing structures.

Mr Platts-Mills relied in particular on the introductory words of the answer to the question: 'When is it cost effective to use the A T & T calling service? For practically all . . .'. He says those words must mean that A T & T are saying that at least 95% or thereabouts of all national and international calls are cheaper using A T & T's services and that this is not true. This passage in the brochure, Mr Platts-Mills accepted, was the high-water mark of his case in relation to the A T & T brochure.

There is a dispute on the evidence about what a call by call comparison for national and international calls actually reveals. This is a matter which in my judgment is inappropriate for resolution on this motion. I propose to proceed on the basis that there is a real dispute as to whether 95% or thereabouts of all national and international calls made by a consumer with A T & T are cheaper than with British Telecom. If therefore I thought that the A T & T brochure would really be understood by a reasonable reader, used to the ways of advertisers, as making that assertion then Mr Platts-Mills would demonstrate that there was a serious question to be tried, that the A T & T brochure was not honest for the purposes of s 10(6) of the 1994 Act. However, I do not think that a reasonable reader would so understand the A T & T brochure.

In my judgment he would understand the brochure, taken as a whole, to be promising substantial savings on the bottom line of the bills that A T & T customers might hope to receive. This seems to me to be the constant theme of the text of the A T & T brochure.

Illustrations . . . of this theme in the brochure are as follows:

(1) Phoning long distance or abroad? Sometimes I think the flight would be cheaper;
(2) One little number . . . great big savings on your international and long distance calls;
(3) Now you can benefit from cheaper rates on international and long distance calls saving up to 40% in some cases;
(4) The easy way to save money when you're phoning overseas or making long distance calls within the UK;
(5) All you need to do is dial 143 . . . you will then automatically access the A T & T network and our competitive rates;
(6) Join our country call plans for up to 40% savings;
(7) If you call one specific country regularly you can make savings up to 40% by paying a minimal membership charge and joining one of our special international country call plans, or if you make international calls worldwide why not sign up for our Call World Plan for extra savings to all our top calling destinations. See the enclosed rates sheet for membership fees and examples of the savings you can make to Country Call destinations.

Then, to receive these benefits just choose the calling plan that's right for you by ticking the relevant box on your application form;

(8) That's all there is to it and once you're registered you will be saving money as soon as you lift the receiver;

(9) You will get cheaper rates on your international and long distance calls from home;

(10) And as the world gets smaller we believe it's time to bring down the cost of staying in touch from your home phone;

(11) Up to 40% savings with our Country Call plans;

(12) When is it cost effective to use the A T & T calling service? For particularly all non-local calls and especially international calls;

(13) Can I place local calls using 143? Yes, you can but all UK calls will be charged at the same rate so we recommend you continue to use B T for local calls and A T & T for long distance and international calls;

(14) How do A T & T Country Call plans work? Joining a Country Call plan, e.g. Call EU, ensures you will have access to the best discounts that A T & T offer to the destination you call most frequently. Calls to all other international countries will receive our standard discount. Please see the enclosed rates sheet for details.

If, as I am satisfied, this is the correct view of the A T & T brochure, then on the evidence as to the bottom line savings to A T & T customers available to the court on this motion, there is nothing seriously misleading or not honest about the claims made by A T & T in relation to national and international calls. It also follows that Mr Platts-Mills' second complaint that a call by call comparison is inappropriate because of differential pricing structures equally falls to the ground.

In the circumstances, I am not satisfied that there is an arguable case that the A T & T brochure offends the honesty test contained in s 10(6) of the 1994 Act.

The welcome pack

This pack is sent to customers when they sign up with A T & T. . . .

Mr Platts-Mills QC complains of the following assertions in the welcome pack:

(1) On the whole our competitive rates work out cheaper per minute than B T for long distance calls in the UK and when you use your chosen Country Call plans we are up to 40% cheaper on international calls;

(2) Welcome to the A T & T calling service, the easy way to save money when you're phoning overseas or elsewhere in the UK from home; and

(3) On our Country Call plans you can save up to 40% on international calls to specific regions.'

In addition to the two complaints made by Mr Platts-Mills in relation to the A T & T brochure which I have mentioned above, and which are repeated in relation to the welcome pack, complaint is made about the expression 'up to 40% on international calls'. There is a dispute on the evidence as to the extent to which savings of 40% or thereabouts (Mr Platts-Mills' suggested test) can be obtained by using A T & T for international calls. Again, if I thought that the welcome pack really would be understood by a reasonable reader as making that assertion then British Telecom would succeed in demonstrating that there was a serious question to be tried as to the honesty of the welcome pack for the purposes of s 10(6) of the 1994 Act. However, I do not think that a reasonable reader, used to the ways of advertisers, would so understand the welcome pack. Again, in my judgment he would understand the welcome pack, taken as a whole, to be promising substantial savings on A T & T's customers' bills.

Illustrations of this . . . are as follows:

(1) Welcome to the A T & T calling service, the easy way to save money when you're phoning overseas or elsewhere in the UK from home;

(2) Save on international and long distance calls. On the whole our competitive rates work out cheaper per minute than BT for long distance calls in the UK and when you use your chosen Country Call plans we are up to 40% cheaper on international calls;

(3) Is it cost effective to us the A T & T calling service? On

average our customers are saving 20% by using A T & T for non-local calls;

(4) Can I place local calls using 143? Yes, you can, but all UK calls will be charged at the same rate so we recommend that you continue to use B T for local calls and A T & T for long distance and international calls;

(5) Making a call. Now you're connected, it's so simple to save money. All you need to do is dial 143 followed by the number you wish to call. Easy payment. Not only are your bills cheaper with the A T & T calling service, they are easy to pay;

(6) Even bigger savings. On our Country Call plans you can save up to 40% on international calls to specific regions, but if you call all over the world why not choose our special Call World Plan giving you the freedom to save wherever you're calling.'

In the circumstances, I am not satisfied that there is an arguable case that the welcome pack offends the honesty test contained in s 10(6) of the 1994 Act.

The leaflet

The leaflet was issued as an A T & T summer promotion entitled 'Summer Madness'. This appears to have expired at the end of July 1996. British Telecom complains of the assertion in the leaflet that the A T & T calling service can still save you up to 40% on international and long distance calls. This complaint, as Mr Platts-Mills recognised, essentially stands or falls with his complaint about the expression, 'up to 40%' which appears in the welcome pack. I have already expressed the view that that expression was not seriously misleading or not honest in the context of the welcome pack viewed as whole. I am of the same view as to the similar statement in the leaflet having regard to the contents of the leaflet as a whole. The leaflet again focuses on savings at the bottom line for prospective customers of A T & T.

In these circumstances British Telecom's complaints in relation to the A T & T brochure, the welcome pack, or the leaflet taken individually or indeed as a whole do not in my judgment amount to a seriously arguable case of trade mark infringement for the purposes of the grant of interlocutory relief.

The balance of convenience

[*Mr Crystal QC then discussed the balance of convenience in relation to the grant of an interlocutory injunction. In the course of refusing an injunction he said:*]

Although Mr Platts-Mills disavowed any desire on British Telecom's part to censor A T & T's literature, an inunction, even in a very limited form, would have the effect of mandating a withdrawal of A T & T's current literature and its replacement with fresh literature. This would occasion, so I was told by Mr Hobbs, QC on behalf of A T & T, a cost of £45,000 or thereabouts. I of course bear in mind the size of A T & T. Furthermore, an injunction would infringe A T & T's rights to free speech. As the law currently stands, this right is no defence to the grant of an injunction in a trade mark infringement case (see *The Gallup Organisation Ltd.* v. *Gallup International Ltd.*, 29 November 1995, *per* Robert Walker J), but it appears that the court can give the right to free speech due weight on the balance of convenience. Here Mr Hobbs QC, for A T & T, submits that his client's statements are true and he will seek to justify them at trial.

. . .

Application dismissed.

8. *Cable & Wireless PLC* v. *British Telecommunications PLC* (Chancery Division, 8 December 1997, Jacob J, [1998] FSR 383)

Facts:

The plaintiff and defendant were operating in a highly competitive market for telephone services. The defendant issued an advertisement in the form of a brochure comparing the cost of its telephone services with those of the plaintiff. The plaintiff brought an action for an interlocutory injunction to restrain distribution of the advertisement.

Held:

'This is yet another battle in the telephone wars. They have come about for several reasons. First, following deregulation, competition started in the telephone business. Secondly, following the passing of the Trade Marks Act 1994, the use of a rival registered trade mark has, within limits, been permitted in advertisements compared with the prior law of registered trade marks when comparative advertising was banned. Thirdly, a telephone service is essentially a telephone service. So what differentiates various providers is essentially price. Providers have been anxious to capture customers, or not to lose them. In order to do so they wish to suggest that they will provide their services cheaper than their rivals.

Here the use of comparisons, whether one service is cheaper than another, is not an easy matter to determine. Prices are complex, depending on a range of different variables, such as basic rental; degree of use; type of use (local, national or international); time on the telephone (short calls, long calls and a mix), and so on. Really sophisticated customers may be able to measure their patterns of use (which are called 'profiles' in the trade) and work out for themselves which service offers the best value. Indeed, they may be able to negotiate special rates for themselves; but lesser users have to take the various tariffs as they find them. To work out for oneself which gives the best value is a near impossible task.

[*Jacob J outlined the history of proceedings in the case and continued:*]

It seemed to me to be right in the circumstances to go in for some sort of case management. Cable and Wireless were suing for infringement of their trade marks, numbers 1564244, registered for telecommunications, and 2117142, registered for printing matter and advertising matter. They were also suing for malicious falsehood. I could not see what the latter cause of action could possibly add to trade mark infringement. It merely adds the burden (and costs) of proof of malice and involves the difficulties of the 'one meaning' rule. It is difficult to imagine a case where, given a valid trade mark registration covering the goods or services concerned, a claim of malicious falsehood can add anything. Including such a claim was, for instance, wasteful in one of the earlier telephone wars: *Vodafone Group Plc* v. *Orange Personal Communications* [1997] FSR 34.

Further, it seemed to me the dispute between the parties as to the validity of the trade mark registration or as to whether the services they registered were covered by the registrations would not lead anywhere. The real and only point was whether BT a defence under section 10(6) of the Trade Marks Act 1994. In the result, Cable and Wireless agreed to limit their claim to the trade mark infringement, and British Telecom to that defence under the Act.

[*Jacob J further outlined the history of proceedings in the case; described the allegedly infringing brochure; set out section 10(6) of the Trade Marks Act; approved the summary of* Barclays Bank Plc v. RBS Advanta [*1996*] *RPC 307 and* Vodafone Group Plc v. Orange Personal Communications Services Ltd. [*1997*] *FSR 34 offered by Mr Crystal QC in* British Telecommunications Plc v. A T & T Communications (UK) Ltd. (*unreported*); *and continued*:]

One point that was debated before me is not quite dealt with in those points, or at least not quite as fully as it might have been. Suppose the advertisement purports to be a serious comparison reached after thorough and serious research, the sort of advertisement considered by Walton J in *De Beers Abrasive Products Ltd.* v. *International General Electric Co. of New York Ltd.* [1975] 1 WLR 972. Suppose the advertisement is false. It is clear that if the defendant has knowingly put it forward, that is to say, knowingly 'dressed up a stupid old moke as a thoroughbred Arabian stallion', as Walton J put it, there will be liability. No one who knowingly puts forward a false claim can be acting in accordance with honest practices.

But what if the defendant has conducted serious research and he genuinely and honestly believes his advertising claim though it later proves to be false? Can he escape liability, at least until he discovers he was wrong, on the grounds that although his claim was false he was honest at the time he made it? Consider the converse position: the man who recklessly, that is to say, with utter disregard for the truth, makes a claim which will be taken seriously and which by chance turns out to be true. Is he liable on the grounds that although what he said was true, he was not acting in accordance with honest practice at the time he made the claim? If so, it would seem he can go on making exactly that claim once he has done the research which justifies the claim

At one point I was attracted by the view that the section did not really involve any inquiry as to what the advertiser had done. One simply asked whether what he had said was or was not true. Neither side has urged that upon me, although it might possibly have that meaning. The phrase, which is a pretty woolly phrase, 'honest practices in industrial and commercial matters' has its origin in Article 10 bis of the Paris Convention dealing with 'Unfair Competition'. It provides as follows:

(2) Any act of competition contrary to honest practices in industrial or commercial matters constitutes an act of unfair competition.
(3) The following in particular shall be prohibited:
    1. all acts of such a nature as to create confusion by any means whatever with the establishment, the goods, or the industrial or commercial activities, of the competitor;
    2. false allegations in the course of trade of such a nature as to discredit the establishment, the goods, or the industrial or commercial activities, of a competitor;
    3. indications or allegations the use of which in the course of trade is liable to mislead the public as to the nature, the manufacturing process, the characteristics, the suitability for their purpose, or the quantity, of the goods.

None of those specific examples seem to involve any investigation of the state of mind of the advertiser. Nonetheless, in the end, I think the parties were right in submitting that the test is objective in this sense: that one should ask whether a reasonable trader could honestly have made the statements he made based upon the information that he had.

This could mean that he had a defence, if it turns out that the information which he had was wrong in some way or other. He would have to stop when further credible information showing he was wrong became available. The defence does not depend upon whether you regard him as honest, but whether others would regard what he was doing as honest. His personal state of mind is actually irrelevant.

In this case, therefore, it does not matter whether BT believed the statements were true. The question is whether an honest man, given the information that BT had, would have been prepared to make the statements.

What information did BT have? They had commissioned serious research from serious consultants. They knew that those consultants were prepared to put their name behind the advertising. The exercise of price comparison was plainly extremely complicated.

BT thought the headline statement was justified, and they still think it is justified. More information has become available because Cable and Wireless had provided BT confidentially with some direct customer usage profile information. Indirect information was only supplied to BT yesterday. Even more remarkably, in my view, it has not been used by Cable and Wireless in their attacks on this advertisement. After all, their principal attack is that BT guessed the profiles in the possession of Cable and Wireless. I am not sure that 'guess' is a fair word. BT have been watching their rivals fairly carefully, each side has been watching each other's advertisements, and each has complained to the Advertising Standards Authority. I think that 'reasonable estimate' would be a fairer phrase.

Cable and Wireless did not have to guess at all. They launched these proceedings in a tremendous hurry. I think it was inappropriate that an application was made for an ex parte injunction. Quite a number of the complaints made before Park J have not been pursued. This is a battle between two large, reputable organisations and to seek ex parte relief on the basis that the advertisement was dishonest would require stronger material, in my view, than Cable and Wireless had. It may be that their extreme hurry led them to overlook the fact that they had in their hands access to much the most important data for challenging BT's claims.

As the state of the evidence has developed, it has become clear that a lot of the dispute between the parties amounts to statistical models. BT say that they have a more appropriate statistical model which does justify the claims, and that Cable and Wireless's model is too crude. Two particular matters are pointed out. One is that the Cable and Wireless model uses an average call length whereas BT break up call lengths into a number of discrete categories. The other criticism is that BT's model is more sensitive because it divides customers into twelve different classes depending on their kind of usage. Mr Bloch manfully tried to demonstrate me from the Deloitte report that these matters had been tested by Deloitte, but I am quite satisfied that they have not, and there is no inconsistency between BT's evidence and the report before me.

For what it is worth, at this stage in the absence of actual evidence on indirect connected customers, the headline message seems to me to be more likely to be found to be true than false. Certainly it is not one which any honest trader, having the information which BT had, would not be prepared to make.

That is not an end of the matter. Mr Bloch attacked some of the detail. I have already dealt with the suggestion that the brochure suggests that BT have worked with the Cable and Wireless customer profile information, and I have indicated that I do not think it does.

The next attack was on the detailed numbers given in the table. The suggestion was that these numbers are not as accurate as the table suggests, given to three significant numbers, but that customers would take them to be such. The difficulty with that argument is that no customer is invited to expect that those particular numbers will apply to him. He cannot so expect because he knows that this is produced by some sort of statistical method, and that he will not be the 'average'. All he can do, given these numbers, is to get some sort of feel for the position. It is to be remembered that he is being asked to appreciate that there is a few per cent saving one way or the other in the context in which Cable and Wireless have been suggesting very enormous savings by providing indications of the savings based simply on call time.

I do not think that there is a reasonable likelihood of significant numbers of people being misled by the details in these tables to any significant degree. I do not think it is established that no honest man would be prepared to put out these Deloitte calculations as part of his advertising.

I have therefore come to the conclusion that there should be no injunction pending trial. As I have indicated in the unusual circumstances of this case, there will be liberty to apply. Any application that is to be made will have to be made on proper notice with a proper opportunity for BT to answer any further evidence that may be put in.

Injunction refused.'

9. *Emaco Ltd.* v *Dyson Appliances Ltd.*, (Chancery Division, 26 January 1999, Parker J, Unreported)

Facts:

The plaintiff and defendant were both manufacturers of vacuum cleaners engaged in an intense advertising war. The defendant published a graph in which it claimed that the vacuum cleaners manufactured by the plaintiff (the 'EPS') were less powerful than one manufactured by the defendant (the 'DC01'). The founder and chairman of the defendant allegedly told a reporter for a trade journal that a 'cassette system' incorporated by the plaintiff in its vacuum cleaners did not 'work'. The plaintiff published a flyer comparing the DC01 unfavourably with the EPS range. The plaintiff and defendant each brought actions for damages for malicious falsehood and trade mark infringement.

Held:

[*Parker J outlined the history of the proceedings and described the technical operation of the relevant vacuum cleaners. He continued:*]

The Law

The claims based on malicious falsehood

As Glidewell LJ said in *Kaye* v. *Robertson* [1991] FSR 62, 67:

> The essentials of [the tort of malicious falsehood] are that the defendant has published about the plaintiff words which are false, that they were published maliciously, and that special damage has followed as the direct and natural result of their publication. As to special damage, the effect of section 3(1) of the Defamation Act 1952 is that it is sufficient if the words published in writing are calculated to cause pecuniary damage to the plaintiff. Malice will be inferred if it is proved that the words were calculated to produce damage and that the defendant knew when he published the words that they were false or was reckless as to whether they were false or not.

In *Horrocks* v. *Lowe* [1975] AC 135, at 150, Lord Diplock contrasted recklessness with 'carelessness, impulsiveness or irrationality in arriving at a positive belief that [the matter complained of] is true'.

It is accepted by both sides that the requirement that publication of the material of which complaint is made should have been 'calculated to cause pecuniary damage' to the other party is an objective one. On the pleadings, however, each side denies that the publication of the material complained of by the other side was calculated to cause pecuniary damage.

Thus, in relation to each of the claims of malicious falsehood four issues arise for decision:

(1) Meaning: What was the meaning of the material of which complaint is made? In addressing this issue, it is in my judgment appropriate to adopt the approach of the Court of Appeal in *Skuse* v. *Granada Television Limited* [1996] EMLR 278 (a libel case), in so far as that approach is applicable to the particular facts of the instant case (Both sides accept that the so-called 'single-meaning rule' in libel cases applies in the context of the claims in malicious falsehood.). Thus:

(i) The words and images complained of are to be given their natural and ordinary meaning, in the sense of the message or messages which they would have conveyed to a reasonable member of the public reading or viewing them in the context in which they were intended to be read or viewed.

(ii) Thus, in the case of the graph and the flyer, the words and images must be read and viewed through the eyes of a potential customer interested in purchasing a vacuum cleaner who is being subjected to sales patter designed to persuade him or her to purchase one machine (either the EPS or the DC01, as the case may be) rather than the other.

(iii) In the case of the words attributed to Mr Dyson, there is an issue on the pleadings as to what precisely he said. Subject to that, the question is how his words would reasonably have been understood by someone in Susan Dean's position: ie. by a reporter for a trade journal. How Susan Dean in fact understood them is, of course, directly relevant to that question.

(iv) In addressing these questions, the Court must avoid on the one hand engaging in an over-elaborate analysis and on the other hand adopting too literal an approach.

(2) Falsity: Giving the material complained of its natural and ordinary meaning, were the messages conveyed (i.e. the representations made) by such material, or any of them, false? The resolution of this issue involves both factual and expert evidence. And

(3) Malice: To the extent that false representations were made, were they made 'maliciously', in the sense that the maker of them either knew that they were untrue or was reckless as to whether they were true or not (see *Kaye* v. *Robertson* [[1991] FSR 62, 67])? This is an issue of fact.

(4) Damage: Was the material complained of calculated (in an objective sense: ie. likely) to cause pecuniary damage to the party complaining of it?

The claims based on infringement of trade mark

[*Parker J summarised the judgments of Jacob J in* Vodafone Group Plc *v.* Orange Personal Communications Services Ltd. [*1997*] *FSR 34 and* Cable & Wireless Plc *v.* British Telecommunications Plc [*1998*] *FSR 383 and continued:*]

In the instant case, both sides invite me to proceed on the footing the the test of 'honest practice' is an objective one, and nothing turns on the question whether the test is fully objective (as suggested in *Vodafone*) or something less than fully objective (as suggested in *Cable & Wireless*). In the circumstances, it is sufficient for me to say that I am content to proceed on the footing that the test is essentially an objective one.

Remedy

As I indicated earlier in this judgment, each party seeks (among other things) injunctive relief and an inquiry as to damages. In relation to the claims of malicious falsehood, since no special damage has been pleaded or proved the damages (if any) will be at large (See Mr Milmo QC in reply [Day11/1369].). In the case of the claims of infringement of trade mark, each party claims loss of profits or, at its option, an account of profits made by the other party by its (ex hypothesi) infringing use of the trade mark.

I drew attention earlier . . . to the fact that this case is concerned essentially with raking over the ashes of past battles (or, perhaps more aptly, skirmishes) in the marketing war between Electrolux and Dyson, rather than with regulating the conduct of that war in the future. On that footing, injunctive relief may well be inappropriate in any event. Moreover, damages (whether in the form of general damages or of damages linked to profits), to the extent that they are more than merely nominal, will plainly be extremely difficult to assess and may ultimately prove to be relatively insignificant in terms of quantum. The fact that these considerations have not deterred the parties from fighting this protracted and expensive litigation vigorously to judgment only serves to confirm that they are more concerned with winning than with the obtaining of any particular remedy. 'Victory, victory at all costs' appears to be the cry, on both sides. As Mr Prescott QC put it, rather more graphically, in the course of his closing speech when referring to Dyson's Counterclaim (Day 9/1111.):

> The position is . . ., this animal having been attacked, it must defend itself. As we see it, that is what this case is really about. . . . [R]ather like nuclear warfare, if the other side are going to maintain their case for trade libel, then we would be most unwise to give ours up, for reasons which are obvious.

These factors must, it seems to me, have a bearing on what (if any) remedy should be granted in the event that either party succeeds in its claims. As I observed at the time (Day9/1112.), each side is aiming its nuclear weapons at each other and each is pressing the button. It is my task, in this judgment, to determine what are the legal and practical consequences of this high-risk strategy. The possibilities range from global conflagration to a damp squib. . . .

The claims in malicious falsehood

[*Parker J then considered each party's claims in relation to malicious falsehood. He found that three of the four claims in the defendant's graph were false, but that none was made maliciously. He found that the comment made by the defendant's chairman to the trade reporter was 'more an expression of opinion, or a subjective judgment, than a representation of fact' upon which an action for malicious falsehood could be founded. He further found that all four of the representations made in the plaintiff's flyer were untrue, but that none was made maliciously. Each party's action in malicious falsehood therefore failed. In the course of considering the actions for malicious falsehood Parker J made the following comments regarding proof of damage in situations of comparative advertising:*]

   In the light of my conclusion that Dyson did not act maliciously in publishing the graph, it is not necessary for me to consider the issue of damage in the context of the claim in malicious falsehood. For completeness, however, I should say that it seems to me that, to the extent that it has any market effect at all (and depending on the circumstances this may be an important qualification), comparative advertising is by its nature calculated (in the sense of likely) to cause pecuniary damage to suppliers of the competing product, if only by reducing the market share of the competing product whilst increasing that of the product which is the subject of the comparative advertising. That, after all, is the purpose of comparative advertising. But where, as in the instant case, damages are sought in respect of a single example of comparative advertising in the context of a continuing marketing war between two suppliers, questions inevitably arise as to whether any substantial damage can properly be attributed to that particular piece of comparative advertising, and, if so, how such damage is to be assessed. I shall have to return to this aspect in the context of the claims based on infringement of trade mark. . . .

The claims of infringement of trade mark

Liability

The reciprocal claims of infringement of trade mark relate to the graph and the flyer respectively.

Although, as I have already held, neither the graph nor the flyer was published maliciously, the fact remains that each was a thoroughly misleading document, containing a number of false representations. Given that the test of an 'honest practice' for the purposes of the proviso to section 10(6) of the Trade Marks Act 1994 is agreed to be an objective one . . . the conclusion is in my judgment inescapable that in each case the use made of the competitor's trade mark was 'otherwise than in accordance with honest practices in industrial or commercial matters' within the meaning of the proviso. To hold the publication of documents such as these to be an 'honest practice' for this purpose would in my view be to render the proviso of negligible practical use or effect.

The next question which arises is whether the use made of the competitor's trade mark, besides being 'otherwise than in accordance with honest practices', was made (a) without due cause, and (b) '[took] unfair advantage of, or [was] detrimental to, the distinctive character or repute of the [competitor's] trade mark'. Plainly, in my judgment, this requirement is met in each case.

The conclusion accordingly follows that in each case the proviso to section 10(6) of the 1994 Act applies, with the consequence that the use of the competitor's trade mark constitutes an infringing use.

In the result, therefore, each party succeeds in its claim of infringement of trade mark.

Remedy

The question what (if any) remedy or remedies should be granted in the event that either party or (as has happened) both parties should succeed in establishing infringement of trade mark was not addressed at any length by either party in the course of the hearing. In the circumstances, I find it necessary to invite further submissions on this question.

My current concerns in relation to the question of remedy are as follows.

As at present advised it seems to me that injunctive relief of any kind may well be inappropriate, given:

(a) that each party has been guilty of infringing the other's trade mark by means of comparative advertising in circumstances which did not amount to an 'honest practice' for the purposes of the proviso to section 10(6) of the 1994 Act;

(b) that, as I understand the position, neither party is threatening to continue to circulate the offending material;

(c) that the specification of at least one of the models (ie. the DC01) has changed since the graph and the flyer were published, with the consequence that the comparisons which the graph and the flyer sought to make are in any event out of date; and

(d) that, as I observed earlier . . ., both sides appear to be more concerned with winning than with the obtaining of any particular remedy.

As to damages, I have three particular concerns.

In the first place, as at present advised it seems to me to be a real possibility that any damage caused by the particular infringements which have been established in this case—ie. by the publication of the graph and the flyer respectively—may be negligible, if not nominal. It occurs to me to wonder how many consumers are significantly influenced by a single piece of promotional material such as the graph or the flyer, to the point where they are deterred from purchasing a particular type of machine and/or persuaded to purchase a different type of machine. It must, after all, be remembered that, as I pointed out earlier . . ., the graph and flyer were but single incidents in the course of a continuing marketing war between Electrolux and Dyson.

In the second place, I am concerned that the parties will be faced with very considerable practical difficulties in attempting to prove that the particular infringements caused any substantial damage. Short of providing the Court with a list of consumers prepared to testify that they were about to buy an EPS (or, as the case may be, a DC01) until deterred from doing so by the flyer (or, as the case may be, the graph) I am, as at present advised, unable to envisage what evidence the parties could usefully put before the Court in support of a claim of loss or profits. The same general considerations apply in relation to any claim for an account of the profits made by the infringing party from its wrongful use of the other party's trade mark (should either party elect for such an account instead of claiming loss of profits).

In this connection, I refer once again to the general observations which I made about damages earlier in this judgment . . . in the context of the malicious falsehood claims: the same observations apply, mutatis mutandis, in the context of the claims of infringement of trade mark.

In third place, I am concerned about the considerable time and expense which any inquiry as to damages in this case would, as I see it, inevitably involve.

In the light of these concerns, before directing any inquiry as to damages I must be satisfied that there is, at the very least, a realistic prospect of the inquiry resulting in the award of a sum which is other than negligible in relation to the time and costs involved. In *Macdonald's Hamburgers Ltd.* v. *Burgerking (UK) Ltd.* [1987] FSR 112 CA, Fox LJ said (at page 118):

> In my view the court must have a degree of discretion to refuse [an inquiry as to damages], with its attendant trouble and expense, if it is satisfied that such an [i]nquiry would be fruitless.

See also *The Sanitas Company Ltd.* v. *Condy* (1887) 4 RPC 530 at 533 *per* Kekewich J, cited by Fox LJ later in his judgment in the *Macdonalds* case (see ibid p 118).

In the instant case no evidence has been led by either party on the question of damages, and as matters stand I am not satisfied that an inquiry as to damages at the suit of either party would be justified. In particular, the mere fact that any party prosecuting such an inquiry would do so at its own risk as to costs does not seem to me (as at present advised) to provide sufficient justification for taking up the court's time in an exercise which may ultimately prove fruitless.

Accordingly, there will have to be a further hearing at which I will hear submissions as to the appropriate remedy or remedies (if any) to be granted on the respective claims of infringement of trade mark.'

APPENDIX II—German Materials

1. §1 *Gesetz gegen den unlauteren Wettbewerb*

§1 *Wer im geschäftlichen Verkehr zu Zwecken des Wettbewerbs Handlungen vornimmt, die gegen die guten Sitten verstoßen, kann auf Unterlassung und Schadensersatz in Anspruch genommen werden.*

[§1 (Any person who, in the course of trade and for purposes of competition, commits acts contrary to honest practices may be enjoined from continuing in those acts and held liable in damages.])

2. *Testpreis-Angebot*[1] (Bundesgerichtshof, I ZR 211/95, 5 February 1998)

Facts:

The plaintiff is the German distribtuor of a well known US sports goods manufacturer specialising in golf and tennis products. The defendant is involved in the distribution of tennis goods products.

In May 1992, two of the plaintiff's employees approached the defendant with a view to obtaining evidence by entrapment. Offers were made to them in letters that also included the following claims:

---

[1] This translation of *Testpreis-Angebot* is largely drawn from a translation by David Wright published in (1999) 30IIC 704. The authors would like to thank the editors of IIC for their kind permission to use this text.

You want to know why its worth becoming a customer of P Tennis? Every P raquet is made of the latest high-tech materials (e.g., HI-modular graphite, ceramics and Kevlar) and embodies state of the art of racquet technology. We would not seriously expect you to buy cheap composite racquets (graphite-fibreglass). Special string test packages are available (see enclosed data sheet)—Each racquet is available at the uniquely attractive test price of DM110 . . .

The plaintiff objected to the statement in the letter 'we would not seriously expect you to buy cheap composite racquets (graphite-fibreglass)' as disparaging comparative advertising and the test-price offer as an infringement of the *Rabattgesetz*[2] . . .

Opinion of the Court:

. . .

B. Defendant's Cross-Appeal on the Law

I. The appeal court held the statement, 'We would not seriously expect you to buy cheap composite racquets (graphite-fibreglass)' to be both a disparaging '*Systemvergleich*' that was prohibited pursuant to §1 of the UWG and also misleading advertising prohibited under §3 of the Act. . . .

II. The defendant's cross-appeal against this decision is dismissed.

The appeal court rightly held the advertising statement, 'We would not seriously expect you to buy cheap composite racquets (graphite-fibreglass),' to be comparative advertising, prohibited under §1 of the UWG. It is true that there are reasons for modifying the principles of comparative advertising case law on which the appeal court based its decision. However, the modification of those principles proposed would not effect the outcome of the current case.

1. In line with this Court's case law, the appeal court assumed that a comparison of one's own goods or services with those of a competitor is generally incompatible with honest practices,

[2] Act on Discounts.

even if the claims made are true and the comparisons drawn are accurate, since any advertising that seeks to highlight a trader's own performance by means of the comparative disparagement of a competitor is incompatible with the principle of competition by a trader's own merits (see *Statt Blumen ONKO-Kaffee*, BGH GRUR 1972, 553 at 554, (1973) 4 IIC 114, *Krankenkassen-Fragebogen*, GRUR 1988, 764 at 767, *Energiekosten-Preisvergleich I*, GRUR 1996, 502 at 506, *Preisvergleich II*, GRUR 1996, 983 at 984). This general prohibition was, however, soon qualified by a general exception under which a comparison of a trader's own goods or services with those of a competitor is regarded as admissible if there is sufficient cause for the comparison, and if the type and extent of the information given remains within the limits both of what is necessary and of truthful and objective discussion (see *40 % können Sie sparen*, BGHZ 49, 325 at 329, *Reperaturversicherung*, BGH GRUR 1974, 666 at 668, *Vorsatz-Fensterflügel* GRUR, 1986, 618 at 620, *Generikum-Preisvergleich*, GRUR 1989, 668 at 669, *Energiekosten-Preisvergleich II*, GRUR 1997, 304 at 305).

2. As a consequence of Directive 97/55/EC of the European Parliament and the Council of 6 October 1997, amending Directive 84/450/EEC concerning misleading advertising so as to include comparative advertising (OJ 1997 L 290/18), this Court is modifying its case law in order to interpret §1 of the UWG in conformity with the directive. This possibility was pointed out to the parties during the oral hearing before this Court.

There is no need to modify the concept of comparative advertising. As before, and in accordance with Article 2(2)(a) of the said Directive, comparative advertising is advertising that explicitly or by implication identifies (at least) a competitor or the goods or services offered by a competitor (established case-law, see *Energiekosten-Preisvergleich I*, GRUR 1996, 502 at 506).

However, the rule-and-exception relationship as assumed by this Court in its previous case law, in the form of a fundamental prohibition of comparative advertising with a general exception, is no longer upheld. Comparative advertising must now be regarded as fundamentally admissible provided the conditions specified in Article 3a(1)(a) to (h) of Directive 97/55/EC are met.)

This Court is not prevented from construing the UWG in conformity with the directive by the fact that the deadline for implementation of the directive on comparative advertising has not yet expired. If conformity with the directive can be established by means of a simple construction of national law, the judges are empowered, at least according to German understanding, to correct the previous interpretation and consider the changed legal and factual conditions (see Larenz, *Methodenlehre der Rechtswissenschaft*, 6th edn. 1991, at 314, 352ff). . . .

The Directive is a harmonisation directive pursuant to articles 100a(1), 100(1) and 189(3) of the European Community Treaty. Such directives for the 'harmonisation of legal and administrative regulations' are primarily directed to the Member States, instructing them to implement the principles specified in a harmonisation directive in national law by means of appropriate legislation. It goes without saying that there is no need for implementing a directive if national law already meets the requirements set. Such is the case of the directive concerning misleading advertising, 84/450/EEC, 10 September 1984, which simply required compliance with a minimum standard already met by German law. §1 of the UWG, as construed by case law with respect to comparative advertising, does not conform with the new Directive 97/55/EC. However, the broad wording of this general clause permits interpretation in accordance with a directive by the courts. The obligation to implement is not only addressed to the legislative bodies. On the contrary, all agencies of state power in the Member States are obliged to take the measures necessary to perform the obligation to implement (Article 5 EC). This also applies to the courts within the limits of their powers; they must construe national law in light of the wording and purpose of a directive (see the decision of the European Court of Justice in *Inter-Environnement Wallonie/Région Wallonne* [1984] ECR 1891, WRP 1998, 290 at 293 n. 40 for further references).

Of course, the courts' obligation to construe the laws in conformity with a directive does not apply immediately after adoption of a directive. Article 189(3) EC grants the Member States discretion in implementing directives that must primarily be exercised by the legislature. The (to this extent subsidiary) obligation of the courts to construe the national laws in conformity with a directive only begins if the legislature has failed to act before expiry of the implementation period and the contents of a directive are unambiguous overall or in the area in question (*Dorsch Consult*, ECJ NJW 1997, 3365 at 3367 n. 43, *Dos*, BGH GRUR 1993, 825 at 826—and for further references, *SAM*, BGH GRUR 1998, 699).

However, in light of the current state of development of the law, this Court deems it appropriate to take account of Directive 97/55/EC even before expiry of the 30-month implementation period. The general clause of §1 of the UWG permits an amendment of German (judge-made) law (see also Erdmann/Bornkamm, GRUR 1991, 877 at 880). This clause bases the evaluation of competitive behaviour on the criteria of honest practices. This permits the courts to adapt the law and apply it in such a way as to take account of the developments of business life, changes in generally accepted standards and long-term changes in public attitudes (see Köhler/Piper, *UWG*, Introduction, para 145). This is shown clearly in the development of case law on comparative advertising (see von Gamm, *Wettbewerbsrecht*, 5th edn. ch. 22 para. 33ff), which has been marked by a gradual relaxation that has now led to the recognition of a general exception going beyond the previous individual exceptions. The principle of prohibition was, in any case, not always applied strictly (see *Cola-Test*, BGH GRUR 1987, 49 at 50 with comment by Sack; *Aussehen mit Brille*, GRUR 1997, 227 at 228, *Kfz-Waschanlagen*, GRUR 1997, 539 at 540ff; see also *Therapeutische Äquivalenz*, BGH GRUR 1992, 625). In the legal literature, the trend was already towards further relaxation in the interests of greater market transparency and information (see Menke, GRUR 1991, 661 at 661ff for further references; Köhler/Piper, *UWG* at §1 para 129). It has also been pointed out

147

that the practical importance of the dispute on whether comparative advertising is admissible or prohibited as a matter of principle should not be overestimated (see Baumbach/ Hefermehl, *Wettbewerbsrecht*, 19th edn., at §1 para 335).

In the course of harmonisation of the rules of fair competition, the general clause of §1 UWG now permits an early adjustment to the developments of European law instead of the imposition of previous (divergent) principles of case law, which in any event would no longer apply after expiry of the implementation period at the latest. This corresponds with the case law of the European Court of Justice, according to which the Member States must refrain from measures which jeopardise the achievement of the objectives of a directive (this view was recently expressed by the European Court of Justice, see WRP 1998, 290 at 290ff): a directive acquires legal effect at the time of notification with respect to the Member States to which it is addressed (Article 191(2) EC). It is true that Member States cannot be reproached for not implementing a directive before expiry of the implementation period, which is intended to allow them the necessary time for the adoption of implementing measures into the legislative system. Nevertheless, they are obliged to adopt the necessary measures during the implementation period to ensure that the objectives prescribed in a directive are achieved upon expiry of this period (ECJ WRP 1998, 290 at 293 nn 41–45).

There is no justification for the objection that interpretation of national legislation by the courts in conformity with a directive before expiry of the implementation period represents an encroachment upon the powers of the legislature (see Brechmann, *Die richtlinienkonforme Auslegung*, (1994) at 265; Ehricke, 59 RabelsZ 1995, 598 at 621; Götz, NJW 1992, 1849 at 1845), provided conformity can be achieved by means of construction of national law (in the present case the general clause of §1 of the UWG), and provided that the legislature enjoys no scope for latitude in implementation. The latter must be assumed in any event where the present case relies on the concept of comparative advertising (Article 2(2)(a)) and the principle established and the conditions for admissibility regulated in Article 3a. It is true that the Directive leaves the choice of the form and means of implementation to the Member States (European Community Treaty article 189(3)), but the contents of an implementing measure must correspond with the binding specifications of the Directive. It is also possible, provided this is seen to be compatible with the objectives of the Directive, for the legislature to prohibit comparative advertising as a matter of principle if the conditions of Article 3a(1)(a) to (h) of the Directive are not met. This might fit better in the previous system of German competition law, but would not alter the fact that the conditions for admissibility that ultimately determine the decision are identical, irrespective of the legal approach selected. It is a different question whether, by *argumentum e contrario* on the rule in Article 3a(1), comparative advertising must always be prohibited if the conditions specified therein are not met (This view is taken by Plassmann, GRUR 1996, 377 at 381; Tilmann, GRUR 1997, 790 at n 9; Funke, WM 1997, 1472 at 1473ff. For the opposite view see Sack, GRUR Int 1998, 263 at 270). Any legislative latitude allowed here would not be preempted by the present decision. This also applies to the question (requiring interpretation) of the requirements of deception to be applied to advertising comparisons. The courts' consideration of Directive 97/55/EC at an early stage means that this and other questions of construction raised by the Directive can be made the subject of a timely submission to the European Court of Justice, the organ ultimately competent for such purpose. This would ensure in good time that the objective prescribed in the Directive, namely the harmonisation of comparative advertising in Member States of the community, can be achieved upon expiry of the implementation period (see ECJ WRP 1998, 290 at 293 n 44).

To this must be added the following aspect: the Directive is not merely an occasion for reconsidering the previous case law on comparative advertising. On the contrary, it also has a direct effect on the concept of dishonest practices that underlies behavior in violation of fair competition. An activity held by the

European legislature to be admissible as a matter of principle, cannot, irrespective of whether the period for the implementation of the directive has not yet expired, be regarded as an infringement of 'honest practices'. The use of the term honest practices permits the national legislature not only to adjust the law to changes in general attitudes, but also creates an opening for value judgements expressed in other provisions of national or European law that must be considered in the construction of this term for the purposes of uniformity within the legal system.

In light of the above, this Court holds it admissible and objectively appropriate now to base its interpretation of the general clause of §1 of the UWG on the criteria of Directive 97/55/EC, and, abandoning the previous prohibition principle, to permit comparative advertising in the future within the limits imposed on the legislature by Article 3a of the Directive. This approach must also be applied to facts from the past, since it does not represent a change in the law but rather an application of the law, namely the construction of the general clause of §1 of the UWG in light of a changed general attitude.

3. In the present case, the contested advertising statement violates fair competition within the meaning of §1 of the UWG even on the basis of a construction in accordance with Directive 97/55/EC. For, according to Article 3a(1)(e) of the Directive, comparative advertising (*inter alia*) is only permissible if it does not disparage the goods of the competitors concerned. According to the findings rightly made by the appeal court, this condition is not met. There is no need to determine whether the advertising statement is also to be seen as misleading, as assumed by the appeal court, with the effect that it also fails to meet the condition for admissibility of Article 3a(1)(a) of the Directive.

(a) The present case concerns comparative advertising because the defendant's advertising sufficiently identifies specific competitors and the goods they supply. The advertising comparison refers to all suppliers of so-called composite racquets (graphite-fibreglass), which class, according to the uncontested findings of the appeal court and as known in the trade, also includes the plaintiff.

(b) The appeal court's assumption that the defendant's advertising statement was a global disparagement of a whole product type, namely by denigrating all tennis racquets of a specifically mentioned construction, is upheld on appeal on the law. In the cross-appeal it is objected that the appeal court gave insufficient consideration to the facts of the case, thus infringing §286 of the *Zivilprozessordnung*,[3] by only taking account of the contested statement and not of the preceding sentence with the addition in brackets 'such as HI-modular graphite, ceramics and Kevlar.' The defendant alleged that it had made it sufficiently clear that cheap racquets in the 'composite racquets (graphite-fibreglass)' category also included high quality products, *i.e.:* a graphite material that was very special ('latest high-tech'), namely highly modulated graphite (HI-modular graphite).

The objection in the cross-appeal against the finding of fact made in the appeal court cannot be allowed. In any event, findings of fact can only be reviewed to a restricted extent in an appeal on the law. It is true that the appeal court did not expressly mention the explanation contained in the parentheses in the sentence above. However, it is apparent that it included this sentence in its assessment. For it based its findings decisively on the contradiction between the two statements and attached an interpretation to it according to which only the racquets offered by the defendant were made of state-of-the-art materials, whilst in contrast, so-called composite racquets made of graphite and fibreglass were outdated and not in line with the latest technology. In any event, this interpretation of fact must be accepted on an appeal on the law. Given the contrast between the two statements, it does not appear obvious on the basis of everyday experience that the public will interpret the statement to mean that there are also high quality racquets made of graphite and fibreglass.

Moreover, the following statement in the contested advertising that the tennis racquet type in question was technically out of date and of lower quality is, according to the appeal court's

[3] Code of Civil Procedure.

findings, incorrect. The defendant itself assumes that this type also includes high-quality racquets.

The appeal court rightly held the global disparagement to be dishonest within the meaning of §1 of the UWG. It is true that not every comparison of goods includes a disparagement (see Baumbach/Hefermehl, *Wettbewerbsrecht*, 19th edn. at §1 para 340), for advertising only makes sense if it praises the advertising enterprise's products and services, which naturally involves a differentiation with respect to those of competitors (*Aussehen mit Brille* BGH GRUR 1997, 227). However, the limit is exceeded if, as must be assumed according to the legally correct findings of the appeal court, the rival products are presented as having inferior quality compared with the advertiser's own (Baumbach/Hefermehl, *Wettbewerbsrecht*, 19th edn. at §1 para 340) . . .

The defendant's cross-appeal is dismissed.'

3. *Preisvergleichsliste II* (Bundesgerichtshof, No. I ZR 2/96, 23 April 98)

Facts:

The plaintiff manufactures components used for assembly and fixing in joineries. It distributes these products through sales representatives throughout the country. The defendants, which trade under the name 'Information and Purchasing Co-operative for Wood and Plastics Processing Industries', asked some joineries to show them invoices paid by them for such products. On this basis they compiled comparative price lists in which they listed products, suppliers and prices with respective invoice dates. The joineries themselves were not named. The defendants sent this list to several joineries with a view to informing them about the best prices and to persuading them to join the co-operative. . . . They also offered to supply the components at the prices quoted with an additional charge of 6 per cent.

The plaintiff objected to this list, which it considered to be a violation of §§1 and 3 of the UWG, since the list was neither objective nor complete. It argued that the most expensive supplier was discriminated against, in particular because only a few articles were mentioned. The choice made by the defendant had a great potential for various manipulations. The conditions under which a price comparison was exceptionally permitted were not met.

The defendants argued that . . . the comparative price lists were correct and that the joiners at which the list was directed knew that the compilation was of necessity incomplete. . . .

Opinion of the Court:

I. The appeal court did not find a violation of §§1 and 3 of the UWG. . . . The court held that the advertising conducted by the defendant did not constitute prohibited comparative advertising. According to established principles of case law a comparison of prices was only prohibited if it was conducted by a trader who offered the goods in question himself. The defendants, however, did not belong to this group because they did not sell components used for assembly and fixing in joineries themselves. They only offered joineries the opportunity to conclude contracts with other suppliers for a charge of 6 per cent. Therefore the defendants had only compared prices charged by other suppliers, not their own prices with prices charged by competitors. A compilation or market survey conducted by a person who did not himself take part in the relevant price competition did not constitute unfair competition. . . .

II. The appeal is sucessful. The judgment of the appeal court is reversed and the case is referred back to the appeal court. . . .

2. . . . Contrary to the view expressed by the appeal court the defendants' conduct does not fall outside the definition of comparative advertising only because they compared prices charged by other suppliers rather than then their own prices with competitors' prices. . . . The defendants did not restrict themselves to neutral information about potential suppliers. They distributed their comparison not only in order to promote other trader's competitive actions but also in order to promote their own business . . . With the intention of making a profit they

153

approached the same group of purchasers that was also addressed by the plaintiff. Therefore they competed with the plaintiff.

3. For these reasons alone, the judgment of the appeal court has to be reversed because it is not in accordance with established principles of comparative advertising case law. According to these principles a price comparison was generally prohibited, but exceptionally allowed if no competitor was either named or unnecessarily identified, if there was a sufficient cause for the comparison and if the type and extent of information given remained within the limits both of what was necessary and of truthful and objective discussion; the public interest in information could constitute a sufficient cause (see *Generikum-Preisvergleich*, BGH GRUR 1989, 668 at 669, *Preisvergleichsliste II*, BGH GRUR 1992, 61 at 62, *Energiekosten-Preisvergleich I*, BGH GRUR 1996, 502 at 506, *Energiekosten-Preisvergleich II*, BGH GRUR 1997, 304 at 305, *Preisvergleich II*, GRUR 1996, 983 at 984).

4. However, since the decision of the appeal court, this Court has abandoned the principle that comparative advertising is generally prohibited and only exceptionally allowed. After Directive 97/55/EC of the European Parliament and the Council of 6 October 1997 amending Directive 84/450/EEC concerning misleading advertising so as to include comparative advertising (OJ 1997 L 290/18) entered into force this Court has changed its legal position in its judgment *Testpreis-Angebot* to ensure an interpretation of §1 of the UWG which is in conformity with the Directive. This was pointed out to the parties in the oral proceedings. Comparative advertising which, as in the present case, identifies competitors is now permitted as long as the conditions specified in Article 3a(1)(a)–(e) are met.

On the basis of the findings of fact made by the appeal court so far, this Court is unable to decide whether these conditions are met in the present case. A further inquiry into the facts must be carried out, consequently the case must be referred back to the appeal court. In the proceedings in the appeal court the parties will be given the opportunity to adapt their submissions to the changed legal requirements. This practice is in conformity with the principles of fair trial and natural justice (Article 103(1) of the *Grundgesetz* BVerfG NJW 1991, 2823, BVerfG NJW 1994, 1274).

In particular, the appeal court will have to examine the condition specified in Article 3a (1)(c) of the Directive, according to which comparative advertising must compare objectively one or more material, relevant, verifiable and representative features of goods, which may include the price. The requirement that comparisons must be objective, which is also stressed in recitals (7) and (15), is primarily to be understood as a reinforcement of the requirement that comparisons must be factual (see Gloy/Bruhn, GRUR 1998, 226 at 237; Tilmann, GRUR 1997, 790 at 796). Furthermore it can become relevant in connection with the criterion of verifiability (see Plassmann, GRUR 1996, 377 at 379). This requirement, which was also made by this Court in its former case law (see *Preisvergleich II*, BGH GRUR 1996, 983 at 984ff), addresses the distinction between statements of fact and statements of opinion (see Gloy/Bruhn, GRUR 1998, 226 at 236; Plassmann, GRUR 1996, 377 at 379). It requires that all statements comparing features of the goods must have a factual content which must be objectively verifiable. Statements of fact will always meet this requirement. But even representations which on their face seem to be statements of opinion may contain a factual core (on the meaning of the word 'representation' see Baumbach/Hefermehl, *Wettbewerbsrecht*, 19th edn. at §3 para 13ff). It must be clear that the comparison can be verified with respect to its factual claims. However, it is not required that the relevant consumers are able to verify the features mentioned in the comparison without any effort (see also Tilmann, GRUR Int 1997, 790 at 796). For a comparison of the type under consideration here it should be sufficient if the addressee is able to obtain the necessary information from the defendant or from the suppliers mentioned in the list. On the other hand it would seem excessive to require the defendant to mention the recipients of the invoices from which the prices were taken by name in order to ensure verifiability.

Another condition to examine would be the requirement of Article 3a(1)(a), according to which comparative advertising must not be misleading according to Articles 2(2), 3 and 7(1) (on this requirement see Gloy/Bruhn, GRUR 1998, 226 at 234ff, Plassmann, GRUR 1996, 377 at 379, Sack, GRUR Int 1998, 263 at 271, Tilmann, GRUR 1997, 790 at 796). . . .

4. *Vergleichen Sie* (Bundesgerichtshof No. I ZR 69/96, 15 October 1998)

Facts:

The parties are competitors in the business of selling costume jewellery. The defendant sells its jewellery through a system consisting of five levels of altogether about 10,000 'consultants'. The jewellery is sold at a profit from one level of consultants to the next level. The consultants are independent traders who choose their own consultants for the subordinate level. On 3 April 1994 one consultant, who was already working for the defendant, wrote a letter to a person potentially interested in becoming a consultant herself. The letter contained the following:

> Today we offer this opportunity on the basis of a different range of products: High-quality designer jewellery at affordable prices. Compare for yourself with the catalogue of P.L.

The plaintiff objected to this statement as prohibited comparative advertising. . . .

Opinion of the Court:

I. According to the appeal court the statement made by the defendant's consultant constituted prohibited comparative advertising pursuant to §1 of the UWG . . .

II. The appeal against this judgment is successful. Accordingly, the judgment of the appeal court is reversed and the action is dismissed. . . .

1. According to the case law of this Court, which has modified its position since the decision of the appeal court, comparative advertising is permissible in principle as long as the conditions specified in Article 3a(1)(a)–(h) of Directive

97/55/EC of the European Parliament and the Council of 6 October 1997 amending Directive 84/450/EEC concerning misleading advertising so as to include comparative advertising (OJ 1997 L 290/18) are met (*Testpreis-Angebot*, BGHZ 138, 55, *Preisvergleichsliste II*, BGH WRP 1998, 1065). . . .

2. The advertising claim in issue, which sets off the products offered by the defendant against those offered by the plaintiff, who is identified by name, comes within the definition of comparative advertising given in Directive 97/55/EC (article 2(2a), see also *Testpreis-Angebot*, BGHZ 138,55 at 59). It is true that a mere general invitation, directed at the public, to compare certain products cannot alway be considered as a comparison (see *TOK-Band* BGH GRUR 1961, 237 at 240, *Divi*, BGH GRUR 1974, 280 at 281, *Cola-Test*, BGH GRUR 1987, 49 at 50 see also Baumbach/ Hefermehl, *Wettbewerbsrecht*, 20th edn. at §1 para. 362, Köhler/ Piper, *UWG* at §1 para 131). However, despite the words 'compare for yourself with the catalogue of . . .' the statement in issue is more than just an invitation to compare. The invitation follows from the previous sentence in which the products offered by the defendant are described as 'high-quality designer jewellery at affordable prices'. Thus the comparison is evidently supposed to be made with respect to the features which the statement considers advantageous for the defendant, namely price and quality. In both respects the defendant's consultant sets the defendant's product off against those offered by the plaintiff. On the one hand, the members of the public at whom the advertisement is directed—in this case persons who might be persuaded to become consultants and to sell the defendant's jewellery—understand the statement as saying that the products offered by the defendant are priced lower than those offered by the plaintiff. Only on this interpretation does an invitation to carry out a comparison which makes the defendant's prices seem 'affordable' make sense. On the other hand, the statement also claims the equivalence of both products, because the relevant section of the public is likely to assume that the defendants would, as a matter of course, only compare their prices with those charged by a competitor who also offers 'high-quality designer jewellery'.

3. Therefore the statement in issue comes within the definition of comparative advertising. However, the conditions of Article 3a(1)(a)–(h) of Directive 97/55/EC, under which comparative advertising is permitted, are met. In this context it is unnecessary to examine the criteria specified in letters (d), (f) and (h) as these are met without any doubt.

(a) First there is no evidence that the statement might be misleading (Article 3a (1)(a) of Directive 97/55/EC). The written and oral submissions of the parties do not give any reason to assume that the claim concerning the price-value relation, i.e. the lower price in comparison to the plaintiff's products on the one hand and the quality of the goods offered by the defendant on the other, are incorrect. The action has been based exclusively on §1 of the UWG, not on §3 [which prohibits misleading advertising]. What is more, the plaintiff has not adduced any evidence as to why the statement might be misleading. This Court therefore sees no reason to direct the appeal court to re-examine this factual question.

(b) Second the statement compares goods meeting the same needs or intended for the same purpose (Article 3a(1)(b) of the Directive). This conclusion is not affected by the fact that the defendant does not compare particular pieces of jewellery with identical pieces offered by the plaintiff. Both the wording of the provision, which only refers to the same needs or the same purpose, and the goal of enhancing consumer information speak in favour of a wide interpretation of this provision which should also render advertising comparisons of non-identical products permissible as long as their function is identical and as long as they appear interchangeable in the eyes of the relevant section of the public (see Plassmann, GRUR 1996, 377 at 379, Menke, WRP 1998, 811 at 822; Gloy/Bruhn, GRUR1998, 226 at 235ff; on the permissibility of a comparison between a branded product and a generic product see OLG Stuttgart, Judgment of 31 July 1998—2 U 12/98). This interpretation does not harm competitors' interests as their position is protected by those further criteria according to which a comparison must not mislead, denigrate or take unfair advantage of their reputation.

It is also not objectionable that the comparison does not relate to particular products but to a class of goods described as 'high-quality designer jewellery' (see also *Testpreis-Angebot*, BGHZ 138, 55. In that case the comparison related to a type of product, namely tennis racquets manufactured by a certain method). The field of costume jewellery is still sufficiently delineated, in particular it can be distinguished from real jewellery. It is not necessary to determine whether the feature 'high-quality', with which the writer of the letter in issue apparently intended to qualify designer jewellery in general, allows a sufficiently clear distinction from simpler kinds of products—and whether this feature is verifiable according to Article 3a(1)(c) of the Directive. . . . The products in issue can certainly be compared by the addressee herself, and the advertisement does not go beyond an invitation to do just that. This is particularly true because the advertisement is not directed at final consumers but at a person who is to be persuaded to become a consultant within the distribution system operated by the defendant. For this particular addressee a comparison which relates to the whole range of products offered by the defendant is even more informative than a comparison of particular pieces of jewellery.

(c) It should not be overlooked that the verification of the features compared, which must be possible according to Article 3a(1)(c) of Directive 97/55/EC, is more difficult if the comparison relates to a class of products. However, this result seems acceptable in the present case. While it must be guaranteed that the comparison can be verified, it is not required that the relevant section of the public must be able to verify the features mentioned in the comparison without any effort (see *Preisvergleichsliste II*, BGH WRP 1998, 1095 at 1098). In this case the reference to the plaintiff's catalogue makes it easier for the addressee to compare the prices of the goods. It can be expected that a person interested in the sale of the whole range of products offered by the defendant will make an effort to compare the prices of the products shown in the plaintiff's catalogue with the prices of similar articles offered by the defendant . . . .

(d) Contrary to the view expressed by the plaintiff, the price comparison cannot be considered as a blanket disparagement (Article 3a(1)(e) of Directive 97/55/EC). By equating discredit and denigration this provision makes it clear that not every disparaging effect which is inherent in a critical comparison is sufficient. Advertising only makes sense if it mentions the advertiser's offer favourably, thereby contrasting it to offers made by competitors (see BGHZ 138, 55 at 66). It is inherent in a price comparison which praises the advertiser's products as being good value that it is unfavourable to those competitors who offer their goods at higher prices. The public, which is used to different prices for comparable goods, is well aware of this fact. It therefore does not consider a price comparison in itself to discredit or denigrate the more expensive competitor, but rather sees such a comparison as the expression of lively competition on the basis of price. Thus there must be circumstances additional to the (negative) effect inherent in every price comparison to make the comparison appear unduly disparaging, denigratory or biassed (see Plassmann, GRUR 1996, 377 at 380, Tilmann, GRUR 1997, 790 at 797, Menke, WRP 1998, 811 at 816, Gloy/Bruhn, GRUR 1998, 226 at 237, Sack, GRUR Int 1998, 263 at 271ff, OLG Stuttgart, judgment of 10 July 1998—2 U 278/97). In this case such factors are neither evident, nor have they been put forward by the plaintiff. They are also not implied by the statement that the defendant offers costume jewellery at affordable prices or by the invitation to compare with the plaintiff's catalogue. A different conclusion might only be reached if this statement were to be understood as suggesting that the prices charged by the plaintiff were unacceptable because they were generally too high and completely outside any reasonable relation between value and money. On a natural reading, however, it cannot be assumed that the public would understand the statement in this way. The statement does not comment explicitly on either the prices or the quality of the plaintiff's products. The comparative advertisement in issue is very reserved in this important aspect. The invitation to compare is obviously not meant to disparage the plaintiff's price-value-relation, it is rather supposed to tell the addressee, who is to be persuaded to become a consultant, that it is financially rewarding to work for the defendant, because compared to those of other vendors of 'high-quality designer jewellery' such as the plaintiff, its products are good or even better value. As this purpose is evident, the statement appears neutral and not disparaging.

(e) Finally the defendant does not take unfair advantage of the plaintiff's reputation (Article 3a (1)(g) of Directive 97/55/EC). The plaintiff's submissions do not point to any evidence in this respect. Independent of the question of what constitutes a 'reputation' in the sense of this provision (see Plassmann, GRUR 1996, 377 at 380), it is obvious that the defendant does not take any unfair advantage. The mere fact that in its invitation to compare the defendant mentions the plaintiff's name is not sufficient. Otherwise all comparative advertising would be illegal, as Article 2(2a) of Directive 97/55/EC presupposes that a competitor or his goods be identified. Rather, similar to the test of denigration . . ., additional circumstances which go beyond the mere reference to a competitor's mark, name or distinguishing sign must be present which support the conclusion that the defendant took unfair advantage of the plaintiff's reputation (see Sack, GRUR Int 1998, 263 at 272). There is no evidence of such factors here. There is no indication to support the assumption that the defendant's consultant intended to take advantage of the plaintiff's reputation and to exploit the plaintiff's goodwill. The purpose of her statement . . . even contradicts this conclusion. . . .'

5. *McDonald's/Burger King* (Landgericht Köln No. 81 O 185/98, 29 January 1999)

Facts:

The plaintiff and the first defendant are competitors in the fast food industry. The second, third and fourth plaintiffs are the first plaintiff's managers. The parties were in dispute over the legality of the following advertisements:

Satte Mehrheit!

62%   38%

62% der Testpersonen schmeckt der WHOPPER besser
als der Big Mac[4]

Ganz krosser Unterschied

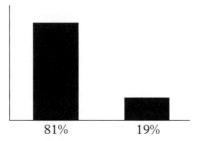

81%   19%

81% der Testpersonen schmecken unsere neuen King
Pommes besser als die Pommes Frites von McDonald's.[5]

The plaintiff argued that these advertisements constituted disparaging comparative advertising prohibited by §1 of the UWG. The comparison was not justified by EC Directive 97/55 on comparative advertising both (i) because taste, which is the standard of comparison used in the advertisements, was not a 'feature' and even less a 'verifiable feature' of the relevant goods or

[4] Full Majority! 62% of those tested preferred the taste of the Whopper to the Big Mac.

[5] Crisp Difference. 81% of all those tested preferred the taste of our new King Pommes to McDonald's french fries.

services and (ii) because their different composition meant that the products compared were not 'intended for the same purpose' within the meaning of the directive. In this context the use of the slogan '*BURGER KING weil's besser schmeckt*' ('BURGER KING because it tastes better'), which was not objectionable as such, had also to be considered as prohibited.

On 14 October 1998 the plaintiff obtained an interlocutory injunction which enjoined the defendants from using the advertisements. . . .

The defendants considered the advertisements permissible. A comparison relating to taste had not even been prohibited under the old law as was evident from the judgment of the Bundesgerichtshof in the *Cola-Test* case (GRUR 1987, 49). The Directive had not changed the law in this respect. However, the advertisements in issue also satisfied the conditions specified in the directive: First, the test was conducted in an objective and neutral manner. Second, the taste of food was not only a material and typical feature, it was also made verifiable by the test reports; the reports would also be made available to consumers. Finally, not the features themselves but rather the test had to be objective; a sensory comparison was not only objective, it was even a type of test carried out by the '*Stiftung Warentest*'.[6] . . .

Opinion of the Court

The application is well-founded. The interlocutory injunction is upheld because the advertisements in issue are disparaging and unjustified and therefore prohibited under §1 of the UWG. They also do not meet the criteria specified in Directive 97/55/EC.

Both advertisements explicitly refer to the defendant. They explicitly refer to its 'Big Mac' and french fries and compare them unfavourably as to taste with the products of the first defendant, also mentioned explicitly. The judges of this Court are members of the relevant section of the consuming public themselves and can therefore make this finding without having

[6] See above at 3.

to examine further evidence. The advertisements are presented as the results of a representative opinion poll (and not without reason they were published in the context of the recent general elections) which, according to the defendants, they really are.
. . .

It is exactly this appearance of a seriously intended objectivity which makes this case differ from the *Cola-Test* case and which brings out the essential message referred to above: a significant or even overwhelming majority of the relevant public not only prefers one of many products ('french fries') of the defendant to the corresponding product of the plaintiff, it also prefers the defendant's flagship product 'Big Mac' to that of the plaintiff, 'Whopper'. In this context the slogan 'because it tastes better', which is pointless as such, is given a distinct factual core which is disparaging to the plaintiff's products. Unlike the *Cola-Test* case the defendants do not restrict themselves to pointing out the difference in taste and to inviting the public to compare themselves; rather, as in the *Testpreis-Angebot* judgement of the Bundesgerichtshof (WRP 1998, 718 at 723), the competitor's products are presented as inferior, here as to taste.

The defendants cannot rely on Directive 97/55/EC for various reasons. First, as far as the hamburgers are concerned, the goods compared are not intended for the same purpose within the meaning of article 3a(1)(b). The parties agreed that both products are designed to satisfy different tastes and therefore composed different. The proposition that different food tastes differently and that therefore different preferences cannot be compared seriously and honestly should not require further justification: One person prefers apples, the other person prefers oranges. The choice of precisely these products—both of them are the parties 'top sellers'—is the product of almost every consideration but taste and confirms the findings made above concerning the disparaging character of the advertisement.

Contrary to the position adopted by the defendants, it must be stated in relation to both advertisements in issue that 'taste' as determined and utilised by the defendants is not a 'feature' and even less a 'verifiable feature' of the food compared in the advertisements. At this point it needs to be explained that this Court does not intend to prohibit every comparison referring to taste. However, the sensory tests conducted by '*Stiftung Warentest*', which the defendants relied on, are organised in a completely different manner (e.g. 'yellowish-liquid product, taste excessively sour', see exhibit 13) to the tests in this case ('tastes . . . better than'). The word 'taste' is ambiguous. On the one hand it indeed refers to features of a product because there are criteria according to which it is possible to tell whether a product is typical of its kind. Testing of this sort which presumably cannot easily be used in advertising is carried out by '*Stiftung Warentest*'. On the other hand, 'taste' as a word for a sensual impression felt by a hungry consumer has only a slight relation to the foodstuffs themselves because this taste is experienced differently. The difference is not only a result of the differences between individuals, it also differs depending on the way a person feels in a particular moment: A 'Whopper' for breakfast tastes different from a 'Whopper' had late in the evening with a glass of beer. Against this background it becomes evident that the results of the opinion polls carried out by the defendants reflect nothing but a momentary impression which cannot be generalised and which even less can count as 'verifiable features' of hamburgers and fries. . . .'

APPENDIX III—European Community Preparatory Materials

1. Explanatory Memorandum to the Draft of 1991, COM(91)147 final—SYN 343, Brussels, 21 June 1991

I. Background

Two basic consumer rights

1.1. On 14 April 1975 the Council adopted a Resolution on the Preliminary Programme of the European Economic Community for a Consumer Protection and Information Policy. The programme, annexed to the Resolution, summed up consumers' economic interests by a statement of five basic consumer rights, amongst them the right to protection of economic interests and the right to information.[1]

1.2. The protection of consumers' economic interests is set out in a number of principles, including the following: 'No form of advertising—visual or aural—should mislead the potential buyer of the product or service. An advertiser in any medium should be able to justify, by appropriate means, the validity of any claims he makes'.[2]

1.3. The consumer's right to information rests on the following principle: 'Sufficient information should be made available to the purchaser of goods or services to enable him to:

---

[1] Point 3 of the Annex to the Council Resolution of 14 Apr. 1975.

[2] *Ibid.*, point 19(iv).

—assess the basic features of the goods and services offered, such as the nature, quality, quantity and price;

—make a rational choice between competing products and services . . .'.[3]

1.4. All these principles were confirmed by the Council Resolution of 19 May 1981 on a 'Second Programme of the European Economic Community for a Consumer Protection and Information Policy', in which the Council noted—as it did in the Preliminary Programme—that the Commission would submit suitable proposals for the effective implementation of the programme.

The global approach

1.5. On 1 March 1978 the Commission sent the Council a proposal for a Council Directive relating to the approximation of the laws, regulations and administrative provisions of the Member States concerning misleading and unfair advertising.[4]

The proposal was a global approach that covered not only misleading and unfair advertising, the pronouncements to be taken into consideration in determining whether advertising is misleading or unfair, and also an article permitting comparative advertising.

All of these issues were discussed during the negotiation of the proposal, not only with the Council, the Parliament and the Economic and Social Committee but also with representatives of commerce and industry, the advertising profession and consumers.

1.6. The reticence of some Member States at that time to deal with unfair advertising and the firm opposition of one of them to dealing with comparative advertising had the effect—at the end of the discussions in the Council—that the provisions on unfair advertising and on comparative advertising were dropped. (It has to be remembered that the Single European Act had not then been adopted and that unanimity was therefore required.)

[3] Point 3 of the Annex to the Council Resolution of 14 Apr. 1975 point 34.
[4] OJ 1978, C70/4.

II. The Step by Step Approach

2.1. Since the provisions on misleading advertising proved acceptable, on 10 September 1984 the Council adopted Directive 84/450/EEC relating to the approximation of the laws, regulations and administrative provisions of the Member States concerning misleading advertising.

In adopting that Directive, the Council inserted a recital stating that 'it is in the interest of the public in general, as well as that of consumers . . . to harmonize in the first instance national provisions against misleading advertising and that, at a second stage, unfair advertising and, as far as necessary, comparative advertising should be dealt with, on the basis of appropriate Commission proposals'.

Misleading advertising

2.2. Directive 84/450/EEC deals with:

(a) The minimum and objective *criteria* for determining whether advertising is misleading. (The characteristics of goods and services; the price and the conditions on which goods are supplied or services provided; the nature, attributes and rights of the advertiser.)

(b) Adequate and effective *means of controlling* misleading advertising, i.e. the possibility of taking legal or administrative action against misleading advertising, as well as the possibility of ordering the cessation or the prohibition thereof either temporarily or permanently, but without excluding voluntary control by self-regulatory bodies.

(c) The *reversal of the burden of proof*, i.e. the advertiser may be required to furnish evidence as to the accuracy of factual claims in advertising.

The Directive has so far been implemented by all the Member States except Italy and Belgium (legislation in force in Belgium must be considered incomplete).

Unfair advertising

2.3. Within its definition of unfair advertising, the above mentioned 1978 proposal included a number of acts which can be considered typical of unfair advertising: to appeal to sentiments of fear; to promote social and religious discrimination; to infringe the principle of the social, economic and cultural equality of the sexes; to exploit the trust, credibility or lack of experience of a consumer or of the public in general in any other improper manner.

2.4. Although unfair advertising has still not been properly dealt with, some of its aspects have already been harmonized, at least as regards television advertisements. The need to take some of those principles into account was recognized in Council Directive 89/552/EEC of 3 October 1989 on the coordination of certain provisions laid down by law, regulation or administrative action in Member States concerning the pursuit of television broadcasting activities.[5]

Comparative advertising

2.5. Unless it meets a certain number of restricting conditions, comparative advertising too can become misleading and/or unfair. However, this is not always the case, despite the implications of certain national laws or the practices of the courts in some Member States. That is why the issue needs to be settled by means of an amendment to Directive 84/450/EEC.

2. The Need for Rules on Comparative Advertising

3.1. There are three main reasons for harmonizing comparative advertising in the Community:

1. The need to harmonize the rules on an important marketing too; and on comparative testing;
2. To improve consumer information.
3. To stimulate competition.

[5] Articles 10, 12, 16.

Consequences of the rapid development of new communication techniques

3.2. Though not all advertising crosses frontiers there is a good deal which certainly does. Advertising crosses frontiers on the packaging of goods. It may be broadcast across borders through the medium of radio or television or in the press. In such cases differences between advertising rules in the Member States can complicate the marketing process and may go so far as to disrupt the free movement of goods and the availability of services in the European single market.

In other words, the proliferation of cross frontier means of communication (especially TV channels) will mean that comparisons in advertising are permitted in some Member States (United Kingdom, Ireland, Denmark, Spain and Portugal—and France too is in the process of authorizing it), thus giving them a competitive advantage, while it is condemned in others which, in the absence of controls or standards, will lack adequate means of redress or, in many cases, the ability to counteract effectively.

3.3. The Court of Justice has on a number of occasions dealt with situations where an advertisement lawful in one Member State has run up against the laws of a neighbouring Member State: in the *GB-INNO* case[6] the Court held that a particular law of this type constituted an obstacle to free movement within the meaning of Article 30 of the Treaty and was not justifiable under Article 36 or other imperative principles.

The need to regulate the use of comparative tests in comparative advertising

3.4. Comparative tests can provide an excellent basis for comparative advertising. Such tests are usually carried out by a third party not itself in competition; it must therefore be ensured that test results are not used in such a way as to cast doubt on the credibility and independence of action of the third party.

[6] Case C–362/88, *GB-INNO-BM* v. *Confédération du Commerce Luxembourgeois*, Judgment of 7 Mar. 1990.

Comparative advertising as a means of improving consumer information

3.5. Consumers in the single European market will be faced with a growing number of products and services from Member States other than their country of residence, displaying variations in composition, size and other objective characteristics. In such a situation, comparative advertising can be a useful source of information for consumers and can facilitate a rational choice in the market place, provided that the advertising meets certain conditions.

3.6. Although, when Directive 84/450/EEC was adopted in 1984, there were still some doubts as to the value or even the need for this type of information, the economic and legal situation has since evolved.

The case law of the European Court of Justice, which states that national regulations prohibiting the marketing of certain goods not corresponding to specific features fixed by the law of a Member State should, in cases of doubt, be replaced by a simple obligation to provide suitable labelling clearly pointing out any difference, has also evolved.[7] Recently the Court of Justice has also stated that in principle any information accompanying the marketing of a product is valuable to the consumer since it is a form of protection and that a national regulation hindering consumer information cannot be justified on the grounds of imperative reasons relating to consumer protection.[8]

In a more general way, completion of the internal market will bring an ever greater diversity of goods. Faced with such diverse information, consumers will benefit more from comparative advertising, which will demonstrate the merits of different goods belonging to the same range, than from other sources of information.

[7] See, for example, the Communication on the free movement of foodstuffs within the Community OJ 1989 C271/3.

[8] Case C–362/88 *GB-INNO-BM* v. *Confédération du Commerce Luxembourgeois*, Judgment of 7 Mar. 1990.

Comparative advertising as a means of stimulating competition

3.7. Authorization of the comparative advertising technique throughout the single market will better equip firms to make an effective challenge to leading brands. The resulting increase in competition will benefit consumers and favour innovative and enterprising firms.

3.8. The present situation where comparative advertising is allowed in some Member States puts advertisers in other Member States at a disadvantage. Because rules vary between Member States, differing even between press, television and radio, considerable distortions of competition occur. For example, a firm wanting to use comparative advertising to promote the sale of its products would be inviting legal action in some other Member States on grounds of unfair competition, even though it may have legitimately used this technique on its home market, launched from a State where comparative advertising is allowed, without effective means of using the same technique itself. Therefore there is a distortion of competition both ways.

IV Ensuring Fairness: Setting Strict Limitations

4.1. In order to prevent any distortions of competition or confusion of the consumer resulting from unfair or misleading advertising, it is important to establish strict limitations on the use of comparative advertising.

4.2. The following limitations will apply:

(1) The elements to be compared should *only* be the *material* ones, which means that they should be relevant, important, decisive.
(2) Those elements of comparison should be *chosen fairly*, which means that they should be comparable and the information provided complete without being silent about other potentially material elements of a significant comparison.

(3) The comparison must be objectively *verifiable*, which means that any advertiser must immediately be able to furnish scientific evidence of the accuracy of his claims.

(4) The comparison should *not mislead*, within the meaning of the Directive on misleading advertising (the criteria by which to determine whether an advertisement is misleading having been established in Article 2(2) of that Directive).

(5) The statement should not cause *confusion* in the market place between the advertiser and his competitors or between the advertiser's trade marks, trade names, goods or services and those of competitors.

(6) It should not *denigrate* competitors, which means that the advertiser must not cause discredit, disparagement or contempt of competitors of their trade marks, trade names, goods, services or activities, except for the unavoidable effects of its advertising action.

(7) Lastly, comparison must not be a means of capitalizing on the reputation of the trade mark of trade name of others.

4.3. The provisions of Articles 4, 5, and 6 of Directive 84/450/EEC on misleading advertising, which this proposal will amend, will continue to apply. This ensures that:

(1) the legal and/or administrative mechanisms for controlling misleading advertising will also apply to comparative advertising;

(2) voluntary control of comparative advertising by self-regulatory bodies is not excluded;

(3) the burden of proof will lie with the advertiser, who must prove compliance with the safeguards and conditions of this proposal.

4.4. In the event of *disputes* the court or other competent bodies will have the final decision. The administrative or legal mechanisms set up in Member States to deal with disputes or conflicts on misleading advertising since the adoption of Directive 84/450/EEC are working successfully, and should be able to deal with any new complaints arising from comparative advertising. In fact, evidence from the Member States which allow comparative advertising does not point to a large number of disputes.

4.5. The general authorisation of comparative advertising requires some explanation of its relation to patent rights, especially the trade mark law [*sic*]; comparative advertising can often only have a significant effect if it involves a clear identification of the object of comparison, i.e. the competitor's product or service marketed under a specific trade mark or trade name.

Member States' laws on trade mark have been harmonized since 1988 by Directive 89/104/EEC of 21 December 1988, which should come into force at the end of 1991. It is therefore permissible to overlook certain peculiarities of the present legislation on this matter in some Member States and to limit oneself to the wording of the Community text, which stipulates that the registered trade mark confers exclusive rights on the proprietor, including the right to prevent all third parties from using in the course of trade any sign which is identical with, or similar to, the trade mark in relation to identical goods and services or even, where appropriate, other goods. Yet it may be indispensable, for comparative advertising to be effective, to identify the goods or services of a competitor, making reference to a trade mark or trade name of which the latter is proprietor. In fact, the use of another's trade mark or trade name in accordance with the conditions established by this proposal does not breach his exclusive right; the aim is not to steal reputations but to distinguish between them.

Although Article 5(3)(d) of Directive 89/104/EEC on trade marks expressly prohibits, *inter alia*, the use of another's trade mark in advertising, this presupposes nonetheless that use of that trade mark is illegal within the meaning of paragraphs 1 and 2 of that Article, which is not the case with comparative advertising when the conditions laid down by the proposal are met.

The limitation of the trade mark law was implicitly understood when the Council adopted Directive 89/104/EEC.

4.6. As emphasized in paragraph 3.4, the use in advertisements of the results of comparative tests on goods and services can be particularly important. Given that the law does not currently provide proper protection for the person carrying out the comparative test, such use must only be allowed if that person expressly agreed. In that case the advertiser should accept responsibility for the test as if it had been performed by himself or under his direction. This will help protect the credibility and independence of action of the third party and permit legal action under the unfair competition rules against the advertiser even if a mistake is made by the third party during the performance of the test; in other words, advertisers willing to benefit from a test which is favourable to their products should also assume liability for it.

V. Conclusions

5.1. It is proposed that the necessary changes be made by amending Directive 84/450/EEC on misleading advertising, which already provides an appropriate regulatory framework. That Directive will then apply to comparative advertising, which will be permitted subject to a number of conditions, and will also apply to the use of comparative tests in comparative advertising.

5.2. The provision of the Directive on misleading advertising enabling Member States to retain or adopt provisions with a view to ensuring more extensive protection for consumers should not apply to comparative advertising, the aim being to allow it under identical conditions in all Member States. The application of a more restrictive rule on this kind of advertising in one Member State that in another is thus prohibited.

VI. The Situation in the Member States

6.1. In *Belgium* comparative advertising is by implication outlawed. The law of 14 July 1971 on commercial practices bans any commercial advertising using comparisons (that are either misleading or denigratory or) identifying other business enterprises, even if not competitors (Article 20(2)).

Under Belgian law, to mention the name of another person in advertising without permission is considered illicit and the Cour d'Appel of Brussels has held such a reference to be 'an act contrary to honest practices'.[9]

However, there are several exceptions to the general rule, such as self-defence, and the use of comparisons orally at the request of customers, as well as the right of criticism.

7.1. In *Denmark* the Marketing Practices Act (No 297 of 14 June 1974) does not prohibit comparative advertising as such. However, it must not be false, misleading or unreasonable. Article 2(2) prohibits practices that, because of their form of reference to irrelevant matter, are 'improper' in relation to traders and consumers. The Commercial and Maritime Court of Copenhagen has repeatedly accepted the lawfulness of comparative advertising.[10]

In 1980 the Danish Advertising Standards Board (*Reklame Rådet*) organised a meeting with representatives of a number of public and private organisations to discuss the opinions of the parties concerned on comparative advertising. Below are some of the conclusions reached at the meeting.

—comparative advertising should be genuinely informative;
—comparative advertising should always be correct, relevant and fair. The information which it contains must be truthful and verifiable. The points of comparison shall be selected in such a way that all relevant items are included—even if this means emphasizing the advantages of the selected competitors—and the comparison shall not contain any derogatory statements;
—any other use of competitors' trade marks must be prohibited.[11]

6.3. In the *Federal Republic of Germany*, the relevant provision is section 1 of the Act against unfair competition of 7 June 1909 (*Gesetz gegen den unlauteren Wettbewerb*). Section 1 states:

[9] 23 Nov. 1953, Jur. Comm. Bruxelles, 1954, 19.
[10] Commercial and Maritime Court of Copenhagen, 13 January 1982 [1982] EIPR D–212.
[11] Reklame Rådet, 'Comparative Advertising', Apr. 1982.

'Anyone who, in the course of competitive business activity, commits acts contrary to honest practices, may be enjoined from continuing such acts and held liable for damages'.

A longstanding case law has considered this provision as the basis for a general prohibition of all direct comparison, even truthful ones. There are some exceptions, such as advertising comparisons for defensive purposes, comparisons of systems which are technically different (but without identification of the respective producers) and comparisons made to display a technological development.

6.4. In *Greece* the basic legislation is Law 146 (1914) on unfair competition, Article 1 of which prohibits any competitive act that is contrary to honest practices. The Law does not appear expressly to prohibit comparative advertising.

Whether advertisements making specific reference to competitors or their products or services is lawful or not will depend on the circumstances of the case, though the trend is to consider it unlawful, especially in cases of denigration. However, when that advertisement only compares the quality of a product to that of another is may be acceptable.

The Advertising Code of the Greek Association of Advertising Agencies allows comparative advertising provided it is not untruthful, misleading or unfair.

6.5. *Spain* has a recent General Advertising Act (*Lay General de Publicidad*) of 11 November 1988, Article 3 of which declares unfair advertising to be illegal. This Act is one of the few that includes a definition of unfair advertising.

According to Article 6 advertising is unfair which:

(a) by its content, appearance or dissemination causes discredit, denigration or direct or indirect contempt of a person, his business or his products, services or activities;

(b) causes confusion with a competitor's business, activities, products, names, trade marks or other distinguishing marks, makes unjustified use of the name, brand or mark of other businesses or institutions, and in general is contrary to honest practices and proper commercial usage;

(c) in the case of comparative advertising, it is not based on essential, similar and objectively verifiable features of products or services, or compares products or services with other which are dissimilar or unknown to those having a limited share of the market.

This law marks a change in Spanish legislation. Traditionally, comparative advertising has been considered illegal. Modern thinking is tending to accept comparative advertising provided that certain conditions (similarity of products, verifiability of statements, etc.) are respected.

6.6. Until recently, the *French* courts generally held comparative advertising to be a form of unfair competition, often of a misleading nature. On April 24 1991 a draft law improving consumer protection was approved at first reading and will soon be adopted. Article 10 of that Law expressly permits comparative advertising, subject to certain conditions being met, conditions which are in fact fairly similar to those of this proposal.

6.7. *Ireland* has no specific legislation on comparative advertising and it is not prohibited unless, likely any other advertising, it is false or misleading within the meaning of the Consumer Information Act of 1979.

6.8. In *Italy*, in the absence of any specific legislation, Article 2598 of the Civil Code applies. Under clause 2 of that Article any reference to a competitor's products is generally considered an act of unfair competition. However, some exceptions are tolerated (puffery, self-defence, etc.).

Article 15 of the Code of Advertising Self-Regulation of the *istituto dell'autodisciplina pubblicitaria* lays down that 'indirect comparison is not allowed unless intended to illustrate from a technical or economic point of view the characteristics and real advantages of the activity or product advertised'.

6.9. In *Luxembourg* Article 17(g) of the Law of 27 November 1986 regulating certain commercial practices and adopting penalties for unfair competition qualifies as unfair competition 'any advertising which consists of comparison with other competitors or with their products or services'.

As in Belgium and the Netherlands, comparisons may also infringe the 1969 Benelux Uniform Law on Trade Marks if they refer to marks without the authorisation of the proprietor.

6.10. The *Netherlands* has no specific legislation on unfair competition. Articles 1401 and 1402 of the Civil Code have been interpreted as prohibiting unfair competitive practices that harm others; comparative advertising may constitute one of these practices. In addition, Article A(2) of the Benelux Uniform Law on Trade Marks allows the proprietor to oppose any unauthorised use of his registered trademark which, without a valid reason, would cause him damage.

Case law seems to be divided about whether truthful comparative advertising is permissible. Comparisons referring to all the relevant features of a product are usually permitted while false statements, not necessarily offensive, are considered illegal.

The Advertising Code Commission [*Stichting Reclame Code*] set up by the Reclameraad, responsible for self-regulation in advertising, considers it permissible to compare 'comparable' products provided that: (1) the comparisons are based on complete, objective and verifiable data, (2) unnecessarily denigratory statements are avoided, and (3) the statements are not misleading. It also allows references to product tests carried out by consumer organizations, if such references are accurate and up to date.

6.11. In *Portugal* Decree–law No 303/83 of 28 June 1983 allows comparative advertising in principle; it is not considered per se to be an act of unfair competition.

Article 18 of the Decree-law states that advertising containing direct or indirect comparisons must not:

(a) mislead consumers as to the quality and the price of the product;
(b) be denigratory;
(c) use messages which may influence the consumer's choice through their hyperbolic or superlative tone;

(d) create confusion between brands, products, services or competing firms;

(e) generally fall within the scope of unfair competition.

The Code of the Portuguese Advertising Agencies Association states that the elements of a comparison must be based on objectively verifiable facts and ought to be chosen fairly.

6.12. In the absence of specific legislation in the *United Kingdom* common law permits comparative advertising that is truthful; it also tolerates puffery and allows the use of scientific comparative test results. Statutory law essentially deals only with misleading practices.

Use of a registered trade mark in comparative advertisements without the authorisation of the proprietor may constitute an infringement of the 1938 Trade Marks Act. Use of a competitor's name, however, appears to be legal.

Section B.21.1 of the British Code of Advertising Practice of the Advertising Standards Authority states that 'in order that vigorous competition may not be hindered, and that public information may be furthered, comparisons between products and their prices, including comparisons in which a competitor of the advertiser or his product are named, are regarded as in conformity with the Code, provided that they do not conflict with the requirements of this or the following three paragraphs [B.22 (denigration) B.23 (Exploitation of goodwill) and B.24 (imitation)]. Section B.21.2 states that in advertisements containing comparisons it 'should be clear with what the advertised product is being compared, and upon what basis'; 'the subject matter of the comparisons and the terms in which it is expressed should not be such as to confer any artificial advantage upon one product as against another'.

VII. The Legal Situation in Non-Member States

7.1. Outside the EEC, comparative advertising is principle allowed in the USA, Canada, Sweden, Norway, Finland and Switzerland.

7.2. In general, common law countries allow comparisons provided that they are truthful; the use of comparative test results is permitted. No action for defamation or injurious falsehood will lie if the statement is true and there is no comparable action for unfair competition.

7.3. Scandinavian countries have similar provisions. Truthful comparisons are allowed if complete and therefore fair.

7.4. In Switzerland, Article 3 of the Federal Act against Unfair Competition of 19 December 1986 stipulates that unfair actions include those by persons who 'in an inaccurate, fallacious, unnecessarily injurious or parasitic manner compare their person, goods, works, performances or prices with those of a competitor or who, through such comparisons, benefit third parties at the expense of their competitors'. It follows that comparative advertising is permitted, provided it does not fall within the categories condemned by the law.

IX. International Rules

8.1. Particularly interesting is the reversal of the rules on self-regulation regularly published by the International Chamber of Commerce. While previous editions of its International Code of fair practice in Advertising stated that comparisons should be avoided, that of 1986 permits them, stating in Article 5 the qualification that 'if advertising includes a comparison it should not mislead the consumer and should comply with the fair competition rules. The elements of comparison should be based upon objectively verifiable facts, which should be chosen fairly.'

Article 7 prohibits denigration of a firm or product, directly or by implication, which causes any sort of discredit.

8.2. The *International League Against Unfair Competition* at its Congress in Antwerp in June 1980 adopted a motion stating, inter alia, that 'in order to safeguard fair competition and in the interests of consumers, comparison with a product or service of a named competitor is permissible when it elicits comparable features and deals with objective matters which are precise, concrete, essential, verifiable, accurate and as representative as possible; such advertising should not mislead either deliberately or by the omission of a vital element; comparative advertising should never consist of a simple denigratory message, damaging by its nature, emotive, or a mere parasitic exercise, i.e. consisting of a reference which cannot be objectively justified to a sign which is legally protected . . .'[12]

Reactions of the Sectors Concerned

(A) Consultation of the advertising industry

Specific meetings have been held with representatives of the European Advertising Tripartite, a body which brings together advertisers, advertising agencies, the advertising media and the Advertising Information Group, which is an informal grouping of national 'tripartite' institutions representing the advertising business and organisations responsible for self-regulatory systems of advertising control. Representatives of the Commerce and Distribution Committee (CCD) were present.

These organizations emphasized three main points:

(1) The need for a directive. There was general agreement on the need for a harmonizing directive, given that the present situation as far as comparative advertising is concerned can be said to lack harmony.
(2) The acceptance of the text itself. The limitations introduced in the proposal were deemed satisfactory. Attention was drawn mainly to the use of trade marks in order to prevent goodwill being 'stolen' by a competitor. The advertising agencies, the media and the CCD came out clearly favour of identifying competitors, thus making comparisons possible.
(3) The need to avoid excess (unfair advertisements). The text of the proposal was deemed capable of dealing with this problem. However it was stressed that tough penalties would be needed to ensure compliance. The

---

[12] *Revue Internationale de la Concurrence*, 141/2/1980.

Commission stated that it was for the Member States to decide about penalties.

(B) Consultation of business

The business circles that have been consulted (Banking Federation of the EEC; European Association of Pharmaceuticals; AGREF; etc.) expressed some reservations at different levels, questioning in particular the 'beneficial effects' that the authorisation of comparative advertising would have for consumers as well as the 'stimulating' effect on competition.

(C) Consultation of Consumers

The Consumers' Consultative Council, at its plenary session of 11 and 12 March 1991, unanimously approved the proposal to allow comparative advertising subject to the following conditions and guarantees.

Comparative advertising should be allowed when, in respect to competing goods and services, it compares precise, objective, verifiable and complete data and is based on decisive features which have been chosen fairly.

Concerning the chosen points of comparison, it must be accurate, fair and relevant even if this highlights the advantages of the goods or services of the other chosen competitors.

Moreover, comparative advertising should not:

—include contemptuous, hurtful, denigratory assertions or assertions which cause confusion;
—compare goods or services not found on the market concerned.

Finally, the use in advertising of comparative tests made by a third party should only be allowed if the party responsible for the test expressly agrees. In such cases the advertiser will be responsible for the test as if it has been performed by himself or under his control.

Observations on the Proposal

1. General

The proposal is based on Article 100a of the EEC Treaty, since the questions of whether or not comparative advertising can legitimately be used will directly affect the marketing prospects of the goods and services on offer and thus affect the functioning of the single European market.

Although the minimal nature of the rules on misleading advertising should be maintained (see Article 7(1)), given that implementation of these rules and actual practice in the Member States is not yet sufficiently uniform the conditions required by Article 100a have been met as regards comparative advertising.

Firstly, the proposal is aimed at the 'approximation of the law, regulations and administrative provisions of the Member States'. Laws on comparative advertising vary from one Member State to the next; some allow it but apply different rules, while others ban it, directly or indirectly.

Secondly, the proposal is aimed at 'the establishment and functioning of the internal market' with a high level of consumer protection. The aim of approximating the relevant laws is to facilitate the free movement of advertising services, which will be subject to the same harmonized rules in all the Member States.

2. Commentary on the Articles

Article 1

Paragraph 1

Given that the proposal aims to amend Directive 84/450/EEC on misleading advertising to include comparative advertising, the title of the amended Directive should reflect this fact.

Paragraph 2

This paragraph contains a definition for incorporation into Article 2 of Directive 84/450/EEC on misleading advertising.

The definition of comparative advertising identifies the feature that distinguishes comparative advertising from advertising in which no mention is made of a competitor or of a competitor's similar goods or services.

Paragraph 3

This paragraph introduces a new Article 3a to Directive 84/450/EEC with the purpose of allowing comparative advertising, identifying what is acceptable in comparative advertising and determining responsibility when the results of comparative tests made by a third party are used in advertisements.

The proposal sets out the following restricting conditions for comparative advertisements:

—The features to be compared should only be the material ones, i.e. the relevant, essential, important, significant aspects of goods and services.

—The comparison should be objectively verifiable, which means that any advertiser should be able immediately to provide scientific evidence of the claim he makes.

—The elements of the comparison should be chosen fairly, which means that they should be comparable and that the information provided must be complete without being silent about the essential elements of the comparison.

By way of prohibitions and limiting conditions the proposal contains the following:

—The comparison must not mislead, within the meaning of Directive 84/450/EEC on misleading advertising.

—The comparison must not cause confusion in the market place between the advertiser and the competitors or between the advertiser's trade marks, trade name, goods or services and those of competitors. This particular condition ensures that the use of another's trade mark or trade name is strictly limited to identification purposes.

—It must not denigrate competitors. An advertisement denigrating a competitor or his trade marks, trade names, goods or service must clearly not be allowed. To this end the proposal states that an advertisement which causes discredit, disparagement or contempt of a competitor or his trade marks, trade names, goods, services or activities is, except for the unavoidable effects of a comparison as such, unfair and is therefore not allowed. The mere fact that a comparison is unfavourable to a competitor is not in itself to be considered unfair if the comparison is accurate.

—On the other hand, comparative advertising must not be carried out in conditions which allow the advertiser to take advantage of a brand's reputation.

In short, comparative advertising cannot validly perform its functions unless it compares material features, in other words, relevant or essential aspects of a product or service which are verifiable. In this context it should be recalled that Article 6 of Directive 84/450/EEC on misleading advertising enables the burden of proof to be reversed, so that the advertiser can be called upon, where appropriate, to substantiate his claims.

It must be pointed out that comparative advertising 'per se' is neither misleading nor unfair. It can provide the consumer with valuable information about goods and services and help him decide what to buy. It can also give competitors the opportunity to demonstrate more clearly the features of their products or services.

As for comparative tests performed by a third party, the use of the results in advertisements can only be allowed if the person responsible for the test expressly agrees. In this case the advertiser will be responsible for the test as if it has been performed by himself or under his direction.

Paragraphs 4, 5 and 6

These paragraphs incorporate into Directive 84/450/EEC the amendments needed to ensure that the same legal and/or administrative means of redress mentioned in Articles 4 and 5 of that Directive may be applied to control comparative advertising which does not meet the requirements of fairness set by the proposal.

Paragraph 7

Article 7 of Directive 84/450/EEC allows Member States to retain or adopt provisions with a view to ensuring more extensive protection for consumers, persons carrying on a trade, business, craft or profession, and the general public. This rule will not apply to comparative advertising, given that the objective of the proposal is to allow such advertising in all Member States under the same conditions.

Article 2

The implementation date is 31 December 1992.

Member States are to communicate to the Commission the texts of all provisions of national law which they adopt in the field covered by the proposal, referring at the same time to this Directive.

Article 3

The Directive is addressed to the Member States.

2. Explanatory Memorandum to the 1994 Draft (COM(94)151 final—COD 343, Brussels, 21 April 1994)

Introduction

Following the opinions delivered by the European Parliament[13] and the Economic and Social Committee[14] on the proposal for a Council Directive concerning comparative advertising and amending Council Directive 84/450/EEC concerning misleading advertising,[15] the Commission is called upon to adopt a modified proposal, in so far as it intends to accept the proposals and, where necessary, to make other changes to its initial proposal.

[13] Opinion of 18 Nov. 1992, PV 38 11 (EP 162 994).
[14] OJ 1991 C49/35.
[15] OJ 1991 C180/14.

Furthermore, as part of the debate on the extent and practical application of the principle of subsidiarity, the Commission has included this proposal among those texts which it undertook at the Council meeting in Edinburgh to examined in greater depth, with a view to withdrawing provisions which would go into excessive detail in relation to the objective pursued and to establishing general principles to be given more detailed form by Member States.[16]

In the case of comparative advertising, the Commission has concluded, following an in-depth discussion, that the essence of the proposal, namely harmonisation of the regulations governing the fairness of comparative advertising, must be maintained and that, in principle, a proposal modified in the light of amendments proposed by the European Parliament, of the opinion of the Economic and Social Committee and of the debates at Council level, may be presented in accordance with Article 189a(2) of the TEU.

1. Grounds for the Proposal in Terms of Subsidiary

(a) What are the objectives of the measure envisaged in relation to the Union's obligation?

> R The objective of the measure is to facilitate the creation and functioning of the internal market at a high level of consumer protection by approximating laws governing comparative advertising, hence the measure will encourage the free movement of advertising services in so far as they will be governed by a harmonised regime in all the Member States.

(b) Is the envisaged measure the exclusive competence of the Union or a competence shared with the Member States?

> R The harmonisation of Members States' laws governing comparative advertising is an exclusive competence of the Union.

[16] Conclusion of the Presidency, The European Council of Edinburgh, 11/12 Dec. 1992. Document SI(92) 1050, section A Annex 2, p. 3.

(c) What is the Community dimension of the problem?

    R The current situation in which comparative advertising is authorised in certain Member States and banned in others not only creates obstacles to the free movement of goods and services but also puts consumers, advertisers and publicity workers in certain Member States at a disadvantage, and the medium used (press, radio or television) leads to substantial distortions in competition.

(d) What is the most effective solution when the Union's instruments are compared with those of the Member States?

    R Harmonisation of legislation relating to comparative advertising in order to ensure the consumer's right to information is respected and that appropriate safeguards are established to avoid disputes between advertisers resulting from incompatible legislation.

(e) What is the concrete added value of the Union's envisaged measure and what would it cost to do nothing?

    R Given the entry into effect of the Treaty on European Union, the envisaged measure should make it possible to provide European consumers with better information, to stimulate competition and to cope with the rapid development of new communication techniques.

    To do nothing would deprive consumers of a useful source of information in making a rational choice and would create obstacles to the free movement of products and services and hence adversely affect free competition.

(f) What instruments are at the Union»s disposal?

    R The directive, because it is a question of amending an already existing directive.

(g) Are uniform rules necessary or is it enough to have a directive laying down general objectives, leaving implementation to the Member States?

    R A directive is sufficient.

2. Elements of the Initial Proposal Contained in the Amended Proposal

The title of the proposal remains unchanged. This also applies to the definition of comparative advertising.

As to the means for controlling advertising (Article 1(4)), given that such means have already been established by all the Member States in accordance with the provisions of Directive 84/45/EEC[17] and that they are functioning properly, it is not considered necessary to amend the text of the initial proposal which extends to comparative advertising the scope of the provisions applied to misleading advertising.

Likewise, Article 1(6) concerning the validity of voluntary control of misleading advertising and comparative advertising by independent bodies remains unchanged.

The Commission considers that systems of the voluntary control of advertising should be encouraged, as recognised in the sixteenth recital of Directive 84/450/EEC; the fact that Article 5 of this Directive will also apply to comparative advertising is proof that the Commission is continuing to encourage such systems, particularly if account is taken of the principles of subsidiarity and proportionality; the Commission therefore considers it necessary to stress this aspect any further in the modified proposal.

The reversal of the burden of proof established by Article 6 of Directive 84/450/EEC also applies to comparative advertising. The Commission considers that maintaining the principle if fundamental, hence the explicit reference made in the new eleventh recital of the modified proposal.

Finally, it has been agreed that the minimal character of the provisions relating to misleading advertising shall not be applicable to provisions governing comparative advertising, for reasons already set out in the explanatory memorandum attached to the initial proposal.

---

[17] OJ 1984 L250/17.

3. The Amendments Introduced

Recitals 3, 6 and 11 have been amended in order to bring them into line with the Parliament's amendments accepted by the Commission, concerning the conditions for authorising comparative advertising.

The amendments contained in recital 4 are designed to refer specifically to obstacles to the principle of free movement and in particular the freedom to provide services relating to comparative advertising.

Recital 12 has been amended because it was considered necessary to emphasise the fact that reversal of the burden of proof—one of the mainstays of Directive 84/450/EEC—also applies to comparative advertising.

Recital 14 has been amended, at Parliament»s request, in order to establish clearly the relationship between comparative advertising and the advertising of certain specific products or services.

As regards recital 15, it summarises the elements taken into consideration in order to bring the proposal into line with the subsidiarity principle.

As regards the articles, the amendments concern Article 1(3) and (7) and Article 2.

4. Comments on the Amendments

(a) Reducing the scope of the text

However, it is not simply a question of modifying the text in accordance with the usual principles. Under the criteria set out in the document submitted to the Edinburgh Council, it was considered necessary to reduce the number of subjects covered in the proposal.

The Commission has observed that the provisions concerning comparative tests, which are only indirectly linked to comparative advertising, may be completely removed from the text, not because they would be without foundation but because they do not appear to be strictly necessary in order to arrive at the legislative goal as set out and justified in the initial proposal.[18]

[18] COM(91)147 of 21 June 1991.

This partial restructuring of the text involves the deletion of the ninth recital and of Article 3a(2) of the initial proposal. Amendments numbers 4 and 14 put forward by Parliament and received favourably at the time by the Commission are now therefore superfluous.

The text is therefore completely in accordance with the requirements of the principle of subsidiarity (see new fifteenth recital).

(b) The limits of comparative advertising

As the European Parliament has pointed out, the use of comparative advertising must be subject to strict limitations. While ensuring that the proposal is not completely stripped of meaning, the Commission has therefore, after an in-depth discussion as announced at the Edinburgh Council, accepted a number of suggestions from Parliament, reinforcing the text to this effect (see annexed tables). In particular, the new wording of Article 3a broadens the criteria set out in the initial proposal in order to ensure fairness in comparative advertising. The new subparagraph (d) has been introduced to clarify an aspect which was also raised by the Economic and Social Committee when a comparative reference is made to a service, it should relate only to the characteristics of the service itself and not to the intellectual qualities of the provider, which cannot be subject to comparison.

A new paragraph 2 has been introduced in Article 3a at the request of Parliament, with the content having been specified by the Economic and Social Committee in its opinion: if 'objective truth' is the guiding principle in the formulation and use of a comparative advertisement, this must also include the full 'actuality' of the statement at the time it is disseminated; this applies particularly in the case of products and services which are the subject of a special offer or where the offer is of limited duration.

(c) Relationship with sectoral advertising

Both the European Parliament and the Economic and Social Committee have stated that they are particularly concerned with problems which might arise owing to the existence of specific regulations concerning advertising for items such as medicaments, tobacco products or foodstuffs. The Commission agrees with the opinion of the two institutions in so far as, in areas in which advertising must also be governed by the same rules. Article 7(3) has been introduced precisely in support of this concept, which was already implicit in the initial proposal.

PARLIAMENT'S OPINION

Amendment No.	Initial proposal	Accepted by the Commission	Integrated (New numbering)
1		Yes	
2	Recital No 3	Yes partly	Recital No 2
3	Recital No 6	Yes partly	Recital No 5
4	Recital No 9	No	
5	Recital No 12	Yes	Recital No 10
6	Recital No 13	No	
7	Recital No 14	No	
8		Yes	Recital No 13
9	Article 1.3	Yes partly	Article 1.3
10	Article 1.3	No	
11	Article 1.3	Yes	Article 1.3
12	Article 1.3	No	
13	Article 1.3	No	
14	Article 1.3	Yes partly	
			Not integrated (subsidiarity)
15	Article 1.3	No	
16	Article 1.3	Yes	
22	Article 1.3	No	Article 1.3
17	Article 1.6	No	
18	Article 1.6	No	
19	Article 1.7	Yes partly	Article 1.7

OPINION OF THE ECONOMIC AND SOCIAL COMMITTEE

Keynotes of the ECS opinion	*Commission's position*
2.6 Precise rules governing means of controlling advertising	Rejected. Directive 84/450/EEC contains adequate provisions
2.7 Conformity of comparative advertising with specific rules on sectoral advertising	Accepted. Article 1.7
Compliance with EEC standards concerning registered trade marks and designations of origin	Accepted as regards trade marks (Recitals 8, 9, and 10)
	As regards designations of origin, the Commission maintains its initial proposal (Article 1(2) and (3))
2.8 Drafting of a self-regulatory code of practice whose frame-work would be defined by Community rules	Rejected. it is not up to the Commission to take action in this domain for reasons of subsidiarity. It is sufficient to encourage voluntary control (Recital 11)
2.10 Setting up of voluntary bodies representing the various interests involved	Rejected for reasons of subsidiarity
3.2 Comparative advertising to be allowed only in the form of explicit references, not implicit ones	Rejected. The Commission maintains its initial text (definition of comparative advertising)
3.3 Ban on the presenting of goods or services as imitations or replicas already protected by the legislation on trade marks	Rejected. This proposal is not the appropriate place to treat this question
3.8 'Objective truth' should also be taken to imply that the information is fully up to date	Accepted (Article 1.3)

3. Opinion of the Commission on the European Parliament's Amendments to the Council's Common Position (COM(96)700 final—COD 343, Brussels, 13 December 1996

I. The Background

On 19 March 1996 the Council of the European Union established a common position with a view to the adoption of a Directive amending Directive 84/450/EEC concerning misleading advertising so as to include comparative advertising.

On 23 October 1996 the European Parliament adopted at its second reading, in the framework of the co-decision procedure, its opinion on the common position (rapporteur Mrs Oomen-Ruijten). This opinion contains 16 amendments, eight of which were accepted by the Commission at its plenary meeting.

Pursuant to Article 189b(2)(d) of the Treaty, the Commission must deliver an opinion to the Council concerning Parliament's amendments. In this particular case the opinion alters the Commission's proposal as provided for in Article 189a(2) of the Treaty.

II. The Commissions Position on the Amendments

At its plenary meeting the Commission agreed to accept amendments 1, 2, 4, 8, 9, 16, 21 and 21. However the Commission cannot accept amendments 3, 6, 12, 13, 15, 17, 18 and 19 for the following reasons.

Amendments 3 and 15 concern comparative tests. At the Edinburgh European Council in 1992, the Commission undertook to revise a series of proposals—including the proposal on comparative advertising—so as to remove certain aspects that sere incompatible with the principle of proportionality. In the case in point the Commission considered that the provisions on comparative tests were not strictly necessary in order to achieve the proposal's objectives.

Amendments 6, 18 and 19 concern voluntary regulatory systems. The creation of a 'European self-regulatory umbrella body' (Amendment 19) is unacceptable because of the potential financial implications for the Community budget. The role of the national self-regulatory bodies (Amendments 6 and 18) is already given due recognition in Article 5 of Directive 84/450/EEC and Amendment 18 could lead to distortions not only with regard to comparative advertising but also with regard to misleading advertising (which is also covered by the same provision).

Amendments 12 and 13 have to be rejected because of the excessive and unreasonable burden they would place on advertisers, bearing in mind the other conditions already contained in the text of the common position (Article 3a).

Amendment 17 modifies the first paragraph of Article 4 of the Directive 84/450/EEC. If accepted, its effect would be to allow Member States to 'require prior recourse to other established means of dealing with complaints, including those referred to in Article 5' (self-regulatory procedures). Such an amendment could prevent or at any rate delay consumer access to ordinary justice, and might well be incompatible with Article 6 of the European Convention on Human Rights.

III. Amended Proposal

In view of the above, and in compliance with the provisions governing the co-decision procedure, the proposal has been amended by the Commission so as to include Amendments 1, 2, 4, 8, 9, 16, 20 and 21 of the European Parliament.

4. The Text of the 1991 Draft, 1994 Draft and Council's Common Position

1991 Draft (OJ 1991 C180/14)	1994 Draft (OJ 1994 C136/4)	Common Position (OJ 1996 C219/14)
THE COUNCIL OF THE EUROPEAN COMMUNITIES	THE EUROPEAN PARLIAMENT AND THE COUNCIL OF THE EUROPEAN UNION	UNCHANGED
Having regard to the Treaty establishing the European Economic Community, and in particular article 100a thereof,	Having regard to the Treaty establishing the European Community, and in particular article 100a thereof,	Unchanged
Having regard to the proposal from the Commission	Unchanged	Unchanged
	Acting in accordance with the procedure referred to in Article 189b of the Treaty,	
In cooperation with the European Parliament,		
Having regard to the opinion of the Economic and Social Committee,	Unchanged	Unchanged
		Acting in accordance with the procedure referred to in Article 189b of the Treaty,

1991 Draft (OJ 1991 C180/14)	1994 Draft (OJ 1994 C136/4)	Common Position (OJ 1996 C219/14)
Whereas one of the Community's main aims is to complete the internal market by 31 December 1992 at the latest; whereas measures must be adopted gradually to establish the internal market; whereas the internal market comprises an area which has no internal frontiers and in which goods, persons, services and capital can move freely;	Whereas one of the Community's main aims is to complete the internal market; whereas measures must be adopted gradually to establish the internal market; whereas the internal market comprises an area which has no internal frontiers and in which goods, persons, services and capital can move freely;	Whereas one of the Community's main aims is to complete the internal market; whereas measures must be adopted to ensure the smooth running of the said market; whereas the market comprises an area which has no internal frontiers and in which goods, persons, services and capital can move freely,
Whereas advertising is a very important means of creating genuine outlets for all goods and services throughout the Community; whereas the basic provisions governing the form and content of advertising must be uniform; whereas, however, this is not currently the case for comparative advertising;	Unchanged	

1991 Draft (OJ 1991 C180/14)	1994 Draft (OJ 1994 C136/4)	Common Position (OJ 1996 C219/14)
Whereas the completion of the internal market will mean an ever wider range of choice; whereas, given that consumers can and must make the best possible use of the internal market, the use of comparative advertising must be authorized in all Member States since this will help demonstrate the merits of the various products within the relevant range; whereas comparative advertising can also stimulate competition between suppliers of goods and services to the consumer's advantage;	Whereas the completion of the internal market will mean an ever wider range of choice; whereas, given that consumers can and must make the best possible use of the internal market, the use of comparative advertising must be authorized under certain very stringent conditions in all the Member States since this will help demonstrate the merits of the various products within the relevant range; whereas under such conditions comparative advertising can stimulate competition between suppliers of goods and services to the consumer's advantage;	Whereas the completion of the internal market will mean an ever wider range of choice; whereas, given that consumers can and must make the best possible use of the internal market, and that advertising is a very important means of creating genuine outlets for all goods and services throughout the Community, the basic provisions governing the form and content of comparative advertising should be uniform and the conditions of the use of comparative advertising in the Member States should be harmonised; whereas this will help demonstrate the merits of the various comparable products; whereas comparative advertising can also stimulate competition between suppliers of goods and services to the consumer's advantage;

1991 Draft (OJ 1991 C180/14)	1994 Draft (OJ 1994 C136/4)	Common Position (OJ 1996 C219/14)
Whereas the laws, regulations and administrative provisions of the Member States concerning comparative advertising differ widely; whereas advertising reaches beyond the frontiers and is received on the territory of other Member States; whereas the acceptance or non-acceptance of comparative advertising according to the various national laws may constitute an obstacle to the free movement of goods and services and create distortions of competition;	Whereas the laws, regulations and administrative provisions of the Member States concerning comparative advertising differ widely; whereas advertising reaches beyond the frontiers and is received on the territory of other Member States; whereas the acceptance of non-acceptance of comparative advertising according to the various national laws may constitute an obstacle to the free movement of goods and services and create distortions of competition; whereas the freedom to provide services relating to comparative advertising must be assured; whereas the union is called on to remedy this situation;	Whereas the laws, regulations and administrative provisions of the Member States concerning comparative advertising differ widely; whereas advertising reaches beyond the frontiers and is received on the territory of other Member States; whereas the acceptance of non-acceptance of comparative advertising according to the various national laws may constitute an obstacle to the free movement of goods and services and create distortions of competition, whereas, in particular, firms may be exposed to forms of advertising developed by competitors to which they cannot reply in equal measure; whereas the freedom to provide services relating to comparative advertising should be

1991 Draft (OJ 1991 C180/14)	1994 Draft (OJ 1994 C136/4)	Common Position (OJ 1996 C219/14)
		assured; whereas the Community is called on to remedy this situation;
Whereas the sixth recital of Council Directive 84/450/EEC of 10 September 1984 relating to the approximation of the laws, regulations and administrative provisions of the Member States concerning misleading advertising states that, after the harmonisation of national provisions against misleading advertising, 'at a second stage . . ., as far as necessary, comparative advertising should be dealt with, on the basis of appropriate Commission proposals',	Unchanged	Unchanged
Whereas point 3(d) of the Annex to the Council resolution of 14 April 1975 on a preliminary programme of the European Economic Community for a	Whereas point 3(d) of the Annex to the Council resolution of 14 April 1975 on a preliminary programme of the European Economic Community for a	Whereas point 3(d) of the Annex to the Council resolution of 14 April 1975 on a preliminary programme of the European Economic Community for a

1991 Draft (OJ 1991 C180/14)	1994 Draft (OJ 1994 C136/4)	Common Position (OJ 1996 C219/14)
consumer protection and information policy includes the right to information among the basic rights of consumers; whereas this right is confirmed by the Council resolution of 9 May 1981 on a second programme of the European Community for a consumer protection and information policy, point 40 of the Annex to which deals specifically with consumer information; whereas comparative advertising, when it compares relevant and verifiable details and is neither misleading nor unfair, is a legitimate means of informing consumers to their advantage;	consumer protection and information policy includes the right to information among the basic rights of consumers; whereas this right is confirmed by the Council resolution of 9 May 1981 on a second programme of the European Community for a consumer protection and information policy, point 40 of the Annex to which deals specifically with consumer information; whereas comparative advertising, when it compares details which are relevant, always verifiable and neither misleading nor unfair, may be a legitimate means of informing consumers to their advantage;	consumer protection and information policy includes the right to information among the basic rights of consumers; whereas this right is confirmed by the Council resolution of 9 May 1981 on a second programme of the European Community for a consumer protection and information policy, point 40 of the Annex to which deals specifically with consumer information; whereas comparative advertising, when it compares relevant, verifiable and representative features and is not misleading, is a legitimate means of informing consumers of their advantage; Whereas it is desirable to provide a broad concept of comparative advertising to cover all modalities of comparative advertising;

1991 Draft (OJ 1991 C180/14)	1994 Draft (OJ 1994 C136/4)	Common Position (OJ 1996 C219/14)
Whereas objective criteria must be established in order to determine which practices relating to comparative advertising are unfair and therefore may distort competition, cause damage to competitors and have an adverse effect on consumer choice;	Unchanged	Whereas conditions of permitted comparative advertising, as far as the comparison is concerned, should be established in order to determine which practices relating to comparative advertising may distort competition, cause damage to competitors and have an adverse effect on consumer choice; whereas such conditions of permitted comparative advertising should include criteria of objective comparison of the features of goods and services;

Whereas the comparison of the price only of goods and services should be possible if this comparison respects certain other conditions, in particular that it shall not be misleading; |
| Whereas, in particular, in order to prevent comparative advertising being used | Unchanged | Whereas, in order to prevent comparative advertising being used in an anti-competitive |

1991 Draft (OJ 1991 C180/14)	1994 Draft (OJ 1994 C136/4)	Common Position (OJ 1996 C219/14)
in an unfair and anti-competitive manner, only comparisons between competing goods and services of the same nature should be allowed;		and unfair manner, only comparisons between competing goods and services meeting the same needs or intended for the same purpose should be permitted;

Whereas comparative tests carried out by third parties can con-stitute a valuable basis for comparative advertising; whereas, however, this independent activity requires clearly defined protection against the unauthor-ized use of results by advertisers; whereas, where such use is lawfully made, advert-isers must themselves assume responsibility for it;

Whereas the conditions of comparative advert-ising should be cumu-lative and respected in their entirety, whereas this shall not prevent Member States from defining modalities of implementation for

1991 Draft (OJ 1991 C180/14)	1994 Draft (OJ 1994 C136/4)	Common Position (OJ 1996 C219/14)
		each of the conditions, in order to find the appropriate solution in each case;
		Whereas these conditions should include, in particular, consideration of the provisions resulting from Council Regulation (EEC) No 2081/92 of 14 July 1992 on the protection of geographical indications and designations of origin for agricultural products and foodstuffs, and in particular Article 13 thereof, and of the other Community provisions adopted in the agricultural sphere;
Whereas Article 5 of Directive 89/104/EEC of 21 December 1988 to approximate the laws of the Member States relating to trade marks confers exclusive rights on the proprietor of a registered trade mark, including the right to prevent all third	Unchanged	Whereas Article 5 of First Council Directive 89/104/EEC of 21 December 1988 to approximate the laws of the Member States relating to trade marks confers exclusive rights on the proprietor of a registered trade mark, including the right to

1991 Draft (OJ 1991 C180/14)	1994 Draft (OJ 1994 C136/4)	Common Position (OJ 1996 C219/14)
parties from using in the course of trade any sign which is identical with, or similar to, the trade mark in relation to identical goods or services or even, where applicable, other goods;		prevent all third parties from using, in the course of trade, any sign which is identical with, or similar to, the trade mark in relation to identical goods or services or even, where appropriate, other goods;
Whereas it may, however, be indispensable, in order to make comparative advertising effective, to identify the goods or services of a competitor making reference to a trade mark or trade name of which the latter is the proprietor;	Unchanged	Unchanged
Whereas such use of another's trade mark or trade name, provided it complies with the conditions laid down by this Directive and, in particular, does not try to capitalize on the reputation of another trade mark, does not breach this exclusive	Whereas such use of another's trade mark or trade name does not breach this exclusive right in cases where it complies with the conditions laid down by this Directive and does not capitalize on the reputation of another trade mark, but is intended solely	Whereas such use of another's trade mark, trade name, or other distinguishing marks does not breach this exclusive right in cases where it complies with the conditions laid down by this Directive, the intended target being solely to distinguish between

1991 Draft (OJ 1991 C180/14)	1994 Draft (OJ 1994 C136/4)	Common Position (OJ 1996 C219/14)
right given that this kind of use is not intended to steal reputations but to distinguish between them and thus objectively highlight differences;	to distinguish between them and thus objectively highlight differences;	them and thus to highlight differences objectively;
Whereas provision must be made for the legal and/or administrative means of redress mentioned in Articles 4 and 5 of Directive 84/450/EEC to be available to control comparative advertising which fails to meet the requirements of fairness laid down by this Directive;	Whereas provision must be made for the legal and/or administrative means of redress mentioned in Articles 4 and 5 of Directive 85/450/EEC to be available to control comparative advertising which fails to meet the requirements of fairness laid down by this Directive; whereas Article 6 applies to comparative advertising in the same way;	Whereas provision must be made for the legal and/or administrative means of redress mentioned in Articles 4 and 4 of Directive 85/450/EEC to be available to control comparative advertising which fails to meet the conditions laid down by this Directive; whereas Article 6 applies to unpermitted comparative advertising in the same way;
Whereas Article 7 of Directive 84/450/EEC allowing Member States to retain or adopt provisions with a view to ensuring more extensive protection for consumers, persons carrying on a trade, business, craft	Unchanged	Whereas Article 7 of Directive 84/450/EEC allowing Member States to retain or adopt provisions with a view to ensuring more extensive protection for consumers, persons carrying on a trade, business, craft

1991 Draft (OJ 1991 C180/14)	1994 Draft (OJ 1994 C136/4)	Common Position (OJ 1996 C219/14)
or profession, and the general public, should not apply to comparative advertising, given that the objective of this amendment is to allow it in all Member States under the same conditions and with a high level of protection;		or profession, and the general public, should not apply to comparative advertising, given that the objective of amending the said Directive is to establish conditions under which comparative advertising is permitted;
		Whereas a comparison which presents goods or services as an imitation or a replica or goods or services bearing a registered trade mark shall not be considered to fulfil the conditions to be met by permitted comparative advertising;
	Whereas this Directive does not in any way affect Community provisions on advertising for certain products and/or services or relating to the advertising content of particular media;	Whereas this Directive in no way affects Community provisions on advertising for specific products and/or services or restrictions or prohibitions on advertising in particular media;

1991 Draft (OJ 1991 C180/14)	1994 Draft (OJ 1994 C136/4)	Common Position (OJ 1996 C219/14)
		Whereas if a Member State, in compliance with the provisions of the Treaty, prohibits advertising regarding certain goods or services. this ban may, whether it is imposed directly or by a body or organization responsible under the law of that Member State for regulating the exercise of a commercial, industrial, craft or professional activity, be extended to comparative advertising;
		Whereas Member States shall not be obliged to permit comparative advertising for goods or services on which they maintain or introduce bans, including bans as regards marketing methods or advertising which targets vulnerable consumer groups;
	Whereas the authorization of comparative advertising is, under the conditions set out	Whereas regulating comparative advertising is, under the conditions set out in

1991 Draft (OJ 1991 C180/14)	1994 Draft (OJ 1994 C136/4)	Common Position (OJ 1996 C219/14)
	in this Directive, necessary for the completion of the internal market and that an action at Community level is required; whereas the adoption of a Direct-ive is the appropriate instrument because it lays down uniform general principles while allowing the Member States to choose the form and appropriate method by which to attain these objectives; whereas it is therefore in accord-ance with the principle of subsidiarity;	this Directive, necessary for the smooth running of the internal market and whereas action at Community level is required; whereas the adoption of a Direct-ive is the appropriate instrument because it lays down uniform general principles while allowing the Member States to choose the form and appropriate method by which to attain these objectives; whereas it is in accordance with the principle of sub-sidiarity;
HAS ADOPTED THIS DIRECTIVE	HAVE ADOPTED THIS DIRECTIVE	UNCHANGED
Article 1 Council Directive 84/450/EEC is hereby amended as follows:	Unchanged	Article 1 Directive 84/450/EEC is hereby amended as follows:
1. the title is replaced by the following title: 'Council Directive of 10 September 1984 concerning misleading and comparative advertising'	Unchanged	Unchanged

1991 Draft (OJ 1991 C180/14)	1994 Draft (OJ 1994 C136/4)	Common Position (OJ 1996 C219/14)
		2. Article 1 shall be replaced by the following: 'Article 1 This purpose of this Directive is to protect consumers, persons carrying on a trade or business or practising a craft or profession and the interests of the public in general against misleading advertising and the unfair consequences thereof and to lay down the conditions under which comparative advertising is permitted.';
2. in Article 2, point 3 is replaced by the following: '3. "comparative advertising" means any advertising which explicitly or by implication identifies a competitor or goods or services of the same kind offered by a competitor; 4. "person" means any natural or legal person";	Unchanged	3. the following point shall be inserted in Article 2: '2(a) "comparative advertising" means any advertising which explicitly or by implication identifies a competitor or goods or services offered by a competitor.'

1991 Draft (OJ 1991 C180/14)	1994 Draft (OJ 1994 C136/4)	Common Position (OJ 1996 C219/14)
3. the following Article 3a is added: 'Article 3a 1. Comparative advertising shall be allowed, provided that it objectively compares the material, relevant, verifiable and fairly chosen features of competing goods or services and that it:	3. the following Article 3a is added: 'Article 3a 1. Comparative advertising shall be allowed, provided that it objectively compares the material, relevant, always verifiable, fairly chosen and representative features of competing goods and services and that it:	4. the following Article shall be added: 'Article 3a 1. Comparative advertising shall, as far as the comparison is concerned, be permitted when the following conditions are met:
(a) does not mislead	Unchanged	(a) it is not misleading according to Articles 2(2), 3 and 7(1);
		(b) it compares goods or services meeting the same needs and intended for the same purpose;
		(c) it objectively compares one or more material, relevant, verifiable and representative features of those goods and services, which may include price;
(b) does not cause confusion in the market place between the advertiser and a	(b) does not create the risk of confusion in the market place between the advert-	(d) it does not create confusion in the market place between the advertiser and a

1991 Draft (OJ 1991 C180/14)	1994 Draft (OJ 1994 C136/4)	Common Position (OJ 1996 C219/14)
competitor or between the advertiser's trade marks, trade names, goods or services and those of a competitor;	iser and a competitor or between the advertiser's trade marks, trade names, other distinguishing marks, goods or services and those of a competitor;	competitor or between the advertiser's trade marks, trade names, other distinguishing marks, goods or services and those of a competitor;
(c) it does not discredit, denigrate, or bring contempt on a competitor or his trade marks, trade names, goods, services or activities or aim principally to capitalize on the reputation of a trade mark or trade name of a competitor.	(c) does not discredit, denigrate or bring contempt on the trade marks, trade names, goods, services or activities of a competitor and does not principally capitalize on the reputation of a trade mark or trade name of a competitor;	(e) it does not discredit or denigrate the trade marks, trade names or other distinguishing marks, goods, services or activities of a competitor;
		(f) for products with designation of origin, it relates in each case to products with the same designation;
		(g) it does not take unfair advantage of the reputation of a trade mark, trade name or other distinguishing marks of a competitor or of the designation of origin of competing products;

1991 Draft (OJ 1991 C180/14)	1994 Draft (OJ 1994 C136/4)	Common Position (OJ 1996 C219/14)
	(d) it does not refer to the personality or personal situation of a competitor.	
2. Reference to or reproduction of the results of comparative tests on goods or services carried out by third parties shall be permitted in advertising only if the person who has carried out the test gives his express consent. In such cases the advertiser shall accept responsibility for the test as if it had been performed by himself or under his direction';		
	2. Comparative advertising must indicate the length of time during which the characteristics of the goods or services compared shall be maintained where these are the subject of a special or limited-duration offer.	2. Any comparison to a special offer shall indicate in a clear and unequivocal way the date on which the offer ends or, where appropriate, that the special offer is subject to the availability of the goods and services, and, where the special offer has not yet begun, the

1991 Draft (OJ 1991 C180/14)	1994 Draft (OJ 1994 C136/4)	Common Position (OJ 1996 C219/14)
		date of the start of the period during which the special price or other specific conditions shall apply';
4. Article 4(1) is replaced by the following: '1. Member States shall ensure that adequate and effective means exist for the control of misleading advertising and comparative advertising in the interests of consumers as well as competitors and the general public. Such means shall include leal provisions under which persons or organizations regarded under national law as having a legitimate interest in prohibiting misleading or comparative advertising may:	Unchanged	5. the first and second subparagraphs of Article 4(1) shall be replaced by the following: '1. Member States shall ensure that adequate and effective means exist for the control of misleading advertising and for the compliance with the provisions on comparative advertising in the interests of consumers as well as competitors and the general public. Such means shall include legal provisions under which persons or organizations regarded under national law as having a legitimate interest in prohibiting misleading advertising or regulating comparative advertising may:

1991 Draft (OJ 1991 C180/14)	1994 Draft (OJ 1994 C136/4)	Common Position (OJ 1996 C219/14)
(a) take legal action against such advertising; and/or	Unchanged	Unchanged
(b) bring such advertising before an administrative authority competent either to decide on complaints or to initiate appropriate legal proceedings.	Unchanged	Unchanged
		6. Article 4(2) is hereby amended as follows: (a) the indents in the first paragraph shall be replaced by the following: '—to order the cessation of, or to institute appropriate legal proceedings for an order for the cessation of, misleading or unpermitted comparative advertising, or —if the misleading or unpermitted comparative advertising has not yet been published but publication is imminent, to order the prohibition of, or to institute

1991 Draft (OJ 1991 C180/14)	1994 Draft (OJ 1994 C136/4)	Common Position (OJ 1996 C219/14)
		appropriate legal proceedings for the prohibition of, such publication'; (b) the introductory wording to the third subparagraph shall be replaced by the following: 'Furthermore, Member States may confer upon the courts or administrative authorities powers enabling them, with a view to eliminating the continuing effects of misleading or unpermitted comparative advertising, the cessation of which has been ordered.
6. Article 5 is replaced by the following: 'Article 5 This Directive does not exclude the voluntary control of misleading or comparative advertising by self-regulatory bodies and recourse to such bodies by the persons or organizations referred to in Article	Unchanged	Unchanged

1991 Draft (OJ 1991 C180/14)	1994 Draft (OJ 1994 C136/4)	Common Position (OJ 1996 C219/14)
4 if proceedings before such bodies are in addition to the court or administrative proceedings referred to in that Article.'		
7. Article 7 is replaced by the following: 'Article 7 1. This Directive shall not preclude Member States from retaining or adopting provisions with a view to ensuring more extensive protection, with regard to misleading advertising, for consumers, persons carrying on a trade, business, craft or profession, and the general public.	Unchanged	8. Unchanged
2. Paragraph 1 shall not apply to comparative advertising.'	Unchanged	2. Paragraph 1 shall not apply to comparative advertising as far as the comparison is concerned.
	3. Community provisions on advertising for specific products and/or services or concerning the advertising content of	3. The provisions of this Directive shall apply without prejudice to Community provisions on advertising for specific

1991 Draft (OJ 1991 C180/14)	1994 Draft (OJ 1994 C136/4)	Common Position (OJ 1996 C219/14)
	particular media shall remain unaffected by this Directive.'	products and/or services or to restrictions on advertising in particular media.
		4. The provisions of this Directive concerning comparative advertising shall not oblige Member States which, in compliance with the provisions of the Treaty, maintain or introduce bans regarding certain goods or services, whether imposed directly or by a body or organization responsible, under the law of the member States, for regulating the exercise of a commercial, industrial, craft or professional activity, to permit comparative advertising regarding those goods or services. Where these bans are limited to particular media, the directive shall apply to the media not covered by these bans.'

1991 Draft (OJ 1991 C180/14)	1994 Draft (OJ 1994 C136/4)	Common Position (OJ 1996 C219/14)
Article 2	Article 2	Article 2
Member States shall bring into force the laws, regulations and administrative provisions necessary to comply with this Directive by 31 December 1992 at the latest. They shall inform the Commission thereof forthwith.	Member States shall bring into force the laws, regulations and administrative provisions necessary to comply with this Directive by 31 December 1995 at the latest. They shall inform the Commission thereof forthwith.	Member States shall bring into force the laws, regulations and administrative provisions necessary to comply with this Directive at the latest 30 months after its publication in the Official Journal of the European Communities. They shall forthwith inform the Commission thereof.
When Member States adopt these provisions, these shall contain a reference to this Directive or shall be accompanied by such reference on the occasion of their official publication. The methods of making such reference shall be laid down by the Member States.	When Member States adopt these provisions, these shall contain a reference to this Directive or shall be accompanied by such reference on the occasion of their official publication. The methods of making such reference shall be laid down by the Member States.	When Member States adopt these measures, these shall contain a reference to this Directive or shall be accompanied by such reference on the occasion of their official publication. The methods of making such reference shall be laid down by the Member States.
	Member States shall communicate to the Commission the text of essential provisions in domestic law which adopted in the domain governed by this Directive.	Member States shall communicate to the Commission the text of the main provisions of domestic law which they adopt in the field governed by this Directive.

1991 Draft (OJ 1991 C180/14)	1994 Draft (OJ 1994 C136/4)	Common Position (OJ 1996 C219/14)
Article 3 This Directive is addressed to the Member States	Article 3 Unchanged	Article 3 Unchanged

APPENDIX IV—Directive 97/55/EC (OJ 1997 L290/18)

THE EUROPEAN PARLIAMENT AND THE COUNCIL OF THE EUROPEAN UNION,

Having regard to the Treaty establishing the European Community, and in particular Article 100a thereof,

Having regard to the proposal from the Commission,[1]

Having regard to the opinion of the Economic and Social Committee,[2]

Acting in accordance with the procedure laid down in Article 189b of the Treaty,[3] in the light of the joint text approved by the Conciliation Committee on 25 June 1997,

1. Whereas one of the Community's main aims is to complete the internal market; whereas measures must be adopted to ensure the smooth running of the said market; whereas the internal market comprises an area which has no internal frontiers and in which goods, persons, services and capital can move freely;

2. Whereas the completion of the internal market will mean an ever wider range of choice; whereas, given that consumers can and must make the best possible use of the internal market, and that advertising is a very important means of creating genuine outlets for all goods and services throughout the Community, the basic provisions governing the form and content of comparative advertising should be uniform and the conditions of the use of comparative advertising in the Member

---

[1] OJ 1991 C180/14 and OJ 1991 C136/4.

[2] OJ 1992 C49/35.

[3] Opinion of the European Parliament of 18 Nov. 1992 (OJ 1992 C337/142), Common Position of the Council of 19 Mar. 1996 (OJ 1996 C219/14) and Decision of the European Parliament of 23 Oct. 1996 (OJ 1996 C347/69). Decisions of the European Parliament of 16 Sept. 1997 and Decision of the Council of 15 Sept. 1997.

States should be harmonised; whereas if these conditions are met, this will help demonstrate objectively the merits of the various comparable products; whereas comparative advertising can also stimulate competition between suppliers of goods and services to the consumer's advantage;

3. Whereas the laws, regulations and administrative provisions of the individual Member States concerning comparative advertising differ widely; whereas advertising reaches beyond the frontiers and is received on the territory of other Member States; whereas the acceptance or non-acceptance of comparative advertising according to the various national laws may constitute an obstacle to the free movement of goods and services and create distortions of competition; whereas, in particular, firms may be exposed to forms of advertising developed by competitors to which they cannot reply in equal measure; whereas the freedom to provide services relating to comparative advertising should be assured; whereas the Community is called on to remedy the situation;

4. Whereas the sixth recital of Council Directive 84/450/EEC of 10 September 1984 relating to the approximation of laws, regulations and administrative provisions of the Member States concerning misleading advertising[4] states that, after the harmonisation of national provisions against misleading advertising, 'at a second stage . . ., as far as necessary, comparative advertising should be dealt with, on the basis of appropriate Commission proposals';

5. Whereas point 3(d) of the Annex to the Council Resolution of 14 April 1975 on a preliminary programme of the European Economic Community for a consumer protection and information policy[5] includes the right to information among the basic rights of consumers; whereas this right is confirmed by the Council Resolution of 19 May 1981 on a second programme of the European Economic Community for a consumer protection and information policy,[6] point 40 of the Annex, which deals

[4] OJ 1984 L250/17.
[5] OJ 1975 C92/1.
[6] OJ 1981 C133/1.

specifically with consumer information; whereas comparative advertising, when it compares material, relevant, verifiable and representative features and is not misleading, may be a legitimate means of informing consumers of their advantage;

6. Whereas it is desirable to provide a broad concept of comparative advertising to cover all modes of comparative advertising;

7. Whereas conditions of permitted comparative advertising, as far as the comparison is concerned, should be established in order to determine which practices relating to comparative advertising may distort competition, be detrimental to competitors and have an adverse effect on consumer choice; whereas such conditions of permitted advertising should include criteria of objective comparison of the features of goods and services;

8. Whereas the comparison of the price only of goods and services should be possible if this comparison respects certain conditions, in particular that it shall not be misleading;

9. Whereas, in order to prevent comparative advertising being used in an anti-competitive and unfair manner, only comparisons between competing goods and services meeting the same needs or intended for the same purpose should be permitted;

10. Whereas the international conventions on copyright as well as the national provisions on contractual and non-contractual liability shall apply when the results of comparative tests carried out by third parties are referred to or reproduced in comparative advertising;

11. Whereas the conditions of comparative advertising should be cumulative and respected in their entirety; whereas, in accordance with the Treaty, the choice of forms and methods for the implementation of these conditions shall be left to the Member States, insofar as those forms and methods are not already determined by this Directive;

12. Whereas these conditions should include, in particular, consideration of the provisions resulting from Council Regulation (EEC) No 2081/92 of 14 July 1992 on the protection of geographical indications and designations of origin for

agricultural products and foodstuffs,[7] and in particular Article 13 thereof, and of the other Community provisions adopted in the agricultural sphere;

13. Whereas Article 5 of First Council Directive 89/104/EEC of 21 December 1988 to approximate the laws of the Member States relating to trade marks[8] confers exclusive rights on the proprietor of a registered trade mark, including the right to prevent all third parties from using, in the course of trade, any sign which is identical with, or similar to, the trade mark in relation to identical goods or services or even, where appropriate, other goods;

14. Whereas it may, however, be indispensable, in order to make comparative advertising effective, to identify the goods or services of a competitor, making reference to a trade mark or trade name of which the latter is the proprietor;

15. Whereas such use of another's trade mark, trade name or other distinguishing marks does not breach this exclusive right in cases where it complies with the conditions laid down by this Directive, the intended target being solely to distinguish between them and thus to highlight differences objectively;

16. Whereas provisions should be made for the legal and/or administrative means of redress mentioned in Articles 4 and 5 of Directive 84/450/EEC to be available to control comparative advertising which fails to meet the conditions laid down by this Directive; whereas according to the 16th recital of the Directive, voluntary control by self-regulatory bodies to eliminate misleading advertising may avoid recourse to administrative or juridical action and ought therefore to be encouraged; whereas Article 6 applies to unpermitted comparative advertising in the same way;

17. Whereas national self-regulatory bodies may coordinate their work through associations or organizations established at Community level and inter alia deal with cross-border complaints;

[7] OJ 1992 L208/1.

[8] OJ 1992 L40/1. Directive as last amended by Decision 92/10/EEC (OJ 1992 L6/35).

18. Whereas Article 7 of Directive 84/450/EEC allowing Member States to retain or adopt provisions with a view to ensuring more extensive protection for consumers, persons carrying on a trade, business, craft or profession, and the general public, should not apply to comparative advertising, given that the objective of amending the said Directive is to establish conditions under which comparative advertising is permitted;

19. Whereas a comparison which presents goods or services as an imitation or a replica of goods or services bearing a protected trade mark or trade name shall not be considered to fulfil the conditions to be met by permitted comparative advertising;

20. Whereas this Directive in no way affects Community provisions on advertising for specific products and/or services or restrictions or prohibitions on advertising in particular media;

21. Whereas, if a Member State, in compliance with the provisions of the Treaty, prohibits advertising regarding certain goods or services, this ban may, whether it is imposed directly or by a body or organization responsible under the law of that Member State for regulating the exercise of a commercial, industrial, craft or professional activity, be extended to comparative advertising;

22. Whereas Member States shall not be obliged to permit comparative advertising for goods or services on which they, in compliance with the provisions of the Treaty, maintain or introduce bans, including bans as regards marketing methods or advertising which targets vulnerable consumer groups; whereas Member States may, in compliance with the provisions of the Treaty, maintain or introduce bans or limitations on the use of comparisons in the advertising of professional services, whether imposed directly or by a body or organization responsible under the law of the Member States for regulating the exercise of a professional activity;

23. Whereas regulating comparative advertising is, under the conditions set out in this Directive, necessary for the smooth running of the internal market and whereas action at Community level is therefore required; whereas the adoption of a Directive is the appropriate instrument because it lays down

uniform general principles while allowing the Member States to choose the form and appropriate method by which to attain these objectives; whereas it is in accordance with the principle of subsidiarity,

HAVE ADOPTED THIS DIRECTIVE:

Article 1

Directive 94/450/EEC is hereby amended as follows:

1. The title shall be replaced by the following:
   'Council Directive of 10 September 1984 concerning misleading and comparative advertising';
2. Article 1 shall be replaced by the following:

'Article 1

The purpose of this Directive is to protect consumers, persons carrying on a trade or business or practising a craft or profession and the interests of the public in general against misleading advertising and the unfair consequences thereof and to lay down the conditions under which comparative advertising is permitted.';

3. The following point shall be inserted in Article 2:
   '2a. 'comparative advertising' means any advertising which explicitly or by implication identifies a competitor or goods or services offered by a competitor;'
4. The following Article shall be added:

'Article 3a

1. Comparative advertising shall, as far as the comparison is concerned, be permitted when the following conditions are met:

   (a) it is not misleading according to Article 2(2), 3 and 7(1);
   (b) it compares goods or services meeting the same needs or intended for the same purpose;
   (c) it objectively compares one or more material, relevant,

verifiable and representative features of those goods and services, which may include price;

(d) it does not create confusion in the market place between the advertiser and a competitor or between the advertiser's trade marks, trade names, other distinguishing marks, goods or services and those of a competitor;

(e) it does not discredit or denigrate the trade marks, trade names, other distinguishing marks, goods, services, activities, or circumstances of a competitor;

(f) for products with designation of origin, it relates in each case to products with the same designation;

(g) it does not take unfair advantage of the reputation of a trade mark, trade name or other distinguishing marks of a competitor or of the designation of origin of competing products;

(h) it does not present goods or services as imitations or replicas of goods or services bearing a protected trade mark or trade name.

2. Any comparison referring to a special offer shall indicate in a clear and unequivocal way the date on which the offer ends or, where appropriate, that the special offer is subject to the availability of the goods and services, and, where the special offer has not yet begun, the date of the start of the period during which the special price or other specific conditions shall apply.';

5. The first and second subparagraphs of Article 4(1) shall be replaced by the following:

'1. Member States shall ensure that adequate and effective means exist to combat misleading advertising and for the compliance with the provisions on comparative advertising in the interests of consumers as well as competitors and the general public. Such means shall include legal provisions under which persons or organizations regarded under national law as having a legitimate interest in prohibiting misleading advertising or regulating comparative advertising may:

(a) take legal action against such advertising; and/or

(b) bring such advertising before an administrative authority competent either to decide on complaints or to initiate appropriate legal proceedings.';

6. Article 4(2) is hereby amended as follows:

(a) the indents in the first subparagraph shall be replaced by the following:

'—to order the cessation of, or to institute appropriate legal proceedings for an order for the cessation of, misleading advertising or unpermitted comparative advertising, or

—if the misleading advertising or unpermitted comparative advertising has not yet been published but publication is imminent, to order the prohibition of, or to institute appropriate legal proceedings for an order for the prohibition of, such publication,';

(b) the introductory wording to the third subparagraph shall be replaced by the following:

'Furthermore, Member States may confer upon the courts or administrative authorities powers enabling them, with a view to eliminating the continuing effects of misleading advertising or unpermitted comparative advertising, the cessation of which has been ordered by a final decision:';

7. Article 5 shall be replaced by the following:

'Article 5

This Directive does not exclude the voluntary control, which Member States may encourage, of misleading or comparative advertising by self-regulatory bodies and recourse before such bodies are in addition to the court of administrative proceedings referred to in that Article.';

8. Article 6(a) shall be replaced by the following:

(a) to require the advertiser to furnish evidence as to the accuracy of factual claims in advertising if, taking into account the legitimate interest of the advertiser and any other party to the proceedings, such a requirement appears appropriate on the basis of the circumstances of the particular case and in the case of comparative advertising to require the advertiser to furnish such evidence in a short period of time; and';

9. Article 7 shall be replaced by the following:

'Article 7

1. This Directive shall not preclude Member States from retaining or adopting provisions with a view to ensuring more extensive protection, with regard to misleading advertising, for consumers, persons carrying on a trade, business, craft or profession, and the general public.

2. Paragraph 1 shall not apply to comparative advertising as far as the comparison is concerned.

3. The provisions of this Directive shall apply without prejudice to Community provisions on advertising for specific products and/or services or to restrictions or prohibitions on advertising in particular media.

4. The provisions of this Directive concerning comparative advertising shall not oblige Member States which, in compliance with the provisions of the Treaty, maintain or introduce advertising bans regarding certain goods or services, whether imposed directly or by a body or organization responsible, under the law of the Member States, for regulating the exercise of a commercial, industrial, craft or professional activity, to permit comparative advertising regarding those goods or services. Where these bans are limited to particular media, the Directive shall apply to the media not covered by these bans.

5. Nothing in this Directive shall prevent Member States from, in compliance with the provisions of the Treaty, maintaining or introducing bans or limitations on the use of comparisons in the advertising of professional services, whether imposed directly or by a body or organization responsible, under the law of the Member States, for regulating the exercise of a professional activity.'

Article 2
Complaints systems

The Commission shall study the feasibility of establishing effective means to deal with cross-border complaints in respect of comparative advertising. Within two years after the entry into force of this Directive the Commission shall submit a report to the European Parliament and the Council on the results of the studies, accompanied if appropriate by proposals.

Article 3

1. Member States shall bring into force the laws, regulations and administrative provisions necessary to comply with this Directive at the latest 30 months after its publication in the Official Journal of the European Communities. They shall forthwith inform the Commission thereof.

2. When Member States adopt these measures, they shall contain a reference to this Directive or shall be accompanied by such reference on the occasion of their official publication. The methods of making such reference shall be laid down by Member States.

3. Member States shall communicate to the Commission the text of the main provisions of domestic law which they adopt in the field governed by this Directive.

Article 4

This Directive is addressed to the Member States.

Done at Brussels, 6 October 1997.

For the European Parliament
The President
J. M. GIL-ROBLES

For the Council
The President
J. POOS